PICTURES ON MY PILLOW

An Oceanographer's Exploration of the Symbols of Self-Transcendence

PATRICK B. CREAN

Agio
PUBLISHING HOUSE

151 Howe Street, Victoria BC Canada V8V 4K5

For rights information and bulk orders, please contact
info@agiopublishing.com *or go to* www.agiopublishing.com

A license to reproduce excerpts from *Four Quartets* by
T.S. Eliot and *Collected Poems 1909-1962* by T.S. Eliot has
been obtained from Faber and Faber Ltd., publishers.

Pictures On My Pillow
ISBN 978-1-897435-61-8 (trade paperback)
Cataloguing information available from
Library and Archives Canada.
Printed on acid-free paper.
Agio Publishing House is a socially responsible company,
measuring success on a triple-bottom-line basis.
10 9 8 7 6 5 4 3 2 1b

DEDICATION

To my sons, Tom and Michael, and their families.

PATRICK BERNARD CREAN

14 AUGUST, 1926 – 8 JULY, 2011

Patrick was a man of unassumed strength. Whichever of his favourite subjects he chose, ocean science or religion, he never faltered in presenting precise, meaningful and logical arguments. A discussion with Patrick on science or religion opened the door for many to see beyond everyday understanding and enter a realm of quiet rationality of what lay beyond.

His unassuming nature gave no hint of the depth of his thinking. But to talk with Patrick was always an engendering experience of a visionary nature, beset with important issues of our time. I shall remember my friendship with Patrick, forever and beyond.

—Timothy Parsons, O.C.

ACKNOWLEDGEMENTS

It is with special thanks and profound gratitude that I acknowledge those with whom the days of my life have been, and continue to be, shared. Over the span of years and on both sides of the Atlantic and Pacific Oceans you are family, friends, professional colleagues, fellow lovers of the sea and ships, fellow hikers of hill, vale and mountain, fellow seekers of the spirit. So many whose own search for personal, professional and spiritual authenticity significantly influenced the human spirit that I have become. You have affirmed the child, the boy, the man, or not. You have challenged and, yes, affirmed nascent worldviews, personal ethics, insights involving 'science, self-knowledge and religion' throughout the depth and breadth of the ages and stages through which we yet navigate.

I also wish to express my love and gratitude to my wife, Wendy McFeely. In the autumn of 2009 she was inspired to pick up this long-shelved project, a future for which neither she nor I held a clear vision. Wendy had long believed that these two manuscripts, written over some twenty years – *Science, Self-Knowledge & Spirituality* and *Pictures On My Pillow* – were crying out from the shelf to be published – together! Her belief in me and in the process of my lengthy search for understanding, for authenticity and subsequent desire to return to community something of the modest wisdom gleaned were compelling and, as she said, not to be ignored. I appreciate beyond words the inner voice to which she listened, as well as the objective and insightful critique she brought to her skilful and thorough editing suggestions. Finally, and not least, it is as *anam cara**, as soul friends, that we came together. As the literal and symbolic blending of our lives evolve, so too our voices, thus the manifestation of such throughout many of these pages, particularly so, the closing chapters.

My appreciation also extends to dear friends and family who offered moral support of the most encouraging and enduring kind in assisting Wendy and myself with the arduous publishing process. In this regard I would like to express particular gratitude to our dear friend, Suzanne Barois. Long a seeker of wisdom herself, a professional in marine sciences, facilitator and writer, she inspires us with her enthusiasm while initiating us to the living of a deeply personal *action circle*. Suzanne has given generously of her time, talent and experience, gracing our home with her presence, her tireless energy, unwavering good nature and commitment to seeing us through to, and beyond, our project's conclusion. Her belief in the value of personal story and the inherent healing and transformative energy found therein for orator and listener alike, sustains us in every way.

For many years I was welcomed to Mt. Angel Abbey in Oregon by the warmth and hospitality of guest master, Father Bernard Sander. His compassionate presence and inclusive spirit remains with me yet, to my profound gratitude.

And finally, I would like to thank Bruce, Marsha and Dan Batchelor of Agio Publishing House, each of whom have contributed their innumerable skills to bring about a high polish to the final product. Their sensitivity and kindness has added so much to the overall teamwork of these many months.

Patrick B. Crean
April 2011

---

anam cara – a person with whom the hidden intimacies of one's life are revealed. From John O'Donohue's book of the same name.

PICTURES ON MY PILLOW

TABLE OF CONTENTS

PROLOGUE

It seems that when we are most greatly beset and exhausted by the exigencies of what has come to be seen as a futile life, there can occur some moment of glimpsed distraction or inspiration that suggests solution, some promise of rescue.

In 1958, some such incident occurred for myself through a chance attendance, having nothing better to do, at a workshop held in St. Mary's University, Halifax, Nova Scotia. It provided an opportunity for those attending a course given by a visiting scholar to ask questions. The audience seemed to consist largely of professional philosophers and theologians, and the level of discussion passed far above my head. I became, however, utterly fascinated by the level of academic virtuosity of the man in the armchair in the middle of the room, with a tape recorder running at his feet.

Perhaps there was a meaning to life that could be found and employed in some catalysis of feeling towards an anticipation that soared brilliantly into an evolutionary future, something beyond the grave for which we are each individually called in participatory preparation! Mind could possibly be a "personalization" of the biological brain in terms of an incredibly complex aggregate of meaningful events, synthesized into a single unity. Certainly the speaker could handle convincingly an extraordinary range of questions, whether in philosophy, mathematics, science, psychology, literature, history, all of which turned out to be but facets of theology.

So I bought a copy of his major work, *Insight: A Study of Human Understanding* and accepted his invitation to an experimental journey into the nature of my own consciousness. It is a journey that continues to grow exponentially with respect to both conviction and prospects that are implied.

There is a basic theme underlying my own personal application of the psychological, philosophical and theological work of Bernard Lonergan, and that is the need to move beyond the categories and metaphors of elementary religious instruction and the self-attentive entry into the realm of consciousness, into the realm of one's own intelligence, into the noosphere. We are each born into some community that has a profoundly formative influence on our subsequent journey through the years of our allotted time. There is some level of meaning that has already been attained. Though most powerfully embodied in human persons, it commonly finds its expression in words that expedite significant sharing in the meaning acquired by other human heads, both of the past and of the present. It is in that history that strong indications of our evolutionary past and evolutionary destiny are to be found.

The educated person in any sphere whose piety remains simple would seem to set a barrier to both personally integrated growth and to secular opportunities of divine communication. The question arises as to whether the approach is in some sense verifiable, whether it can stand up to the concrete test of performance. This can only be done through some accessible fund of common experience. My own experience may be of some interest in this regard, involving as it did a rudimentary grasp of Lonergan's basic analysis of the norms of human conscious procedures as a practical "feedback" model, the use of prayer and meditation as a moderator of negative and limiting feeling states, and the need for action which would lead to higher levels of understanding and spontaneities of positive feelings. This would engender not only a slowly growing appreciation of the universe as it really is, but a concomitant sense of excitement at the nature and destiny of the human spirit.

It would seem increasingly probable that, at the end of each human life, there is an aggregate of contents once conscious, which has become an individual. I would describe such an aggregate as a unity in the realm of spirit that, as such, enters into full complementarity with the aggregate of collective human consciousness contents that has already preceded us – a realm of spirit which still awaits the full realization of being in the universe, the totality of all that is known with all that remains to be known.

The following constitutes merely one account of a myriad such journeys that have occurred or are yet still to occur. For myself, the outcome to date has revealed an extraordinarily exciting evolutionary vision of the universe, a vision in which consciousness of the human type is now considered to be the leading off-shoot, at least in the solar system if not our galaxy. It would seem that this account of my own journey is consonant with the increasingly rapid movement into the information age.

As the ability of the energy resources of the universe appear to be coming less and less accessible to produce change, there is a concomitant evolution of diversification, order, complexity, system. At the forefront of this development is that which can reflect upon itself – ourselves. Human heads produce meaning which can be communicated from one head to another, which is accumulative and progressive, at least if emergent in the context of the norms of its own procedures. It is probably emergent at other locations in the universe where the fundamental laws that govern our own emergence would seem to be equally applicable.

At the close of each human life there would seem to be some unity, some aggregate of meaning that one accepts as uniquely as oneself. Does it terminate with the dissolution of its biological substrate? There seems to be some intelligible overall direction to evolution, the emergence of higher levels that are unpredictable from lower levels. It is increasingly probable that the next step would seem to involve a role for each of us, as discrete 'interactable' increments of meaning in the next higher phase of evolution. That probability would seem in proportion to the amount of effort put into genuinely living out our own increment of a titanic drama. Eventually that probability can become so overwhelming that it becomes a love affair with some totality of the intelligible universe itself, the immanence of a sublime beauty that has to be earned by our own work. For T. S. Eliot, as for Julian of Norwich:

> *All shall be well*
> *All manner thing shall be well*
> *When the tongues of flame are infolded into the crowned knot of fire*
> *And the fire and the rose are one.*

The significance of recounting such a journey lies, however, not merely in a narrative of events, but in some delineation of the accompanying affects, of feelings associated with the stream of sensory impressions, in particular those attended to in consciousness and raised to the level of symbol by an affective response that arises spontaneously from within, beckoning towards some course of action. Symbols invite thought. Thought gives rise to meaning, meaning which is laden with feelings, feelings that constitute immediately sensible energy.

It is in the role of relations with others that we encounter the greatest evolutionary flexibility of diversification arising from spontaneities of feeling.

Others can themselves constitute symbols of performance that powerfully conduce to doing likewise ourselves. Thus can the human mind, for good evolutionary purpose, seek to acquire and exercise power over others through authentic leadership. If such an endeavour, for purposes of selfish satisfaction, fundamentally frustrates the freedom of others to seek the emerging truly good that is appropriate for their own development, their own expansion of consciousness, then there is an encounter with the dark side of human nature, the emergence of moral evil, the social concomitant of the innate perversities of the physical world that insist on finding solutions to the changing problems of human survival.

Over the years, there should occur a shift in our symbols of transformation and transvaluation, such that what once moved no longer moves, what once failed to move now moves, of an inner restlessness that cannot be stayed until at last there is an intelligent, affective and enduring awakening to spiritual reality. Failure in such transformation of symbols points to a blockage in development. It is well to confirm the authenticity of that journey in instances of similarly experienced growth of meaning in the immensely varied resources of literature now available. This would seem to require a constructive eclecticism that functions in terms of the questions that feel really important and give rise to a unique increment of meaning that is all that is asked of us. In the words of T. S. Eliot:

> *We are born with the dead*
> *See they return, and bring us with them.*

To condense some eight decades of experience into a few pages may perhaps imply an almost certain simplicity in the working out of these matters. In point of fact, there is required much patience and persistence for the scripturally pledged outcome leaves open the time scale of petition and response. It is, however, to tell a story, and stories should start somewhere about the beginning. As so strongly emphasized by Carl Gustav Jung, our early years, and family background, have a profound formative influence on the subsequent development of that aggregate of 'once-conscious materials' that eventually becomes each unique individual human person.

PART ONE

GROWING UP IN ENGLAND

CHAPTER I

FAMILY HISTORY

Just west of Dublin, beyond the Phoenix Park, by the humpbacked railway and canal bridges carrying the road between Castleknock and Blanchardstown, there once stood an old house, Roselawn, owned by my maternal grandfather Henry Morris. The house, as I remember it, was then going to ruin, though there still remained one prominent memento of better days. In the billiard room that looked out onto a small walled garden, there was an ornate clock presented to him, according to the corroded inscription, by the officers of some regiment stationed in Dublin. It had long since failed to keep the hours that measured the dissolution of its setting. Henry Morris had owned a livery stable in Parkgate, appropriately enough the Dublin entrance to the park. With the rise of the automobile and departure of the British Army with its cavalry and games of polo, the horse business failed. He himself died in 1909.

The family had once had extensive estates of fertile farmland in County Meath. Family tradition had it that originally the family were Cromwellian settlers from Wales. My great grandfather, Robert Brabazon Morris was born in 1804 and reputedly became the first Catholic in the family. The same tradition had it that there was a gambler in the family and that one should never go to law. His forebears occupied extensive estates in County Meath associated with such names as Mullagha, Tankardstown, Skreen, Collierstown, and

Gaulstown. His great grandfather, Brabazon Morris, lived at Tankardstown and had a thousand acres under plough. He and his brother were the first to introduce threshing machines, at the General Quarter Sessions of the Peace held at Trim on the 18th January 1772, where his commission as a Justice of the Peace from George the Third was read, requiring him to "keep our Peace in the County of Meath, and keep and cause to be kept all Ordinances and Statutes made for the good of our Peace and for the conservation of the same and for quiet Rule ... and to Chastise and Punish all offending ... and to inquire into all manner of Treasons, Murders, Burnings, Robberies, Witchcrafts, Enchantments, Sorceries, etcetera."

It was in Roselawn that my mother and her twin sister, Monnie, were born. Monnie had a quick tongue and usually led in any adventure. Once, when illegally riding their lampless bicycles back through the main drive of the Phoenix Park at night, a large policeman stepped out with peremptory demand, "Where's your light?" With a gay greeting from Monnie of, "It is a nice night, officer," they sped off into the dark.

With the decline in family fortunes, it was necessary to find careers. My mother became a shorthand typist and was later singled out to record the proceedings of the 1923 Imperial Economic Conference in London, hailed in the press as a significant contribution to the promotion of cooperation among the English Speaking Peoples. Monnie trained as a nurse and served in casualty clearing stations behind the front lines in the First World War. Against all regulations, she actually got up into the front line herself, and later, charmed a young officer into letting her drive one of the first tanks.

There were three others sisters: Aunt Rosalie, who entered the Sacred Heart Convent, High Park, in Drumcondra, a suburb of Dublin, and where grand-aunt Catherine Morris had died in 1917 (two other grand-aunts entered religious orders with the Sisters of Charity of St. Vincent de Paul, one dying in Paris in 1888, the other dying in Sedan in 1899); Aunt Madge, who suffered from a chronic injury received in a riding accident; and Aunt May, who seems to have spent her life looking after Madge. May was reputedly a talented musician, though when Madge married she remained with the couple and supposedly never developed this musical talent.

Three brothers made up the Morris clan. Uncle Joey who, with the failure of the horse trade, emigrated to America to find work. He was a gentle, kindly man. I was a small boy when he visited us in Twickenham, and I well remember his taking me for long walks by the river to Richmond. A tall stooped figure with his flat cap, open rain coat and hands in his trouser pockets, glancing down at me as he chatted away about his life in far away Cleveland. There he would die of cancer, with an unused plane ticket to return home found among his effects.

Uncle Harry and Uncle Edmund held a very special place for me because they were marine engineers and I loved the sea and engines. They had apparently served their apprenticeships at the steam locomotive works at Inchicore. The hours were long and involved a walk of four miles back and forth from the house to the works. Harry I never met for, on the 17th April 1917, his ship, an Elder Dempster passenger cargo vessel the *S.S. Aburi,* en route to West Africa from Liverpool, was sunk in an underwater torpedo attack by the *U61*, 125 miles north-west of Tory Island. According to my mother, he had just come off watch when the torpedo struck below his cabin. He was killed instantly, at the age of twenty-six.

Uncle Edmund joined the Bibby line and an enthusiastic postcard, treasured by my mother, dated 8th February 1906 shows a picture of the *S.S. Worcestershire*, then "off Marseilles, bound for Rangoon with seventy first class passengers." Much later I would meet him, as an engineer with the British and Irish Steam Packet Company, aboard the *Lady Meath*, a cattle boat plying between Dublin and Liverpool. My first visit to her engine room amounted to something of a frightening, but nonetheless profoundly symbolic, if not mystical, experience. The heat, the smell of oil, the glittering steel of the engines, the sense of immense controlled power fascinated and entranced me more than anything else in the world. I knew that I wanted to work with such engines.

There was also a delightful human element to offset the implacable majesty of that machinery of power. When the cows came on board, some of them would be milked and a churn, driven by the propeller shaft, would provide fresh butter for all by the time she docked in Liverpool. That delighted me. It was just the sort of thing machinery was for. However, much later we would hear that along with the butter churn and many head of cattle, a merciless explosion of a drifting Nazi mine sunk the ship off Holyhead in the Irish Sea. Uncle Edmund survived, but later, in another distressed ship, he would be terribly scalded by live steam as he urgently closed the throttle valves to the main engines and found his way in the roaring darkness up the ladders and out on deck, only to realize the extent of his injuries.

I have always thought of my mother's side of the family as courteous and gentle and in symbolic terms, ranging from that stillness of listening attention characteristic of the cloister, to the skilled practicalities of meeting the challenge of the sea and surviving, doing one's job to the best of one's ability simply because it's the sort of thing one does.

I knew much less about my father's side of the family, perhaps because there was little discussion of them, yet, in other quite profound and deeply forming ways, my father and his immediate family would leave an indelible imprint on my psyche that would take me many decades to live through and come to understand. In time I would learn from my mother that there was something of a long played out tragedy being enacted in the lives of my paternal grandmother and aunts, many aspects of which I would later witness for myself during my undergraduate days in Dublin. In autobiographical time, the appropriation of my own storied layers resides in the telling of such unfolding insights.

It seemed that I had three granduncles; Jim, Michael, and Hugh. Jim, whom I used to visit during my student days in Dublin, knew much of the family history and from him I gleaned more. They came originally from County Sligo, where an earlier James Crean is recorded as being High Sheriff of the County in 1590, also an Andrew Crean in the mid 1600s. A branch of the family had moved to County Kerry where, according to Jim, they had developed their own leather money. He was immensely proud of them. Michael and Hugh I knew less about. My only salient memory is Michael's possession of a pipe presented by Admiral Lord Nelson to some member of the family who had been one of his captains.

Tom Crean (1877 to 1938), a distant relative, had achieved distinction in Antarctica for extraordinary stamina and courage. He had been with the last support party to see Scott off on his fatal journey to the South Pole. On the return with Lashley and Evans, the incapacitation of the latter by illness led to Crean's extraordinary eighteen-hour, terrible journey, through ice field, crevasses and soft snow. He later received the highest civilian award for gallantry, the Albert Medal. Later he survived a journey of 800 miles in a ship's boat and was one of the exhausted trio who with Shackleton and Worsley, managed to reach the whaling station at Stromness and bring rescue to the remaining crew of the *Endurance* that foundered after being crushed by ice in the Weddell Sea. Another member of the family had received an award for gallantry while serving in the Boer War.

The story of Tom Crean was always a source of inspiration, of getting on with what one had to do no matter how appalling the circumstances of that doing. That courage was rooted in a faith, in turn to be found in my own Irish roots, themselves born of untold historical national hardship and suffering.

Perhaps, most of all, it was symbolized in that last desperate effort to cross the high mountains of South Georgia and reach the whaling station at Stromness, the only accessible outpost of civilization, and the independently sensed presence to Shackleton, Worsley and Crean of a "fourth man," a discarnate intelligence, willing and guiding the successful outcome of that terrible journey.

According to my mother, my paternal grandfather Patrick Crean was a man that she greatly liked and respected and who had welcomed her into the family. For all that, there seemed to be an aura of mystery that surrounded him, my grandmother, and the family as a whole. He was apparently born in 1874 and, in his late teens, joined the Royal Irish Constabulary. He had married, "outside of regulations," a young woman of the same age called Catherine Dawson. He was dismissed from the force and when my father was born in 1894, the birth certificate described my grandfather as a "traveler." In any event, he eventually became a detective and went to Cardiff, South Wales. My grandmother elected to stay in Dublin with my father and his two sisters, Mary and Martha. The family lived in a four-bedroom terraced house, standing well back from the road on Upper Mountpleasant Avenue in Rathmines, an agreeable residential area of Dublin, well placed for convenient access to the city. On the 3rd March 1925, at the age of fifty-one, my grandfather came off duty, saying he felt unwell as he made his way up to his bedroom. During the night, he died of influenza.

I visited the house on Upper Mountpleasant Avenue during my student days in Dublin and found the squalor of my grandmother's and aunts' surroundings repugnant. Though innured to rather Spartan accommodation myself, this house constituted something unique in my experience. My mother told me that the menage ruled over by my paternal grandmother constituted the great tragedy of my father's life, as did the impoverishment wrought on the lives of his two sisters, Mary and Martha. It was only many years later that I would discover an account among my father's papers of the tragedy that finally unfolded in that household – a part of his life of which he had never spoken a word to me.

My father attended a Christian Brothers school, which, as he told me later, he detested. According to my mother, his very poor eyesight was at least in part due to his mother's refusal to provide light for his homework and he had to make do on winter evenings with the light from the fire. He would later train as a teacher in a training college in Dublin, teaching then in a slum school. It was there that he developed a loathing of alcohol because of the terrible poverty and suffering that it caused in families.

I was fascinated by some of my father's stories concerning the rebellion and civil war in Ireland. On Easter Sunday, 1916, an armed force of insurgents seized the General Post Office, on what is now called O'Connell Street, in Dublin and proclaimed Irish Independence from English Rule. A British cavalry troop approached but were driven off by small arms fire. Reinforcements took up positions in the cover of surrounding buildings. Outside the city rumours were flying, and my father cycled off down beside the Liffey Quays to find out what was happening. The only thing he saw were some soldiers manhandling a field gun in a side street, so he turned up O'Connell Street to see what was going on there. He cycled to a stop outside the General Post Office and, with one foot resting on the pavement, had a look around. There were some dead horses in the street and all sorts of noise and shouting from the building with men shoving furniture up into the window openings. Curiosity satisfied, he peddled off to report to the Morris family out near Castleknock. It was only later that he realized the nature of his vantage point, square in the firing line between the aiming British troops awaiting orders to commence firing on the one side and similarly inclined insurgents on the other. He said, "I was the biggest bloody fool on God's earth!"

Another story I loved was of the time he was visiting my mother's sisters at their home in Grove Park in Rathmines, where they lived with Madge's husband, Jack Roche. He was having a bath at the back of the house when he heard one of the Black and Tans' Crossley tenders and a lot of commotion. Unwisely, he peeked around the corner of the window and was ordered to stand up, stark naked in the window, before the irate soldiery, with weapons aimed from the back of the tender, were satisfied!

My father came to London to work as a teacher with the London County Council and to complete an external part-time degree at the University of London. Subsequently he continued to complete, over seven years, an external doctorate. My earliest memory of him is of drifting off to sleep to the scratching of his fountain pen, as he sat at a small table in the corner of the bedroom, working on his Ph.D. thesis by the light of a heavily shaded reading lamp. The topic involved the English stage in the 18th century and, since some of the major figures involved were associated with Twickenham, he was a mine of information on local history. A letter to the *Times Literary Supplement* dated the 30th November 1930 requested permission to see any letters or other documents pertaining to Kitty Clive, an eighteenth century actress. His supervisor, Professor Allardyce Nichol, was of the University of London and one day I was brought to meet the great man. I was fascinated by his miniature stage with its performing puppets. My father's degree was awarded in 1933.

My father's school, where he was to become headmaster, was located on Macklin Street in that confining tangle of narrow roads and high buildings in the angle of the Kingsway, the Strand, New Oxford Street and Covent Garden in central London. It was a Catholic school run by the London County Council. Many of the children came from immigrant families who were living in the poorer back streets. He appears to have been a major source of assistance in helping them to deal with the various local authorities. Some women from the Sisters of Mercy convent in Tavistock Square, from which the convent in Twickenham had been founded, also taught at the school.

Occasionally he would bring me up to his school and Sister Camillus would bring me into the stock room and give me a pencil. Oddly enough, the school provided me with my first introduction to America. In the school library were to be found the adventures of *The Hardy Boys*. The Hardy boys had the use of such undreamed of marvels as motor bikes and motor boats, and had tremendous adventures in a fantastic land called America. I could borrow the books and take off into this extraordinary world only to come back down to earth in boring old Twickenham!

A favourite project of my father's was his extra-curricular elocution class. This was, after all, a society where accent immediately disclosed not only one's social standing but also one's prospects. Every Saturday some group of older students would come down to spend the day with us in the rural atmosphere of Thames-side Twickenham and Pope's Lodge and garden.

Such was the formative background, perhaps more unconsciously significant than in any explicit sense. There were both Catholic and Protestant threads to that ancestral weave from the past. The stories I like best in that regard, were of the Catholic High Sheriff who risked life and fortune in trying to get his Protestant friends to the safety of the nearest English garrison at Boyle from Sligo, and the wealthy Protestant landlord who built a "very good range of houses" for his Catholic labourers!

CHAPTER II

CHILDHOOD

In my end is my beginning.
—T. S. Eliot

TWICKENHAM, LONDON BOROUGH OF RICHMOND
UPON THAMES (1926–1936)

The room was high ceiling'd and contained several other cots. It was my first recallable adventure into consciousness, an awareness of myself through what was other than myself, and, according to my mother was, as far as it went, substantially correct. It was the nursing home on Stockwell Road not far from the house in Durand Gardens where my parents rented a small flat.

I must have been about two when I remember my mother bringing me on a search for more adequate accommodation. The only place I really liked had a small garden pond that, at the time, had the dimensions of a lake promising all sorts of adventures. But then there came the most wonderful place of all, the gardener's cottage in the grounds of the Sisters of Mercy convent on the banks of the River Thames at Twickenham. The gardener's cottage was across the road from the riverside convent, where the path from the grotto sloped upward to the level of the garden. The grotto under the road, that had once known the social elite of England in the early part of the 18th century, would eventually provide me with convenient access back and forth to class.

Packy very quickly became my favourite! More formally, Sister Patrick of the Sisters of Mercy. After recital of the Divine Office in the convent chapel and breakfast in the refectory, she would boil a large pot of potatoes and then make her way through the grotto under the road to feed them to the chickens.

From 1926 to 1939 I lived with my family in Alexander Pope's Coach House which eventually became the gardener's cottage for the Sisters of Mercy convent by the River Thames across the road. Pope constructed a grotto under the road between Tedington and Twickenham for private access to his garden, which many years later became a daily path I trod throughout my primary school years. Behind Pope's Lodge was the home belonging to the Yardley family of cosmetic fame.

Kitty is holding me here at about two years of age with Sister Camillus and Miss Corcoran looking on, both of whom taught at my father's Macklin Street Elementary School in central London.

I could usually manage an intercept and augment my own start to the day with a hot boiled potato! Packy would soon be joined by Sister Maurus, a young twenty-four-year-old postulant. Those formative days of my childhood lay the foundations on which the conscious events of a lifetime are built and I still think of Maurus, even after her death in her ninety-first year, as the "new one." Within the convent walls the classic domestic strata of Victorian upstairs/ downstairs was retained. The former consisting of the teachers and senior staff, the latter of sisters like Packy and Maurus, recruited from impoverished rural Ireland. There was no doubt whatsoever as to where my primary affections and allegiance lay.

The convent itself was located on that great bend in the River Thames that lies between Twickenham and Teddington where the locks then marked the tidal limit of the river. Originally the site of Alexander Pope's celebrated river-side home, it was separated from his garden by the public road that paralleled the river between Twickenham and Teddington. He had excavated a grotto, which, much embellished with rock and stone, provided private access to the garden. Two flanking chambers at the riverside end afforded a view of the passing river in the heat of summer. In my time, that was all that remained. The house itself had been bought and enlarged after Pope's death in 1774 by Sir William Stanhope who had also made improvements in the garden, though as such, he would appear to have been alone in that opinion. Subsequently purchased by Lady Howe, the house was torn down because of the sustained interest on the part of visitors whose literary susceptibilities she did not share. Thus she would go down in local history under the unflattering soubriquet, "Queen of the Goths."

Her house was also demolished and in its place was built the house that would become the convent, purchased by the Sisters of Mercy in 1919. It was built by a wealthy Victorian tea merchant and has been described as a combination of Elizabethan half-timber and Stuart Renaissance with the addition of Swiss, Italian, and Chinese features. A school was added in 1928 as a major extension, with two large stories of classrooms being partially superimposed on an arched playground at ground level by the spacious gymnasium.

My favourite place was the high clock tower, with its little iron balcony immediately below the large dial with gold-painted lettering. The view was wonderful! I could see all the way from the treed embankment at Twickenham, looking across to Eel Pie Island with its moored flotilla of river steamers, and along on our own side past Radnor Gardens, with its big house and weeping willows, across to the wooded tow path and Ham Fields, along the river bank, to Teddington with its church surmounted by a high green patinated roof. In front lay the constant traffic of the river, tugs fussing along with their barges, river steamers with their rows of passengers looking back up at me, perspiring gentlemen in their shirtsleeves rowing ladies, languidly steering graceful shiny-varnished skiffs.

The garden itself was divided in two parts and surrounded in its entirety by a high brick wall. The lower part near the convent enclosed a large grass hockey pitch and tennis court. These were further surrounded by a gravel path leaving space between it and the wall for a narrow perimeter of trees and shrubbery. This proved highly effective in the provision of privacy from the prying eyes of neighbours in adjoining suburban houses. Thus could members of the community pace the path undisturbed in their reading of daily prayer as mandated for religious orders in *The Office of the Hours.*

The upper garden, which could be entered through a central gate in a large dividing wall, was of roughly comparable size and was divided into four plots by two gravel paths intersecting at right angles. In the intersection was a crude oval concrete fountain. The fountain itself, rarely turned on, consisted of the perforated spray head from a watering can fixed to the water pipe. The plots were alive with rows of carefully tended vegetables, fruit bushes and apple, pear and plum trees. The edges of the paths were neatly picked out by well trimmed little box hedges. In summer one could always find a plump gooseberry, a juicy apple or a tomato in the greenhouse.

This was Packy's territory. She was weather beaten, at least as far as her regulation coif allowed, a wiry little countrywoman from Toomyvara in County Tipperary. She spent her days with her garden fork turning over the dark soil, planting and weeding, turning up endless fragments of broken clay pipes from generations that had tilled the same land before her. She always had time and an apple, or something, for a cheeky little boy who took for granted the extraordinary depth of gentleness and love in those kindly eyes. She could, of course, be much exasperated by the occasional perversities of nature and then it was an explosive "Bad cess to it!" – whatever that might be!

Our kitchen was a primary port of call for the community and visitors were frequent. My mother was a great favourite with the nuns who always called her Kitty and so for me, Kitty she became. The kitchen itself had actually been a stable in Victorian days. Over the ancient gas stove was that characteristic piece of curved timber that swept down from above the hayrack and out to just above where the half-door of the original horsebox once stood. It still contained a large staple and ring once used to tether the horse. There was no shortage of eager babysitters, notably Packy. One night the lead water pipe down the kitchen wall to the sink sprang a leak and there was Packy, frantically hopping about trying to stop it with her thumb while groping for something to stem the flow. Then, of course, "Bad cess to it!"

At the furthest end of the upper garden was Stanhope's Corner. A cluster of trees and thick undergrowth contained a path leading down to the entrance of what had once been another grotto. This had led under the little used public road to another property that Stanhope had acquired, but had long since been sealed off. The arch of rough stonework remained and contained a broken plaster bust in a niche that it shared with a large birds' nest. The tablet below the bust bore the inscription:

> *This humble roof, the gardens scanty line,*
> *ill-spoke the genius of a bard divine,*
> *But fancy now displays a fairer scope,*
> *as Stanhope's plans unfold the soul of Pope.*

I had no idea of what it meant, but it seemed appropriate in that place which conveyed such a profound sense of mystery, of earlier presences that somehow watched, understood and shared it with me. There was a large irregular stone slab where, in the heat of summer, there was coolness and I could lie and watch overhead what I have always thought to be one of the most beautiful sights in the world, the tracery of high green foliage against the endless blue of a sky to which one could set no bound.

I suppose it was in the winter of 1928, at the age of two, that my newfound wonderful little world nearly came to an end. My mother told me that I contracted whooping cough, diphtheria and pneumonia. All I remember is my upstairs bedroom in the Lodge, the coughing and gasping, the shadows cast by a night light in a little open sided stove with a metal cup that gave off a pungent odour for assistance in breathing, the leisurely flicker of shadows on the ceiling through the long restless nights. My father would often sit by me to sing me to sleep. Well do I remember the opening lines of his favourite song:

> *Oft in the stilly night, when slumber's chains hath bound me*
> *Fond memory brings the light of other days around me*
> *The joys the tears of boyhood years, the words of love then spoken.*

Little did I know of the torrent of prayer that was being poured out into the immensities of the universe from the community across the road. Sister Camillus always insisted that it was she who was holding me when, against all probability, the moment of crisis passed.

It was then thought that it would be warmer for me to sleep downstairs in the kitchen because of the heat from the large iron fireplace that was set into the outer wall. During the day I would play in front of it or look at my favourite picture book about "Dr. Owl." One night I woke up coughing to find the place full of smoke. My father rushed down to pull out the large sheet iron fire place and find that the half-timbering in the wall behind had caught alight. He doused it with buckets of water. I felt very proud when he told me that I had saved all our lives.

My mother brought me down to the seaside to recuperate and, in the little rented back kitchen, would prepare one of my favourite delicacies, egg-in-a-cup with lots of crumbled bread and butter. Then we would head off down to the beach with my little shrimp net. Other times I would race down along the sea front on my little tricycle, singing away to myself. Life was back on track.

Well, not quite perhaps, for one morning Kitty told me that we were going to visit a hospital. We went into a large ward and before I knew what was happening, I was seized by a large matron and bundled into pajamas with the jacket put on backwards and buttoned up so I could not get at them. Then Kitty left and I found myself alone in a little black iron bed in the middle of this large ward. Some people appeared with a trolley and I was wheeled off into some little room where I was surrounded by masked figures all dressed in white without the slightest idea of what was happening.

Watched by all these eyes from above the masks, something was put over my face and I could only gasp in some nauseating vapour. It seemed to be some ultimate moment of extinction. However, I regained consciousness to find only pain and vomiting. So it was that I had my tonsils removed. Then Kitty brought me home and there was a big fire in the living room of the Lodge and before it a large bright red toy fire engine. Kitty said she had not told me what was going to happen because I would refuse to go with her. It still seems that some sort of prior warning might have helped. I was certainly left with a sense of utter terror at the thought of hospitals and the medical profession.

One day in April 1930, I was playing by the kitchen door when the ancient motorcycle and sidecar that was my father's pride and joy pulled in. Kitty was holding with her in the sidecar a small warmly wrapped bundle. Even for a three and a half year old, my response was less than cordial; "What does she have to come for?" Each member of the community contributed to a list of possible names which I subsequently found among Kitty's papers. Packy's selection was Kathleen and so Kathleen she became.

Sibling rivalry would not be uncommon. It seemed from the beginning, that there was such a dissimilarity of temperament and interests that we had very little to do with each other. Later Kathleen would attend evening classes at Daphne de Lisle dancing school a short distance down the road and became a star performer excelling particularly in gymnastics. I would go down to bring her home. But dolls and dancing were not prominent on my agenda! The gap between us was further widened by the adroitness with which emotional distress could be employed. This seemed to me to be quite unfair, especially when the matter involved some escapade of my own, as I would usually come out the villain! Over time there would grow an attitude of distrust between us.

Choice is a determinant in personal development and by free acts we make ourselves. Indeed, the series of choices over my lifetime gave me the character that I have. According to the Jewish psychiatrist, Viktor Frankl, imprisoned for three appalling years in Auschwitz and other Nazi camps, the ultimate human freedom is the ability to choose our attitude in a given set of circumstances, to choose our own way. It was known to the writer of the Book of Job as expressed in the initial Divine injunction to Satan, "Keep your hands off his person," person being that unique "information unity" that one thinks of as a "me." In any event, many years later, Sister Maurus, who knew of both Kathleen and myself so well over the years, was adamant in her conviction that, "Psychologically, Kathleen and myself were totally different people." Certainly, there was a significant sense in which my choices were very different, a fact that would become all too clear many years later.

My father would bring me for long walks along the towpath to Richmond and then lift me up so I could watch the skaters on the big indoor ice rink near the Richmond Bridge. Then we would walk back on the other side of the river by Petersham Churchyard, where Captain Vancouver lies buried, and return to be rowed back across the river by the Twickenham Ferry. Sometimes, when he came back from work, we would play football, keeping goal in the net of the grass hockey pitch. As I mustered all my strength to kick the ball, he would start hopping up and down, his hands dangling in front of him and kicking his legs alternately left and right. I would laugh so hard I couldn't kick the ball!

There is little doubt, however. that diligence in schoolwork and filial obedience were not among my strong points. On occasion, when greatly exasperated, he would say something that would much disturb me; "You will not always have your Daddy!" There was such a thing as death. Watching from my bedroom window across the road, I had seen the ambulance men carrying the shrouded figure of my old catechism teacher, Sister Augustine, from the front door of the convent. I never saw her again. But the prospect of life without my father was too appalling to even wonder about.

The upstairs/downstairs division of the community across the road seemed to accord with some sort of division in my own thoughts. The upstairs crowd were concerned with school, homework, making something of oneself. In my wanderings around the grounds I would keep a wary eye out in case of an inadvertent encounter that would culminate in prolonged high moral exhortation. The worst, but to give her due, one of the nicest, was Sister Gertrude. Slight, rosy-cheeked, tall, bespectacled, and immensely serious, with closed eyes and hands folded in her spacious sleeves, she became unstoppable. On one occasion, I quietly tiptoed away and left her to it. In the meantime my father came round the corner. When she opened her eyes, she was startled to find him the puzzled recipient of her morally uplifting soliloquy. After that I was always firmly moored by a button or shirt collar resolutely grasped between finger and thumb!

The downstairs crowd better accorded with some much deeper inner level of consciousness, of intentions, personal images, and emotional intensities where I could be myself. There was always an enormous welcome in their kitchen and some such delighted cry from Sister Ethelburga as when there appeared round the corner a small curly head roughly level with the table top, accompanied by an old bag containing a couple of my father's rusty spanners; "Here's Pat, come to mend the gas stove!" My life-long fascination with the symbolism of tools still remains, as does the influence of, and my respect for, such warmly authentic manifestations of the feminine.

These loving and hard-working Irish women were always my great supporters as, for example, at the school concert, when rattling off by rote the speech from the dock by the Irish patriot Robert Emmet after he was sentenced to death, loud whispers floated up from the darkness at the back of the hall with a, "Good man, Pat." All of them were only too familiar with the attempted brutal military pacification of Ireland by the notorious Black and Tans.

On another occasion, when the boys from the junior class were not allowed to play football with the girls from a senior class in a covered playground by the river, I waited my chance and booted the ball into the river, then took off like a scalded cat through Pope's Grotto for the concealment and relative safety of Stanhope's Corner. The kitchen crowd immediately mobilized, some getting a long ladder, someone else the long handled broom for removing cobwebs from the lofty ceiling of the gymnasium. It was low water and the turn of the tide. While Sister Maurus held the ladder down the timbered frontage of the embankment, Packy successfully negotiated the ladder, retrieving the ball bobbing about just within reach of the long broom!

A new tennis court had been installed in the lower garden by the big copper beech guarding the gate leading to the upper garden. The day the workmen were painting the ironwork dark green, I found their empty tea mugs and judged them to be in a deplorable state. To cheer them all up, I painted them green! It was, of course, the downstairs crowd who provided them with new mugs and spared me their considerable wrath.

Sunday afternoons a pair of the kitchen sisters would head off with baskets of food to visit the "soldier's wives." I had no idea of what this was about, of the enormity of carnage, of the human suffering endured by armies and their dependents during and after the First World War. It was simply what the sisters did on Sunday afternoons.

My own overwhelming preoccupation was with discovering, experimenting, exploring. On occasion this could have unfortunate consequences. Thus for example, I discovered the contents of a can, deliberately put out of my reach on a shelf in Packy's tool shed in the upper garden, by tipping the contents over my head. It was creosote!

On another occasion I satisfied my curiosity as to what happened when a large cloud of flammable gas was ignited, instead of in the accustomed manner of the lighting of the gas jets and mantle in the Lodge. There had long been standing an old tin of calcium carbide in the garage, left over from the days of acetylene lamps for bicycles. It was a simple matter to empty it into an old pot, let it fizz up and bubble and then apply a match. The result was a great white flash, the loss of some hair, and the hand holding the match going numb. Perhaps it was better to stick to mantles.

While digging a hole in the garden near the chicken run, I discovered a small oval-shaped iron bottle that aroused great curiosity. Perhaps it was only an old weight from a cuckoo clock. On the other hand it had a small stopper that was firmly rusted in. I brought it along to the garage and clamped it into the vice. I was hammering the stopper with an old chisel when my father found me and became immensely upset. He ran off with my bottle through the grotto and threw it into the river. A few years later, when our instructor showed us a No. 36 Mill's Hand Grenade the outline was all too familiar. In fact, a month after the childhood incident, a short paragraph in *The Richmond and Twickenham Times* reported that the police had found a hand grenade at low water, a few hundred yards downstream from the convent. It had been taken by the military and exploded, though not, I warrant, with a hammer and chisel!

My fondest possessions were kept on a shelf in the garage. These included a small stationary steam engine with its little boiler and spirit lamp. I also had a small dynamo and an electric motor. The most treasured of the lot was a small bulbous heavy stone jar of liquid mercury. Whatever present concerns about its toxic qualities, I loved to hold a little of it, transferring it from one hand to the other. There was something profoundly moving about a metal that had the properties of a liquid. Then one day I found the jar empty and a broad path of tiny silvery particles leading from the bench to the drain. There was little doubt as to the culprit, however strenuous the denials. It served to deepen my dismay and, unfortunately, my distrust.

In 1935, there was great excitement as work commenced on the construction of a new wing to the central building of the convent, including extended sleeping quarters for the community but, most importantly of all, a beautiful lofty new chapel, with elegant rows of choir stalls facing inward from the graceful background of hardwood paneling. When the workmen left every evening I would explore their day's efforts clambering delightedly over ladder and scaffolding. The grotto now opened out onto a breezeway across which it faced the entrance to the new science laboratory.

A new dimension of life opened up when my father brought me for my first visit to the Luxor Cinema that used to stand at the corner where Cross Deep joined Twickenham High Street. I was totally mesmerized by the events unfolding on the great silver screen that concerned events in the life of someone called Tarzan. But the dangers seemed all too real and left me terrified.

Thereafter, I had a horror of jungles and their rivers, the ready immanence of impromptu death by edibility.

However, when my father asked me if I would like to see a picture about the sea, I was enthusiastic. It was a 1937 film based on Rudyard Kipling's 1897 story, *Captain Courageous*. Again, I was completely transported into another world – that of a fishing schooner on the Grand Banks of Newfoundland. I was wide-eyed with anxious anticipation when great seas poured over the vessel! I wept when the kindly Portuguese dory man who had chastised, reformed and then befriended the spoiled brat who had fallen overboard from a transatlantic liner, was fatally injured in a tangle of gear fallen from aloft, and then accepting of his own drowning.

One of the major annual events was the "School Journey." As part of the Macklin Street school curriculum, my father and some of the other teachers would take the senior form to some holiday resort for a week. One year it was the Isle of Wight, where the diminutive size of the local railway trains encouraged some of the more daring spirits to descend from the platform and wander about on the track, at least, until discouraged in no uncertain terms by my father. Another year we went to Teignmouth and one of the most memorable outings was to the beautiful Benedictine Abbey at Buckfast, where the river comes tumbling down from the moors over its rocky bed. It turned out that one of the monks was an old school friend of my father. Kitty bought me a small monstrance, of the type used to expose the Blessed Sacrament, with which I was well pleased, also some pots of honey for which the monks' apiary was widely known. The monk said that someone had broken into the shop during noonday prayer and emptied the till which seemed a crime appalling beyond belief.

Then there was the trip to Cromer, where the shingle banks and salt marshes of Norfolk come to the low cliffs and resort town on the coast of the

North Sea. The really important thing here was that I was allowed to sit in the large lifeboat as it slid down its launching ramp on a short exhibition run for the public. As a souvenir, I was given a small model lifeboat of some sort of coated cardboard construction. Now lifeboats joined lighthouses and ships near the top of my list of most favourite things.

I became the server, in my black cassock and white surplus, before the altar of the convent chapel. I enjoyed swinging the thurible! My estimate of priestly worth depended on the amount of incense that would be dropped onto the burning charcoal at the appropriate moment in the service of Benediction, designed to "honour" the Blessed Sacrament – watching us from the glittering elegance of the elaborate monstrance. "Honour" away I would, to see if I could completely enclose the proceedings in a worshipful aura of holy smoke, while the community worked its way through the decades of the rosary. For this, it was my duty to kneel on the altar steps to the right of the priest.

On one occasion, I realized to my consternation that I was kneeling on the steps behind the priest instead of on his right. The solution was simple, I could inch my way over to the proper position and nobody would notice. All went well, though the responses of the community lacked the usual vigour, until it seemed that the matter was being pretty much carried through by the Reverend Mother and the unsuspecting priest. I was surprised to learn much later that the explanation lay in the efforts of the community to stifle their mutually escalating hysterics of laughter at my innocent progress!

The motorcar and sidecar disappeared in mysterious circumstances. My father had lent it to the mechanic at Abbott's garage, a few hundred yards down the road, with its glass roof over the petrol pumps, just across the road from the imposing bulk of Radnor House with its Italianate tower. Apparently the bike had been found burnt out and abandoned. Shortly after it was replaced by an ancient Morris Oxford with its heavy semi-spherical chrome 'bullnose' radiator. Out of it stuck a little temperature indicator with its little needle mounted between the two glass faces. It was a heavy dull brown in colour and had little latches on the doors like garden gates. There was a huge knobbly rain hood and panels of leather-bound celluloid window panels that could be stuck on two little metal spikes that fitted into holes in the doors. Heavy chrome levers for adjusting the timing and the mixture were mounted in the centre of the steering wheel. My father explained all this to me, as well as occasionally letting me sit in his lap to steer the car in the driveway. He had bought the car from Father Welchman for eleven pounds.

It now became possible for an occasional family outing down to visit Kitty's twin sister Monnie – a remarkable character in her own right who was trained as a nurse at the Rotunda Hospital at the top of O'Connell Street in Dublin where they herded the prisoners from the General Post Office at the time of the Easter Rising in 1916. She had become a nurse and companion to Lord and Lady Boston who lived in their magnificent house, Monk's Hatch, at the top of an interminable, tree-lined driveway leading up to it from the Hogs Back near Guilford. The house looked out over an elegant lawn to command a beautiful vista of rolling countryside in the front, and a steeply rising timbered hillside in the back. A sweep of gravel drive led to the imposing front door with the biggest doorknob I had ever seen! I was under strict instructions to stay away from the family quarters, particularly the front lawn. Nevertheless, I set off exploring in the forbidden area and met an old man on the lawn who offered me a half-crown. I refused, because I was not supposed to take money from strangers, even, as it turned out, from a peer of the realm!

I had actually been sent to stay with Monnie at the time of the coronation in 1936. From her room with its little balcony I could see the celebratory bon-fires on distant hilltops. That night someone else celebrated in their own way by sawing off the magnificent brass knob from the front door! During my visit

I became great friends with the chauffeur and liked to help polish the beautiful big Rolls Royce parked outside the garage below his living quarters.

It must have been about the summer of 1936 when we all took off in the ancient Morris 'bullnose' on what became the greatest of my childhood adventures into an unseen and unsuspected world. We drove to the docks in Liverpool. The car was then driven onto a large cargo net, and hoisted by derrick up onto a hatch cover of one of the British and Irish passenger cargo boats. The following morning the car was unloaded at the North Wall in Dublin. After visiting with my Morris aunts in Dublin, we drove down to the little cottage that my parents had rented on a steep slope leading down to the beach and the waters of Dingle Bay in County Kerry. One Sunday, a local man, a level-crossing keeper, brought the older members of the family on a climb up a local mountain while my sister and myself were looked after by his wife. I was put on the railway track to play since there were no trains on Sunday!

The lanes with their low stone walls, the hedge rows with bright red Fuchsia blossoms, the vistas of headland and sparkling sea, all came together in some mosaic of untrammelled delight. Then there were the drives such as round the Ring of Kerry, or to Valentia where, in 1866, the eastern terminus was located for the first successfully laid Trans Atlantic telegraph cable.

I had my first experience of crime when the neat aluminum cap with its little pouring spigot, that Kitty had bought to fit the top of the glass milk bottle, was stolen while we were walking down on some broad silver strand!

On one occasion I met a blind man on a donkey who asked me if I would like a ride. Off I went, proud as Punch! Unfortunately, by the time someone found me, I was almost in the next county because he hadn't told me how to turn it around!

Most of all I loved my little secret stream that murmured quietly to itself over its rocky bed close to the cottage. It was almost completely overgrown by

While on holiday, riding through the Gap of Dunloe, County Kerry, Ireland
with my parents, my sister Kathleen and Aunt Monie, Kitty's twin sister.

bushes but these presented no problem to a 10-year-old, only sheer fascination and delight. Surely Ireland was the most marvellous place in the world. No wonder my friends, the kitchen sisters, all loved it and missed it so. I still agree with them!

Eventually it had to come to an end and we headed for Galway farther up on the west coast. We camped overnight by a deserted road. Busy with the evening meal, we heard some sounds in the darkness and two figures appeared in the light of our paraffin lantern. One was wheeling the other who had no legs using a wooden packing case fitted with two pram wheels and a pair of shafts for pushing. Of course there was food and tea to be shared and, as is the way in Ireland, we all had to find out about our respective journeys. They were returning from the Galway Races to Ennis, a walk for the man at the shafts of some fifty miles! I listened enthralled, though I never had much interest in horses.

That I had no natural talent in equestrian matters had been made clear the previous week, when I was put up on the back of a horse to ride with the rest of the family through the Gap of Dunloe. The horse stopped for a drink in a river. To the surprise of the horse, and the consternation of all, I finished up with my arms round the horse's neck and the rest of me dangling in the river. Actually, I would make one further attempt to stay up on a horse. That time I fell off at the other end! It had, of course, to happen in front of a delighted group of seminary students waiting to go into class.

We finally got back to Dublin in the early hours of the morning to dark deserted streets and the indelible image of a long facade of Georgian houses, from the lower window of one of them, incongruously surmounted by a barber's red and white striped pole, a great sheet of flame burst skyward, just as we were coming up towards it. The clattering bell of an approaching fire engine sped us on our way. I could imagine no more terrible awakening than by the sudden immediate onset of fire in the night. Well I remembered waking up to a kitchen full of smoke not that many years before.

WIMBLEDON JESUIT COLLEGE, LONDON (1936–1939)

Though my sister Kathleen could continue at the convent school, there was an age limit of ten for boys and my parents had to find an alternative school for myself. My father was a great admirer of Jesuit scholarship and it was arranged that I should attend a Jesuit College at Wimbledon, some half-hour away by train. So it was that I found myself, with no little trepidation, sitting on a bench in my new school uniform at nearby Strawberry Hill Station, waiting for the train in the care of a gentle and kindly older boy, John McShane, who was already attending the college. As a young army officer, he was later killed in action during the advance of the Allies up the Italian peninsula.

The junior school, Donhead, was agreeable enough. I liked Father Miller, the headmaster, who always had a smile for me and used to call me "Podge." Our teacher, Miss Manning, kept us all well in hand and on occasion, would call in the back-up, Mr. Farwell, who would deliver a couple of acceptable whacks from a strap. I came to regard this as an almost welcome break in a boring day!

In the senior school the tenor of events changed with a vengeance. For the first time I encountered snobbery, bullying and a rigorous code in which any admission of feeling was totally unacceptable. Emotions had to be under the rigid command of ruthless self-discipline. 'Blubbering' was beneath contempt and any complaint was out of the question for 'whining' or 'sneaking' were the most appalling crimes of all. Any perceived or imagined instances of these would lead to ostracism, broken only by communal harassment.

For each boy social status was largely determined, it seemed, by family wealth. One of the indicators of this was the sort of car that appeared when delivering someone to school. One of the prefects actually drove himself in an ancient Rolls Royce. On the odd occasion when my father gave me a lift to school in the old Morris "Bullnose," I would ask him to let me off well clear of the school gates to avoid the inevitable sneering repercussions.

The attitude that resulted involved a complete distrust of feelings, which must be rigidly disciplined. What was imperative was a stoic acceptance of situations and then simply getting on with it. All that mattered was doing one's duty. Any questions that arose in that connection could immediately be settled by recourse to the supreme authority – the nearest priest.

Religious instruction now dwelt much on sin and the agonies of hell. In that mind of childhood, these considerations became indissolubly linked with the administering of severe physical punishment for even minor offenses or errors in homework. Such was usually delivered with prolonged delays between its ordering and its imposition. The worst was Father B., and I dreaded his afternoon Latin class that resolved that year into a matrix of anticipatory fear or the realization of its object.

The ground floor windows of the gloomy classroom opened onto a covered walkway along one side of the playground. The windows on the opposite side looked down onto the rows of battered desks, while in front, stood the ominous figure in a black soutane, long flaps hanging down the back from each shoulder, pale blue eyes behind the horn rimmed glasses, set in that sallow face with its forelock of dark hair. Trying to shrink into my desk, eyes boring into an opened page of *De Bello Gallico*, I waited for that imperious snarl that would summon the next victim. Oh God! Oh God! Oh God! If someone else, there would be unmitigated relief and the hope that this would get us to the end of the class. If, instead, the snarl was "Crean!" there would be the pang of terror, a hopeless, petrified fumbling to construe some paragraph under that sardonic gaze, the inevitable dismissive snarl, "Get six!" Oh Mary, Queen of Heaven, help me!

This required going on the morning break, the following day, to a special room in the Jesuit's quarters that contained a solitary desk, a chair, and the man who would administer the ordered number of blows to the hands with the ferula. The result left them swollen and paralyzed and I would head for the cold water basins in the toilets to ease the stinging pain. If it was ordered on a Friday afternoon I had to wait until the Monday morning. I remember all too clearly sitting up in my bed at night trying not to go to sleep so it would be longer until that dreaded Monday morning. In fact, in the course of a television interview years later, one of my distinguished alumni predecessors, Alfred

Hitchcock, attributed his lifelong interest in terror and suspense to precisely these punitive practices.

I particularly resented having to spend my Wednesday and Saturday afternoons playing rugger in winter, or cricket in summer. Excelling in these pursuits could of course lead to status among the other inmates of the school. For me, however, there were infinitely better things to do in terms of discovering or exploring whether by myself or with a friend. Climbing in the mountains or sailing the sea in company of good friends was a marvellously rewarding collaborative effort. Competitive sports of any kind seemed, on the contrary, a silly waste of time and effort.

Why I should be ordered into a group trying to force some silly shaped sort of ball into some place where an opposing group didn't want it, while they were trying do the same to us, was a mystery. The whole process was carried out in equally silly distinctive underwear in winter, and often in pouring rain. Someone would run a few steps with the ball and then a heap of bodies would pile up in the mud with no better result than to get up and do it again! On one occasion, after some match, boys started throwing lumps of mud from their discarded boots in the locker room. Getting a large lump in the face, I was returning the compliment when, caught by the unexpected appearance of our form master, I was singled out for punishment. I had to first take a bus and then change to a second bus and then walk up Edgehill Road to the College and report for punishment – at which time I was duly beaten by the headmaster. Then I had to take another bus to Raynes Park Station and then the train home. When I finally arrived, my parents were frantic with worry as to what had happened to me.

Cricket was a similar abomination except less chilly. I managed a degree of ineptitude and boredom that meant that I was put in a position in the field where the ball was least likely to arrive. This worked well except when, through an oversight, I had been assigned close to the scene of action, the so-called slips. Lapsing into my accustomed reverie, a hard fast-moving ball landed squarely between my eyes in a welter of stars and blood and tears. However, for a little while, I was thought to be some sort of hero.

The record of events that becomes uniquely oneself is intensely and enduringly affected by the day-to-day feeling-ladeness of circumstances in which they are experienced. For myself, it would take decades to exorcise an unconscious, and consequently, an irrational and uncritical respect for ecclesiastical authority. The suppressed need to resolve the surd of a religion grounded in love, enforced by the ferula, and the most terrible conception that can be put into the mind of a child – an unendurable agony that never ever ends. Between my first hospital experience and Father B.'s Latin classes, there was little left for the imagination to make a start on the nature of eternal hell fire. There is an ineradicable trace imposed by such powerful childhood experiences. In fact, when attending lunch at the cafeteria in a Jesuit College in Dublin some fifty years later, the sight of the familiar black soutane with its long black shoulder flaps immediately evoked a spontaneous image of the refectory in Wimbledon and sharp pangs of fear.

In the last school year before the war, the annual play selected for performance by the sixth form was *Journey's End* by R. C. Sherriff, based on his letter's home from the front during World War One. The latter was ever-present, for as we filed into and out of the college chapel, we passed the long list of names incised into the oak panel memorial to old boys whose short lives had so prematurely ended in the horrors of Flanders or the Somme. In the play the young schoolboy officer has wangled a posting to the company commanded by his earlier cricketing hero. Only then does he learn that after two years of trench warfare, the only way the latter can keep his feelings in check is through the daily consumption of inordinate amounts of whisky. But then the young officer gets a bit of a "knock in the back" and is carried down into the dugout where, unaware that his spine has been severed by shrapnel, the last words to his old friend are, "Could we have a light? It's so frightfully cold and dark!" That summed up for me my life at the Sacred Heart College, Wimbledon, of being helplessly caught up into some vast merciless process that left me helpless and hopeless.

Matters seemed to come to some sort of dreadful focus when, one morning waiting for the train to school on the platform of Twickenham Station, I watched the crowd on the other platform across the tracks, bound for the day's work in the city. They were young and old, with newspapers and brief cases and umbrellas, pale impassive faces, freshly washed and now presentable on that grey morning. From behind my back came the inexorable, powerful whine through the open doors of the converter plant that, so I had been told, provided electrical energy in a form suitable for the trains. A distant sound down the track grew swiftly into the approaching train, another face briefly glimpsed at the driver's window as it slid to a noisy halt to stand with its clattering compressors and banging doors, the fast train up to town, non-stop from Richmond to Waterloo. It all formed some seminal moment of childhood memory. There was a clatter of banging doors and throbbing air compressors, a whistle and the rising tone of drive motors, a form swiftly diminishing down the track, and then an empty platform.

It seemed that I was looking at an overall vignette of human life, some phased presentation of my own life indeed, the inexorable pacing of an uninspiring routine until age, infirmity and death intervened. Presumably at innumerable stations around the greater London area I would find essentially similar groups. Yet, there I was in my little school uniform, leather satchel with a few battered books and ink-stained copy books, headed for school as the first stage of entrapment in some such circumstances that I could no more control than the flow of energy from the converter station, of entry into a world in which I had to live, to survive, to find some sense of meaning, if such a thing could ever exist.

Our pasts make us what we are, and so there was set in place for me a deeply rooted fear of authority, ecclesiastical and otherwise. Later there would occur a whimsical association with that catchy verse of W. S. Gilbert:

> *Stick close to your desks, and never go to sea,*
> *And you all may be Rulers of the Queen's Navee!*

In practical terms, the solution was simple enough. Check any proposed course of action first for clerical approval. It would eventually become a recipe for a slow descent into the realm of incipient neurosis. Security is wedded to mediocrity. That is not what is required of us by the evolutionary universe which has given rise to intelligent life, us!

My parent's expensive and well-intended effort to instil in me the life-enriching rudiments of a classical education left me totally baffled as to what possible relevance works by Caesar and Virgil had to the modern world I had to live in. What really mattered was the realm of engineering and science – that which could be based on the experimentally verifiable and prove to be useful.

Religious instruction dwelt interminably on the unlimited spectrum of human aberration from minor venial sins to a range of unspeakably horrible mortal sins. Great emphasis was placed on unspeakable pain that never ever ended. Pain I knew about, like the pain of having my tonsils out, coming out of the ether, vomiting, and the raw pain of the site from which they had been cut; picking up the wrong end of the poker just removed from the fire; the red swollen palms and fingers left by the ferula. In case there was any doubt about eternity, some such illustration would be provided such as imagining a cube of granite a mile high, and a little bird wiping its beak on the granite every day for a million years. The punch line being that by the time the granite was worn away to nothing, eternity would not have even started. Some mortal sins, which all merited eternal damnation such as, for example, missing Mass on Sunday, could be carefully complied with. There was, however, a much more dangerously elusive source of flouting the divine plan in the pubescent offing.

It seemed that such a state of mortal sin could easily come about in connection with something so terrible as to be unmentionable – this I later discovered to be called sex. This was a great mystery, but the only remedy, in case of error of thought or feeling in this connection, seemed to be to confess to a priest and obtain absolution as quickly as possible in case I inadvertently died. The meaning of the word would eventually be revealed on my pressing a school friend for an explanation of a large scrawl of obscenity and profanity, written in huge whitewashed letters, on a back fence overlooked by the railway line that brought us to school. When, much embarrassed, he finally obliged me, I howled with laughter at anything so absurd! It eventually transpired that something of that nature was the case yet was apparently so disgusting that it could never be referred to in respectable company. The net result was a morbid scrupulosity tantalizingly allied with complete biological and psychological mystification with respect to the opposite sex!

My own little perception of the cosmos, of the real world, included a major contradiction, a self-proclaimed authoritative institution of highest sanctity and learning that could produce at one extreme the unstinting love and generosity of my old friends the downstairs sisters in Twickenham, and, at the other, the fear inspired by Father B., and the man at the desk in that bare room who wielded the ferula.

That old Twickenham Southern Railway Station and its converter plant have long since gone and been replaced. But the question would remain and bring about consequences that were at the heart of living – the discovery of the meaning of meaning, a journey that does not end with the dissolution of one's biological self, a journey far beyond my wildest imaginings.

Another gloomy foreboding was the role of family life when one became grown up. This seemed to be what those who had not been called to the much higher vocation of religious life did. The break in the year-long subjection to the local railway timetable was the summer holiday by the seaside. This seemed to me to be characterized in terms of the remembered image of a large fat man towing a string of bawling children, strung out hand in hand, through the tawdry blandishments of some amusement arcade on the sea front. Was that what life was really about? What was the meaning of it all? Did it have any meaning, something that could be grasped and give some point to it, some direction? It seemed that one had something called an "immortal soul," but how did it work?

I was told that something called "heaven" would constitute the reward after one's death if one made a superhuman effort to "love" everybody, including Father B. If the highest vocation was the priesthood, I was clearly not up to it. Somehow I had to escape to something that really fascinated me and carried, as far as I was aware, no immediate threat of eternal divine retribution. There was no doubt as to its nature. I truly loved the sea, the ships that sailed upon it, and the steam engines that powered them – not a mortal sin in sight!

Such influences had come about through my father bringing me to visit my Uncle Edmund's ship in Liverpool Docks as a rather frightened little boy. Steel ladders and gratings are designed for adults! When my uncle opened the throttle valve to turn the engine over, exquisite obedience, the silent rhythmic dance of such an interconnected complexity of shining steel parts, in perfect unity and harmony, left an indelible impression of how things ought to be. Here was a meaning worthy of one's best efforts to understand. I had found my dream.

Sometimes from the ciphered testament of thought and feeling, an event will evoke an affective response of far-reaching personal significance. If I always had an immense curiosity as to how things worked, such an event was that visit to the engine room of my uncle's ship, bringing to the fore, as it did, a life-long fascination with things of the sea, with heat engines, the mechanical, the technical, the scientific. These would become empowering and directing symbols that, as they transformed to incite to further and higher levels of meaning, still endure into an authentic and formal role in the great spiritual adventure of human life.

This was the dream that was further augmented by my father bringing me on my first visit to the Science Museum in South Kensington. It has always remained for me a place of high pilgrimage. A recent television program on the cosmos brought into a single, magnificent perspective, Fermilab's lofty structure and the extraordinary technical achievement of its huge underground circular particle accelerator, together with the choir stalls of Beauvais Cathedral. It would be many decades before I could enjoy such a spontaneity of intense feeling response as two sides of the same coin in which are invested the ongoing progression of a truly human destiny.

It was a major frustration that there was no opportunity for classes in science because of wartime teaching shortages. I had to content myself with such books as I could find such as Professor E.N. da C. Andrade's book on engines. A prize possession was a tradesman's book on steam fitting. This one really was for adults!

Shortly before the war, my father brought me to visit Cammell Laird Shipyard at Birkenhead across the Mersey from the immense extent of Liverpool Docks. Here I saw two ill-fated ships under construction, the *H.M.S. Ark Royal*, and a submarine up on the stocks that would be called *H.M.S. Thetis*. The former would succumb to enemy torpedoes, and the latter would founder on diving trials in Liverpool Bay. Apparently someone checked the drain cock on a torpedo tube and when no water came out, assumed the bow door was closed and opened the inner door, flooding the boat and causing it to dive bow first to the bottom. The stern, with its propellers, remained sticking out above the surface but some eighty crew and shipyard workers were drowned.

Still, in that mind of boyhood, great engineering works became for me something of the nature of shrines of human endeavour much to be reverenced. Such symbols transform and trans-value over life, as indeed they should. The same wonder now remains, if not much enhanced, by the outline of a giant radio telescope reaching out to the furthermost depths of the universe. Now I also can well imagine the pressures and demands on those in the control room, the pressures and demands of funding and research grants, the anxieties of advancing a career among the stiffest of competition.

Somehow I had to escape to a much greater world that stretched infinitely beyond the familiar confines of Twickenham. Sometimes, when the great winds from the Atlantic were exploring every exposed nook and cranny of our streets, the scudding clouds speeding just above the rooflines, snatching smoke from the chimney pots, there was a great surge of longing to set forth upon the sea to uncover new horizons, to embarque upon a journey into meaning that would only emerge into a coherent perspective of meaning in some fullness of time. Meaning is what we have made in our heads of something that wasn't there in the beginning, but has come about as some unity at the end.

Then the impossible happened. Just as term was about to commence, I was told that I would not be going back. I could not credit my good fortune! It was the 1st September 1939. I can heartily identify with the prayer of thanksgiving shouted out by the schoolboy being driven to school by his grandfather in the movie *Hope and Glory*, only to find it had been bombed out during the previous night: "Oh, thank you, Adolf!"

So little can great events cast their shadow in the minds of the young, though actually I had experienced one moment of apprehension. I had been to the cinema and the news reel had included some pictures of fighting in China. It included an unforgettable graphic shot of a soldier lying behind the turret on the top of a tank, look round to see where his foot had just been just blown off. Walking home through the darkened streets to the Lodge, a poster on a Pillar Post Box showed a German bomber swooping down over a burning city and urged people to volunteer for duty during air raid warnings. Perhaps such a thing was possible. Could it happen to staid, solid Twickenham? Of course not!!!

From early on, I was quite fascinated by dreams. My father was fond of recalling an occasion when he came into my bedroom to wake me up and my response was, "Daddy, I saw pictures on my pillow!" It seemed extraordinary that the same "me" that loved my egg-in-a-cup with bits of bread and butter, that loved to play in the garden or lie in Stanhope's Corner looking up through the summer foliage in wonder at the endless blue sky above, that same "me" could also experience such exotic adventures while still in bed!

Such nightly imaginings had no place, however, in my formal religious education. In fact it seemed that feelings had to be ruthlessly subjected to the clear light of reason. It would be decades before I was able to grasp the important role of dreams as a "gauge" of conscious attitude as reasonable or unreasonable in the very personal and unique journey into the realm of my life's meaning. There remains much mystery about the realm of dreams, the way in which one psychic content gives rise to another, in affording glimpses of the fundamental dynamics of consciousness in process when the directing concerns of waking moments are replaced by some sort of complete spontaneity. Eventually, they would prove the key to a transforming of attitude that led from an encroaching darkness into the glorious light of what, for something better, we call the real world.

CHAPTER III

WAR YEARS

SCHOOL DAYS, BERKSHIRE & WILTSHIRE (1939–1943)

There would be one last visit to the College in order to be issued with a cardboard box that could be hung over one's shoulder on a piece of string and which contained a gas mask. Trying it on, it smelt rubbery and had a little window that soon became opaque with condensed vapour. On the other hand, we soon found out that if you blew hard enough the resultant noise had a hilarious similarity to sounds not usually associated with the upper part of the torso!

We were told to appear, with one suitcase each, at Paddington Station for evacuation, in company with my father's school, to some unknown location. All of us children had firmly affixed a large brown identifying label and our now inevitable companion, the gas mask. We boarded the train and, as it headed off for the West Country, every time it stopped, we waited anxiously to hear if this was going to be our new location.

Actually it turned out to be Newbury in Berkshire where we were all transferred to a large red brick school building and distributed among the class-rooms. The windows were all painted black and there was tea and corned beef sandwiches while volunteer drivers delivered the evacuees to their billets. As the headmaster's family, we were the last and found ourselves delivered to the pleasant bungalow of a Mrs. Wills who made us welcome despite such a massive intrusion of strangers into her little home. I was delighted with the garden which ended on the edge of a shallow railway cutting where I could watch the frequent passage of the great steam locomotives with their strings of passenger coaches or goods wagons.

A few weeks later the school was moved to Hungerford, several miles further to the west. My parents found a gamekeeper's cottage with a hand-pump in the yard for water, candles for lighting except for the pressurized oil lamp that hissed away on the table in the living room. It stood at the end of a long driveway lined on either side by tall trees, which led up from the little country road running up the hillside through ploughed fields to some big country house hidden in trees on the low ridge. Immediately opposite was the entrance, with its tall pillars and ornamental ironwork which led to another big house called Inglewood. The house itself was a little distance in through tall trees and fronted by a broad sweep of gravel drive. The house had become a training college for the Catholic teaching order of the De La Salle Brothers in their black soutanes and little white bibs.

For the first few months of the war, in view of the circumstances, I was allowed to attend their classes. Here there was no physical punishment and, in blithe disregard for such frivolities as homework, I indulged to the full my passion for exploring the local countryside. Again I found myself with the run of a magnificent estate with its beautiful gardens and woods, outbuildings, huge walled Victorian kitchen garden with its many plots, tasteful walkways and greenhouses. It had its own power plant with a large oil engine that drove a large dynamo with a large belt. In the woods on the hill above was a large concrete swimming pool, actually used to provide a water reservoir in case of fire. Again, I found my own level with the "downstairs" crowd, particularly Brother Herman, who worked the kitchen garden. Every now and then, Kitty would send me over with a carton of cigarettes.

The army had taken over the driveway, and the porch of our cottage became a sentry post to guard the long column of army lorries now parked underneath the trees of the driveway. That first winter of the war was one of the coldest on record and my father fitted up a partial shelter with a ground sheet to give some protection from the wind for the sentry in the porch. Kitty was in and out at all hours with mugs of hot sweet tea. One morning however, the sentry was found unconscious, they said from undernourishment and cold, and he was brought away in an army ambulance.

Further down the road from the cottage at the far end of the Inglewood estate lived Father Casey. His housekeeper, Miss Hall, would sometimes come to visit Kitty and the two of them would enjoy a game of cards. One night Kitty asked me to walk her home. The trees were heavy with a massive coating of ice from freezing rain. I was extremely nervous on the way down past the long wall of the estate with its dark threatening backdrop of tall woods. I had been reading Conan Doyle's *Hound of the Baskervilles* and my fertile imagination had no difficulty in conjuring up the violent appearance of the great luminous homicidal hound out of the darkness over the wall. I happened to be looking up at the immense ice-thickened branch of a great elm tree overhanging the road when there was an ear-splitting report like the discharge of a cannon and it started to come down on me. Terrified, I took to my heels for the cottage while in the dark behind me there was a tremendous crashing, cracking and splintering. My parents had difficulty finding out what had happened to me, but then my father went out and found the road completely blocked!

My father, Patrick Joseph Crean, in a picture taken in 1944 by his good friend Father Rees, while walking on Inkpen Beacon.

Rural life continued its agreeable tenor with little indication of the mighty events impending. One afternoon, however, I saw a convoy of army lorries winding up the road past the cottage with the dirtiest lot of soldiers I had ever seen. In fact, the army didn't know what to do with them and that night we had two sleeping in the living room and two in a tent in the garden. One of them gave me a pocketknife and said they had come from some place called Dunkirk. The two in the garden seemed to like it there and first thing every morning I would rush over to the window and make sure that the large stocking'd feet of my new friend were sticking out from the end of the tent.

In addition to his work for school, my father had become a civil defence

My sister Kathleen and myself, with our bicycles, in front of the cottage. In 1939 we were evacuated from Pope's Lodge in Twickenham to a gamekeeper's cottage on an estate near Kintbury in Berkshire where we lived until 1941. For part of this time I attended the Presentation Brothers' Training College across the road at Inglewood House.

training officer for the county of Berkshire. I remember him by the oil lamp alternating his preparations for lectures on incendiary bombs, mustard gas and the like, with work on a project he had been asked to undertake and which he much preferred. *A Short Life of Our Lord* was first published in 1945, a scripture textbook for use in schools, and which subsequently ran to many editions.

My love for exploring extended to some of the neighbouring great estates despite dogs and gamekeepers. For most of my childhood I had scrupulously bowed to the menace in such signs as, "Trespassers will be prosecuted," due to my having confused the meaning of the word "prosecuted" with that of "executed."

Once I realized that such activity did not constitute a capital offence, provided no damage of any kind was done, the challenge was irresistible.

On one occasion my friend Kevin Jeremy and myself had spent an idyllic summer afternoon wading in the highly exclusive trout streams and wandering through the exquisite parkland of one such estate. We had just returned to the public road when I saw an old lady approaching the gate. I opened the gate for her and she thanked me and smiled saying, "You may walk through my land, if you wish." It was Lady Wills herself of a vast tobacco fortune!

For my 14th birthday, my father brought me into Hungerford for the most exciting present I could have conceived of – a beautiful new B.S.A. bicycle! Now I could explore some of the most beautiful and interesting parts of rural England, from Old Sarum to Avebury, or Salisbury Cathedral to Inkpen Beacon and Coombe Gibbet. I loved the little parish churches with such records of history going back over many hundreds of years.

Not far from the cottage was the River Kennet. At one location there was an area that was popularly used for swimming. One day I met two other boys there who were wearing scout uniforms. They told me that they belonged to the Shalbourne Scout Troop, the village at the foot of the downs near the Salisbury Road, a few miles south of Hungerford.

I cycled over and went up to the great oak door of the old manor house and pulled the long wrought iron handled bell pull. A lady answered the door and I said: "Please, Miss, I want to be a boy scout." She brought me in through the spacious main hall, with its large staircase and stately grandfather clock, down a short corridor with mullioned windows looking out to a walled garden on one side, with ancient age-blackened rough oak timbers and panelling on the other. She talked to me about scouting and gave me a form to be filled in including my parent's permission. Little did I realize that it was the start of a treasured friendship that would endure over some five-and-a-half decades.

Shalbourne Manor rose garden near the village centre of Shalbourne. Marguerite de Beaumont gave a home to many evacuees from London during the blitz of World War II and ran her scout troop from a loft over the manor's garage. Throughout the many years of our friendship I received warm welcomes to her hearth and home.

The old manor house in which she lived had stood for some five centuries, sheltered within a fold of the downs. The extensive stables were managed by Marguerite de Beaumont, a distinguished breeder of prize-winning horses, while her friend and companion, Doris Mason, ran the farm. The dining room of the manor was turned into an emergency surgery that they equipped at their own expense to help treat any wartime casualties in the village.

The house became home for a group of a dozen evacuees from the tough East End dock area of London. Their hosts took no nonsense and the children worshipped them. The worst of them, under their remarkable care, would subsequently become a senior Detective Inspector in Scotland Yard!

Marguerite de Beaumont and Doris Mason in a meadow,
Shalbourne Manor, with some of their beloved animals.

According to a family biography, Marguerite was descended from an illustrious French family whose origins could be traced back over a millennium. Her father was a medical doctor who had also served with distinction in the Franco-Prussian war of 1870. Subsequently, he followed his fascination with theology, philosophy and biology and entered the Jesuit Order. He was involved with the setting up of the Royal University in Dublin where he became associated with the distinguished Catholic family of Lord O'Hagan, Lord Lieutenant of Ireland, the daughter of whom was charmed by this brilliant young French scholar.

It transpired from the confession of a dying nursemaid, who had been entrusted with Marguerite's father's baptism as a baby due to his mother's illness and his father's absence on military duty, that she had failed to have the baptism performed. He informed his superiors at the Jesuit House on Farm Street in London and that, in consequence, this invalidated all the subsequent sacraments, including his ordination. Despite their readiness to baptize him on the spot, he left the order. He married Kathleen O'Hagan, who so admired "his constant and uninterrupted religious quest and devotion wherein intellectual achievement was subordinate to spiritual insight and inspiration," that the baptism had not been performed.

In 1909, Marguerite, her sister and her mother turned up at the Crystal Palace Scout Jamboree in London in their own home-made scout uniforms. Sir Robert Baden-Powell wanted to know who they were and welcomed them to join in. Subsequently they would influence the founding of the Girl Guide movement by Lady Baden-Powell.

Marguerite de Beaumont ran the scout troop in the large loft over the garage. Our Wednesday night troop meetings would always finish with a "yarn," some sort of story with a moral. The emphasis was on positive things involving notions of honour, duty, courage, loyalty, respect for others, which seemed so much more worthwhile than that interminable preoccupation with sin which seemed to lie at the heart of my more accustomed catechetical instruction. The scouts were officially designated as messengers for the Home Guard and I was enormously proud of the bright red badge on my khaki scout shirt with an inscribed crown and letters N.S. for national service in simulated gold thread – a shirt, the cloth faded and somewhat stiff with the years, hanging yet in my closet.

During the summer holidays, I would work with the summer harvest on the farm. Our first job was to stack the sheaves into stooks as the tractor drawn reaper and binder circled the field leaving an ever-diminishing enclosure of crop at the centre. Shotguns would appear to try for a rabbit or two in order to augment the meagre wartime meat rations. The sheaves would later be pitch-forked up onto a big trailer and then loaded onto a conveyor to be stacked into ricks. At midday, in the shade of a hedgerow, I would eat Kitty's sandwiches, washed down with lemonade, and listen in fascination as Alf and Ernie reminisced about the First World War battles of Ypres or Gallipoli. In mid-afternoon when there would come the welcome sight of two horses with panniers carrying loads of jam sandwiches and flasks of hot sweet milky tea, I felt very much a part of a vast and meaningful endeavour, something that made life enormously worthwhile, something we were all in together.

Thus it was that Marguerite de Beaumont became one of the most powerful and enduring influences from those early years of the war. Her patience and affection elicited a trust and response from the horses that was remarkable to watch. Perhaps I should let her speak for herself through quoting a passage from the Introduction in one of her books, *The Way Of A Horse*, published in 1953: "In introducing this book to my readers I hope they will get a picture such as meets the eye when one enters a field where mares and foals are grazing. There is an atmosphere of peace and contentment that is what I hope to convey in these pages. The spirit of horsemanship throughout the ages has been an inspiration to many, and although it is something quite intangible it has a great influence on all those who deal with horses even to the present day. It was the thought of the spirit of horsemanship that made me decide to write this book – the idea of handing on this tradition appeals to me very much. I have had much to do with young people and young horses, both are very similar and in many ways it is necessary to approach them in the same manner."

She had an extraordinary depth of insight into human nature and certainly knew more about me than I have ever known myself. It can't all have been bad for Shalbourne Manor, with its leaded windows in wrought iron frames, looking out over yew hedges, lawns and rose beds. It would become a home away from home for me, and would stand as some enduring place of psychic refuge, some source of inspiration as to what could be. It remains most vividly personified for me in those moments of some communion, deeper than any discourse, when I, absorbed in the flickers of flame among the logs on that great Tudor hearth, the dogs stretched in sleep before it at the end of the day, would sense her eyes upon me – and she would speak to me of my thoughts. I have always associated that sensitivity of feeling, and acuity of perception, with a particularly feminine excellence.

On one of those evenings she told me that I was a mystic, one who yearns for some sort of unity with an ultimate reality. At the time I supposed it involved withdrawal into a life of stringent asceticism and prayer, setting forth upon the classic way of the purgative, the illuminative, the unitive. Nothing could have been further from my natural inclinations, involving steam engines and sailing the sea and the like. Yet there are a myriad ways in which the exigencies of life can impose its mandate of an inevitable sequence imposed upon our living and dying – as I would indeed find out for myself!

There were occasional intense fleeting vignettes of the war. Once while standing beside the old disused well outside the kitchen of the manor house, a low flying German bomber sped into view and I could see the sequence of black dots as the bombs were jettisoned to land on the other side of the ridge across from the house that carried the Salisbury road. One lad in the scout troop, an irrepressible Cockney from London, had the corner blown off his bedroom, though apparently it didn't disturb his slumbers. He became the hero of the troop with his: "When I woke up I could see the sky!" He had a large jagged shard of bomb casing that he later discovered in his bedclothes.

The most exciting occasion of all was when Marguerite's nephew, also one of her scouts, Robin de Beaumont, and myself brought a group of cub scouts on a hike up over the high ridge of Rivar Down with its wonderful view of distant rolling farmlands out over, and beyond, the village. There was a sudden tremendous roar of engines and we found ourselves looking down on the great harsh outline of a German bomber with its black crosses and swastikas. It lifted up just over our heads and for an unforgettable fleeting instant, I looked at a face framed in a dark flying helmet between the barrels of twin machine guns. The reason for his extreme low level path appeared almost immediately and we cheered frantically as a solitary pursuing Spitfire flashed into view. The bomber was shot down a few miles further on and the following day I went off to find the smouldering wreckage. A policeman was stopping people going through the gate into the field where the plane had crashed. On either side of the gate, however, sightseers poured through the gaps in the hedge. It was said that someone found a hand and that the watch on the wrist was still going. I delightedly made my way home with a part of the airframe as a souvenir to add to my growing collection of shrapnel.

Another occasion would teach me a very different lesson. Not far from the cottage, the main railway line from London to the west of England crossed the Kennet and Avon Canal by a long bridge occasioned by the very shallow angle of its crossing. One bright moonlight night we were startled by the sound of low-flying engines and the unmistakable scream of falling bombs followed by their explosions. Apparently the pilot had been aiming for the bridge but the bombs had fallen short near some farm buildings. One of them had landed close to a stable made of timber built on low brick foundation walls. There were a few signs of splintering but otherwise the building appeared undamaged. Inside there was a very different story. One horse had apparently thrown its head up and the full length of its throat had been ripped open by shrapnel. Everywhere there was a hideous carnage of blood and gore. The terrible reality of war left no room for simplistic illusions.

By a curious chance another of the bombs had landed in the soft earth of a cabbage patch and exploded deep underground. The net effect was to leave a large hump in the ground still with its ordered and appropriately angled cabbage stalks. I walked up on the hump but was later chagrined to learn that in exactly similar circumstances, the hump had collapsed and the unfortunate sightseer had been instantly suffocated in the residual gases of the explosion below.

Not surprisingly, the days of my rural retreat and country rambles would come to an end, and I was sent to a boarding school run by the Presentation Brothers in Reading. I was reluctant to give up my intoxicating freedom and used to refer to the school as the "concentration camp!" Kathleen was sent to a convent boarding school in Abingdon but apparently, after two weeks of inconsolable grief, was retrieved by Kitty and enrolled in a nearby day school.

In spite of my initial objections, Presentation College was a very different proposition from my earlier Jesuit College experiences. There was none of the snobbery or bullying. Most important of all, there was none of the sadistic practices of ordering and administering corporal punishment!

Instead, the Brothers usually carried a strip of coiled rubber that, on relatively rare occasions, could be expertly unpocketed to administer retributive justice on the spot. For myself, such discipline met a need and I am grateful to those who plied their calling to such effect that I would gain sufficient honours in the Oxford School Certificate Examinations to qualify for admission to university.

What had once been a large residence provided the living quarters for the Brothers and about twenty boarders. The two upper floors provided dormitories for these students and housed the school chapel where night prayer would involve recitation of the rosary, paced by the deep sonorous booming voice of kindly Brother Jerome. The staff shortages of the war years led to our involvement in varied domestic tasks such as washing dishes, cleaning and polishing, for which we received a modest remuneration of pocket money.

The winter of 1940 saw the mounting fury of the blitz. One night the Brothers brought us up onto the roof of the school, where we could see the flash of shell bursts and roving beams of searchlights to the east over London, to the north over Birmingham, to the west over Bath and Bristol, to the south over Portsmouth and Southampton. One of the most tiresome facets of these months was the middle-of-the-night scramble to pick up our mattresses and bedding and bringing the lot to the central hallway on the ground floor by the refectory. However, instead of leaving us to sleep out the rest of the night in peace, when the "all clear" sounded, we had to cart our bedding back upstairs and remake our beds!

Reading itself escaped lightly from the bombing. It was said that the mists of the Thames River Valley provided some measure of concealment. There was however the terrible incident of the "People's Pantry," one of the wartime restaurants set up by the authorities to provide a simple menu of inexpensive fare.

That Wednesday afternoon I had obtained permission to go to the cinema with one of the other boarders. As we headed down the driveway, someone ran after us and said that I was required for a football match scheduled with the local Bluecoat School in our playing field. Football, though less disgusting and boring than rugby, was certainly not on my list of preferred activities. However, I was the only one of adequate size to fill in. I performed as usual, running up and down the field after the action but far enough away to make any involvement in it fairly unlikely!

Suddenly at the end of the match, there were loud shouts from the Brothers to get under the trees as a German plane banked sharply over the field and headed towards the town. Rumours started flying but it eventually emerged that the plane had dropped three bombs. One had landed in Wellsteeds Department Store which was fortunately shut on Wednesday afternoon. The crowd had come out from the cinema we had planned to attend. Many had made for the People's Pantry across the street, as we invariably did as a relief from school food. One bomb landed beside the queue that had formed outside, the other behind the serving counter at the back of the building. One hundred and twenty people were killed and many more injured.

On one occasion the senior form was called out to harvest a large field of mangolds used for cattle food, which would otherwise rot in the ground because of the shortage of agricultural labour.

Because of our 'domestic' chores, the religion classes that were meant to begin each day were sacrificed to 'household' orderliness. In retrospect, I think this was no great loss! The years would continue to reveal that rigid fundamentalism of what was described at the Second Vatican Council as clericalism, juridicism and triumphalism. Nonetheless, the institutional church has thus far retained its bureaucratic supremacy to foster career oriented ambition through cooption and manipulation of the gullible by a Christianity in the guise of myth rather than in terms of its immense depth of true meaning and evolutionary purpose, ranking it high among the authentic spirituality at the core of all the great world religions.

For the present however, even without the religion classes, I was left with a rigid fundamentalism. Thus, for example, if I did not enter religious life I would have to be content with some mundane alternative. Miss mass on Sunday or commit rape and murder, and, if a priest couldn't be found in time, that was it forever! If St. Paul said, "better to marry than to burn," the morbid scrupulosity that resulted was firmly based on the inevitable prospect of an eternity of incineration. I knew what this meant because I had once picked up a poker, just removed by Kitty from the fire, by the wrong end! With respect to the assertions of God's alleged love for us, I would be ill advised to hold my breath in anticipation. I had only to recall the merciless enforcement of learning by His devout servant, Fr. B., in his Latin classes – that terrible year of what amounted to sustained, ongoing terror.

On the other hand, the parents of Kevin Jeremy, a friend who was one of the day boys, were very kind to me, and our rambles together would usually finish up with a very welcome tea before returning to the spartan commons of a boarder. There were many fascinating places to visit that provided symbolic evidence of the past. One such was Medmenham Hall beside the Thames, once the home of Sir Francis Dashwood and his notorious Hell Fire Club much patronized by the young rakes of London in the 18th century. The motto above the door remained, translatable, if memory serves me well, as "all things for evil." Further up the river at Mapledurham was a church, two thirds of which remained in Protestant use while one third remained, because of some old legal provision, Roman Catholic. The two Christian denominations were separated by only an ancient high barred railing, its flagstones bare and empty save for the thick dust.

Our family eventually moved from the gamekeeper's cottage into Hungerford and we could revel in such luxuries as electric light and indoor plumbing. In December 1941, the Americans entered into the war in Europe. With appearance of their forces there would be much uncertainty, when cycling, as to which side of the road would be safest when being approached by a large U.S. army vehicle. I saw my first American soldier sitting by himself at the front of the upper deck of the bus that ran along the Bath Road from Reading to Newbury. He had a guitar and was singing softly to himself: "You are my sunshine." Two large American paratroopers used to attend our little church in Hungerford and my parents would always bring them home for whatever we could muster in the line of breakfast. Then suddenly they stopped coming and it was rumoured that they had been flown straight to North Africa and dropped into action.

Life at school could be rendered tolerable by counting the days to the end of the term and the wonderful freedoms of the holidays, or working with the harvest at Shalbourne. My courses were the bare minimum for school leaving examinations, arithmetic, algebra, geometry, geography, English, French and history. My favourite was geography taught by Brother Canice. He had completed a degree in science and fired my imagination about university courses of practical experiments that would be so much more fun than just books. English I usually did well at, though English literature had little attraction. The only phrase that ever really made a deep impression came from Shakespeare's *Tempest*, written towards the end of his life, in which he proclaimed:

> *We are such stuff as dreams are made on,*
> *and our little life is rounded with a sleep.*

I didn't think about it much, but I was vaguely aware that sometime, in the far distant future, we all have to die and the place of my "pillow pictures" seemed a good place to finish up!

In the summer of 1943, I sat the Oxford School Leaving Certificate examinations at the University of Reading. The preparations were intensive on the part of our teachers and one of my clearest recollections is that of Brother Benedict marching up and down the tennis court with the lawn-mower, myself in the summer house with my books, and with every passage of the mower another question on Euclidean Geometry. Looking back over the years, it is salutary to remember those who worked so hard to further the education of the likes of myself who little appreciated the future significance to themselves, of their efforts. Brother Canice remains for me a remarkable instance of true religious dedication, of responsibility and compassion. Later he would be transferred to a college in the West Indies, also run by the Presentation Brothers. For his courage and leadership on an occasion of a major fire, he would be awarded a distinguished state decoration in London. Sadly, still as a very young man, he would succumb to a brain tumour in a Texas Hospital.

The reference letter given me by my headmaster affords a glimpse of myself as another saw me then, something that one cannot see for oneself at the time. It contains the following: "Results since to hand (from the Examinations referred to above) show that he has passed very creditably and taken his Matriculation as well. He is a lad of irreproachable character, painstaking and enterprising with a special flair for things mechanical and scientific. I might add that he is well above the average in ability." Certainly the latter statement, in my own estimation, must have strained the generosity of the writer. Surely my perpetual inundation by unanswered questions could only signify an exceptional level of ingrained stupidity!

It would be decades before I linked the attributes of moral character and intelligence to a prediction by my mother's sister, Aunt Rosalie, who was a superior of a convent that operated a large laundry. To the best of my recollection, girls who had got into trouble with the authorities in Liverpool were assigned to work in the laundry. Her expressed opinion that, "Pat would find life difficult," would reflect a prescience. Gentle, kindly Rosalie knew far more about human nature than I could even dream existed!

So it was that I set forth into the great secular world firmly equipped with the formal indoctrination of institutional Roman Catholicism of that day. I had a sort of "hand-me-down Decalogue" which provided the basic working model for dealing with life. The first four commandments, which had to do with God, were taken care of by the church: mass on Sundays and holy days of obligation, no meat on Friday, or any other fast days, confession once a year, and reception of communion about Easter time. The other six amounted to being faithful to parental tradition and avoiding murder, fornication, theft, lying, and greed. The source of all ultimate power descended from the Pope through the bishops and priests and the prescriptions of canon law enforced by penalties. The most terrible of these was an eternity of unspeakable suffering that never, never ended. The church was in constant battle with Satan and the powers of evil; the great majority of mankind would be eternally damned for not being Catholic; issues of any nature, about which I had doubts, could be resolved by my parish priest. By and large then, the only people I could unreservedly trust were fellow Catholics. There were, of course, lots of questions, but these would have been regarded as a deficiency in faith, whatever that might be!

KING'S COLLEGE STUDENT/MARINE
ENGINEERING APPRENTICE, LONDON (1943–1944)

My big chance would come in the third year of the war when I became an engineering student at King's College in the University of London, located on the Strand and overlooking a broad sweep of the Thames. For that winter term of 1943, I found lodging in a house on St George's Square run as a hostel by Westminster Cathedral. The square actually opened onto the road that ran along the embankment and I would enjoy crossing over to the riverside Pimlico Gardens to watch for the low lying grey-painted colliers with their hinged funnels that enabled them to pass under the bridges on the way to Battersea Power Station with its towering bulk and great chimneys.

Watching these vessels enjoying what I thought must be a relief from the hazardous routine of east coast convoy traffic, it excited me to have such symbolic testimony to the proximity of the open sea. On the other hand, my bedroom at the back looked out on the large residential complex of Dolphin Square. It was the Free French Headquarters and its destruction by the Luftwaffe had been promised in a German propaganda broadcast by Lord Haw-Haw!

It was an easy bus trip, past the Houses of Parliament and Whitehall,

Charing Cross and along the Strand, to King's College. The translation from my boarding school days into the adult realm was dizzying enough, but into my wonderful dream world of engines as well – it was all too good to be true! Built in 1776 for the Duke of Somerset, the impression made by King's stately and lofty interior elegance was immeasurably enhanced by the brightly lit engineering laboratories at the basement level, the glittering steel and shiny enamel paintwork of the test engines, and all the experimental equipment. Next year, it was all waiting for me.

It was immensely exciting to find myself at last coming to grips with science courses – courses not offered at my boarding school because of the wartime staff shortages. Be that as it may, the distractions were many, for it was the time of what came to be called the mini-blitz, apparently occasioned by the heavy night raids on Germany by the R.A.F. and the heavy day raids by the U.S.A.F. Mini or not, if there is a Nazi bomber overhead in the full thunder of the anti-aircraft fire and weaving beams of the searchlights, the only target he is looking for is, of course, oneself!

One night a week we slept in the dormitory near the main entrance. We would take a two-hour watch in pairs, alert to the possibility of incendiary bombs on the college roof. A professional firewatcher trained us for this, which was not as simple as it seemed. A significant proportion of each bomb was explosive so that, when you thought you had dealt satisfactorily with its igneous menace, it killed you. Thus one had to position a sandbag, lie down behind it in your steel helmet, wearing armoured goggles consisting of crossed slits in a steel plate. Your partner supplied you with water to squirt around the fire, either through a rarely convenient hose or with a stirrup pump from a bucket. The training officer would leave a small hurricane lamp, turned down to a mere glimmer because of the blackout. To illuminate our endeavours, each pair was equipped with an official lantern. This consisted of a heavy wooden box with a big handle and a fat lens that emitted a paltry glow that ensured an enormous battery life since the demands in terms of luminosity made upon it were negligible.

I soon aroused the serious displeasure of our trainer. The top floor of the college housed the medical department and gave cause for much unease in some of our more sensitive watchers. This was because, near the scene of our watch keeping on the top floor of the college, the serried ranks of the variously dismembered dead in the large dissecting room greatly outnumbered our selves. More to the point, in the main passage, a number of exhibits included a mounted assembled skeleton. While blundering about in the dark with a hose, I caused it to be no longer mounted or assembled.

My partner was an engineering student by the name of Weissen. He was quite content to put his feet up in the little watch room and leave me to call him if the need required. I would wander off among the chimney pots in the great silence of the night over London, broken only by the pacing of the quarters and the hours by the chiming of Big Ben. One night when looking down from an angle of the building into a large sloping window on the floor below, I was startled to see by the moonlight a face framed in dark hair watching me, only to realize that the owner was laid out on a mortuary slab.

On other occasions, the sudden wail of sirens would rend the night and I would wait for the distant thunder to the east that the barrage was centreing on the approaching bombers. As it drew closer, I tried to shrink as best I could under the protective limited shelter of my steel helmet. I was rewarded with a startlingly good view of the proceedings.

One morning after some such night, Weissen was called out of our first lecture. Apparently his father had been driving home in the small family Fiat and a bomb had landed beside the car killing him instantly. He later showed me a Yale key that had been in his father's pocket. It had been both bent and twisted.

There were, however, lighter moments. On one occasion we had a newcomer in Home Guard uniform with big hobnailed boots, standing in for a friend. The only toilets anywhere near the dormitory were on the basement floor below and, while having some outside windows, always remained like the rest of the building in Stygian darkness due to the blackout requirements. We had to descend a flight of stone stairs and feel our way to the right opening. On this occasion, I heard hobnail boots approaching and stood back against the wall to facilitate safe passage. It didn't occur to me to say anything since one didn't talk to people to whom one had not been formally introduced! Eventually I heard the rattle of a box of matches in my immediate vicinity. A sudden flare of light revealed a pair of eyes some two feet from my own. There was a startled cry as the match went out and the crash of boots on the flagstones at the other side of the passage!

It was not sufficient to protect the college from incendiarism. It was also necessary, if called upon, to vigorously repulse any intended violent intrusion by the enemy. So it was that I drew my uniform from the stores at Imperial College, South Kensington and became a member of the University of London Senior Training Corps. This largely involved spending one day a week, in heavy boots and ill-fitting khaki, marching and counter marching in the central quadrangle of Somerset House to the scathing comments of our drill sergeants from the Coldstream Guards. Thus everything had to be done with immense alacrity and precision. This made great demands on some of the more reflective members of our community, usually associated with the Faculty of Arts, who, with the best of intentions, were apt to perform highly unmilitary and original variations on the raucously prescribed drill enjoined upon us. There were also lectures on various and sundry weaponry. The only such lecture I really enjoyed was when, being shown how to present arms, the corporal drove the muzzle of his rifle straight up through the large green light shade above his head, showering himself with broken glass.

By the Christmas of 1943, the evacuees had largely returned to London. My father was transferred back from the now almost exclusively titular official school location. The family, including myself, took up residence in a house on Gloucester Road in Teddington, a short walk from Twickenham. From the humble confines of a hall at the back of a church in Hungerford, my father now found himself transposed as headmaster of a school of evacuees from Gibraltar, located in the lofty and imposing surroundings of the Victoria and Albert Museum. The school consisted of a series of classrooms and offices separated by screening partitions. When visiting, I sometimes felt myself to be observed and, looking up to the gallery inside the high dome overhead, might glimpse the face of one of the museum's staff. For myself, I now took the train up to Waterloo Station and joined the morning crowd flowing over the bridge spanning the Thames to the Strand, checking the time against what looked like a gargantuan bedside clock sitting atop Shell-Mex House to get to my first lecture.

The first topic was a quick whip round the class to find out where the bombs had landed the night before. My standard bedtime attire was corduroy trousers, socks and sweater, with shoes ready with open laces, overcoat and steel helmet on a chair by the bed. When the sirens woke me up, there would first be the wait to see what would materialize. A very distant faint thunder would be the warning to get ready and head for the front door. As the cone of fire from the guns grew closer, I would recognize when our own neighbouring batteries opened up. Then we made for the nearby underground public shelter.

One night I volunteered to help in a search for a local unexploded bomb. As I went from house to house, there is an endlessly repetitive story. "It's not in our garden because we've looked but we are sure it is in the garden next door!" This followed by a recital of what fell off the wall or the mantle piece; who said what; until I had to cut it short and move on to hear a similar account next door. With a lightening of the sky in the east, there came a tremendous explosion from a nearby park that settled the matter.

Such matters would all take their toll, and it was with growing dismay that I realized my inability to cope with so much new work. Extra tuition was arranged but the flood of unfinished assignments became a deluge. Thus there were sown the seeds of self-doubt as to whether I was capable of succeeding in a field of work that held such a powerful attraction.

I was bitterly disappointed, though not altogether surprised, when called before the Dean of Engineering. I was told that since I was unable to benefit by the lectures, I should withdraw. In a letter to my father from the lecturer in mathematics, he noted that wartime conditions had unfortunately led to a number of students who, like myself, were faced with the same problem of having none of the normal school course preparation required due to the teacher shortages. I was, however, permitted to finish out the academic year. In a few months I would attain my 18th birthday and be conscripted into the army or sent down the mines as a "Bevin Boy."

During this period, two of my father's friends took an interest in me and invited me out for tea. It would be many years before I realized the remarkable good fortune of being allowed those times spent with The Honourable Mrs. Charlotte Baynes, O.B.E., and Father W. Rees. Mrs. Baynes was a self-taught scholar who, over the course of a long life, had participated in a number of distinguished archaeological studies and had remarkable connections in academic circles. She gave me a number of introductory works dealing with contemporary physics and cosmology and would discuss the emergent view of the universe enabled by recent scientific discoveries.

Father Rees had apparently been an Oxford scholar who, on converting to Catholicism and becoming a priest, was rejected by his distinguished family. He had exchanged the gracious confines of an Oxford College for a shabby little church, partly under a railway arch, where the windows had to be covered with wire netting to protect them from vandals in the impoverished east end of London. Tall, stooped, with thin fair hair he was very short sighted and, in the absence of his very thick spectacles, I was never quite sure whether he could actually see me or not. He was a great friend of my father and companion on long country walks, exploring local history, which they both enjoyed so much. When he brought me out to tea I never knew what to talk about. I really didn't have any idea what scholarship actually was except it had nothing to do with engines. That acquisition of meaning that progresses throughout life is not limited to the mere acquisition of facts. Of far greater significance is that subtle and unarticulated benediction of meaning coming from a person of singular character and integrity. I have always thought myself singularly blessed by the interest my father's two friends showed in myself.

One night in June, the familiar sound of the air raid sirens was followed by a long silence broken only by the sound of sporadic distant explosions. The only explanation we could think of was that the gasholders adjoining municipal gas works were being blown up! On the 13th June 1944 it was announced that London was under attack by pilotless aircraft.

Though I finished off the year as best I could I had to find a way of somehow following my interests. With the approach of my eighteenth birthday and conscription, determined to follow my fascination with engines and the sea, I applied to the General Register and Record Office for Shipping and Seamen in Cardiff for allocation to engine room duties, later to the Wallasey Sea Training School near Liverpool for training in firing marine boilers. I was refused on both counts as being under age. Perhaps it was just as well for it would later transpire that engine room crew in the merchant service had a higher casualty rate than any of the fighting services! A subsequent application to The Marconi International Marine Communication Company was also refused. However, a friend of Mrs. Baynes who was an engineering superintendent with the Blue Funnel Line found me a position as a marine engineering apprentice in a shipyard working on Admiralty contracts. I thereby acquired a classification that would ensure allocation to Naval service. I was interviewed and accepted by J.S. White, Shipbuilders and Engineers, located at Cowes on the Isle of Wight.

This was now the height of the flying bomb period. When getting on the bus for Surbiton Station and the train for Southampton, the conductress was very shaken for on pulling out from Twickenham High Street, a V1 had landed close enough to the stop to destroy the bus that had pulled into the stop they had just left. When the Southampton train pulled in to Surbiton Station, windows had been broken by another V1 though nobody had been injured. On arriving in Southampton, I found myself in the midst of the vast embarkation arrangements for the invasion of Europe. For my first visit to the yard I was issued a special pass for passage from Southampton on board a naval launch to Cowes, Isle of Wight for it was June 1944.

Overhead, from horizon to horizon, with thundering engines, the bomber formations formed a long column heading towards their targets, while to the east there was a similar stream of those returning. The long estuary of Southampton Water eventually divided into the great expanse of open water between the south coast and the Isle of Wight. The Solent affords south-west immediate access to the open sea, or alternatively, to the south-east past the great naval base of Portsmouth and through Spithead. It was here that tide and wind frustrated the Spanish Armada's efforts to access shelter almost four hundred years earlier. But now a very different fleet was massed. All around were ships of the invasion fleet, of every design and purpose, as far as the eye could see throughout the Solent and Spithead – straining at their cables, brightly coloured ensigns snapping smartly in the stiff breeze and bright morning sunshine, the launch leaping and plunging in the lively seas. There was a tremendous sense of purpose. I longed to be part of that great adventure.

The small town of Cowes, internationally famous as a sailing centre, is divided by the River Medina into West Cowes and East Cowes. The engine works, with its powerful "hammer-headed" crane and fitting out berth dated from 1889, and its Victorian building construction, was in West Cowes. The boiler shop where I worked, with its own big overhead crane running on tracks the length of the building, was of corrugated iron with a dirt floor and high raised roof crown. The latter was quite impartial within, affording egress for smoke and fumes or ingress for rain and even, on the odd unwelcome occasion, snow.

The shipyard lay on the opposite bank in East Cowes and afforded much improved facilities. This was because, in a surprise dawn raid by Nazi dive bombers, they had themselves been unpleasantly surprised by the over night arrival of a heavily armed Polish destroyer due for refit and lying alongside the fitting out berth alert and ready for business! The resulting loss of hostile intent towards the nearby engine works did not extend to the shipyard, which, in consequence, had to be extensively rebuilt.

On the 23rd June 1944, I started work in the turbine shop. The novelty of feeding long strips of reaction turbine blading into a die to be cut off by the guillotine soon started to pall. The impulse blading was marginally more interesting since it had to be wheeled off to the machine shop. Be that as it may, I entered into the first couple of months with gusto, taking full advantage of my new surroundings. In any event, it would only be for a couple of months until I would be off to join the Royal Navy.

That winter I grew reluctantly accustomed to the early morning routine of the anxious clatter of my hobnailed boots on usually wet pavement through the damp morning darkness, listening for the works whistle. I became mutely obedient to the tyranny of the time clock. Thus, as I got the card from the right hand rack, inserted it in the slot, pushed the lever – *ching* – pulled it out and put it in the left hand rack, my place and time became known to others. There was, however, or so it seemed, little interest in apprentices other than as a source of cheap labour. I started a campaign for transfer to more challenging and instructive work.

Occasionally on weekends I would renew my propensity for exploration of a large local estate. This time, of royalty! Osborne House had been a favourite of Queen Victoria and no wonder, for it afforded that most magnificent coming together of wooded parkland and some three miles of exquisitely varied beach and rock along the Solent. It was where she died in 1901. It seemed a pity to let it go to waste! I would scale the wall in East Cowes, just out of sight of the nearby Bofors anti-aircraft gun crew. I then had some four miles of exquisitely varied shoreline that, to the awe-inspiring backdrop of the mighty invasion fleet at anchor in the South Hampton Roads, I had all to myself. I never met a soul.

At the further end of the estate was Wootton Creek. Carrying on across the road bridge at the end of the creek I would come to the beautiful confines of the Great Benedictine Abbey of Quarr. After a cup of tea and attending Evening Prayer, I would head home to Cowes by bus. The contrast of the Abbey and the elusive enchantment of Evening Prayer with life in the shipyard left a deep impression. There was some ineluctable sense of "goodness," of a deeper purpose behind it all, the sun, the land, the sea, the ships of the invasion fleet assembled to vanquish the evils of Nazi bestiality which would all too soon become manifest in the newly liberated death camps such as Auschwitz or Belsen.

To equip an animal with intelligence and reason is to make possible the most sublime and the most horrific events in human history. Each of us is called to some part of it, whether through the disciplined and exquisite cadences of the monks in choir, or as the young men who faced maiming or death by gunfire but a short distance away on the Normandy Coast. Over the course of life it would gradually become clear to me that we can only escape the price to be paid for our own destiny at the cost of a terrible and enduring sterility.

Early on I got to know an Irish electrician who told me something of the background of J. S. White's as he found it at the height of the hostilities in the early part of the war. He had heard of the mighty efforts on the part of British industry to provide the fighting men with the weapons of war and he was ill prepared for the realization that this did not seem to include J. S. White's. His first job was to fit an armature in an electric motor that, in accordance with union contract, called for the cooperation of a fitter. He went down to the destroyer lying at the fitting-out berth but couldn't find a soul.

The next night he watched the night shift go aboard but again could find nobody. He resolved to search the ship form stem to stern and eventually saw a chink of light coming from the air boxes around the burners on No. 2 boiler. The fire space is quite large, consisting of close-spaced banks of water tubes sloping upward on either side from the water drums to the steam drum overhead. Most of the night shift were asleep except for a small group playing cards and one man making tea for sale using the large blazing coke brazier used to prevent water condensation on the outer surfaces of the boiler.

The lodging house where I stayed was located on the hill overlooking the engine works and beyond, across the river, to the shipyard. It had three floors and scullery jutting out behind the kitchen with a steep set of steps to an additional bedroom above. This latter was connected by a door to the master bedroom above it. If the small bedroom was occupied by a distinguished elderly aircraft inspector, the arrangement turned out not to be fortuitous. Apparently an additional service was supplied in which the landlord and the aircraft inspector would swap places. This was accidentally discovered by two petty officers, standing by the destroyer at our fitting out berth, who couldn't rouse the landlady for breakfast and climbed up and looked in the window! All in all, the local ambience was profoundly perplexing to the innocence of my Catholic nurturing. The notion of an eternity of hell-fire did not seem to be a topic of concern for others. Indeed, I sometimes wondered if my present surroundings weren't something of the nature of what it might be like!

The landlord was also a fitter in the yard and they purchased the hull of a sixty-foot, steel-hulled Russian schooner lying in the mud of Wootton Creek for the sum of twenty pounds. A tree-secluded pre-war nudist camp sloped down to the waterfront. This consisted of firm grassy tussocks separated by soft slimy mud. By leaping form tussock to tussock, one could get out to the hull of the schooner, its main deck clear above high water though its interior was largely mud. The exigencies of war had seen the camp's inhabitants replaced by a more robustly employed battalion of Canadian Commandos. A New Year's celebration had reached its climax by sinking the schooner with grenades, which resigned itself, gracefully upright, to an apparently mud-embalmed future.

None of these matters presented any problems to our household. Shrapnel holes were speedily sealed off with rubber gasket material held in position by inner and outer steel plates and through hull bolt, courtesy of the Royal Navy, I suppose. The hull was pumped out by a little Seagull outboard motor mounted on a vertical stand and with its normal propeller replaced by a centrifugal pump. The mud was removed by bucket and all that remained was to pull her off the mud. At this point I underwent a radical loss of interest. This was occasioned by a small, but costly misjudgement, in jumping between tussocks. In brief, one leg, followed by the rest of me, shot down into the soft slimy mud landing on a broken bottle that sliced across the sole of my foot.

In due course, a powerful Air/Sea Rescue launch mysteriously appeared with the elderly aircraft inspector onboard, courtesy of the Royal Air Force, I suppose. The hull was towed around to Cowes where it was triumphantly welcomed by the household, saving only my injured self. I was, however, well enough to enjoy the sequel for I had found the character of my hosts increasingly less endearing. Apparently, the nudist camp caretaker had sold them the boat – though he didn't happen to own it! The real owner was now delighted at having it returned to its homeport in reasonably seaworthy condition, free of charge!

Shortly after my eighteenth birthday, I was ordered to appear for a medical examination. I was delighted when passed A-1 for sea duty and found that my national service number had not ended in one of three digits that would have meant being sent down the mines as a so-called "Bevin Boy." However, the situation had changed by then and I was told we were being held for assignment to the Far East. Eventually, however, with the advent of the atomic bomb and the end of hostilities, a Far Eastern assignment became unnecessary. Now, bound under the *Essential Works Order*, I found myself trapped in an environment where the only moral precept seemed to be, "Don't get caught." I found myself becoming more and more of a pariah in the works. Further, relations between the landlady and myself came to the breaking point and I was told to get out.

It was extremely difficult to find accommodation, and, thanks to the generosity of my Irish electrician friend, his wife and family, I took up residence under their kitchen table. The table in question was not of the more currently familiar flimsy construction of brightly coloured plastic and chromed light metal pipe. It was in fact, a four poster designed to keep the rest of the house off in the event of some direct hostile intervention in my host's domestic arrangements by the Luftwaffe. The top was half-inch boiler plate mounted on massive angle iron supports at each corner. It contained a large double mattress. As was common with much of the paint work in Cowes, it tastefully matched that of the destroyer lying at the fitting out berth. It had apparently "come" with the house. It would certainly "go" with the house, saving some skilled attention with an oxy-acetylene torch. The only real disadvantage was the need for alacrity in the morning or risk being enclosed by a palisade of legs as the early-rising family got down to breakfast.

I eventually found another lodging in a large square house owned by a retired master mariner. The upper floor was rented to my new landlady. The slate roof, with its tall chimneys, sloped up on all four sides to a little glass windowed look-out which commanded an extraordinary panorama. Beyond the little town below lay the great panorama of the Solent, bearing the vast profusion and variety of the invasion fleet while in the distance I could see the entrance to Southampton Water with all its busy traffic to the port. My room was a little garret with its sloped ceiling immediately under the roof and which precluded my sitting up in bed. On those nights when stormy winds were active about the little lookout and the chimney pots, I would hear the slates clicking just above and pray for the soundness of the chimney brickwork. The great saving grace of my new home was that the little staircase up to the lookout was all mine!

I was finally transferred to the boiler shop. I worked in the big corrugated iron shop with its overhead crane running the length of its parallel tracks. There was a line of large three-drum Admiralty boilers in various stages of construction, surrounded by scaffolding, mounted on heavy wooden blocks on the dirt floor. An initial nervousness with respect to heights was rapidly superseded by the nonchalant ability to balance myself on bare horizontals while scampering between verticals. The high roof crown was raised to provide ready egress for smoke and fumes. As mentioned, by the same token, it impartially admitted any inclemency of an elemental nature. One morning that winter I was disagreeably surprised to find my workbench and tools hidden in snow.

Works safety was of little concern until a major accident occurred, as for example when someone handling a heavy steel plate on the deck of a hull on the stocks of the shipyard was nudged over the side to his death on the slipway below. These were the days before hard hats and safety boots had even been thought of. On one occasion, while filing a flange in the vice on the bench, there was a heavy thump in the dirt floor behind me. Above me was a very apologetic crane operator who had loosened the heavy motor guard fitting that now lay just behind my boots. On another occasion, standing on a solitary plank some twenty feet above a large jagged heap of scrap metal, I was guiding a massive bound bundle of super heater tubing from the storage racks and it pivoted free from my hands. Fortunately, it missed the plank, and plunged down into the scrap heap below.

My practical shop-floor introduction to the trade union movement was now provided by the fitter to whom I was assigned – Jimmy, small, voluble and neat in his freshly laundered brown boiler suit, originally a car motor mechanic. Jimmy was also a shop steward. He once told me that he had an excellent marital relationship because his wife knew that, "if ever she did anything to him, she knew that he would do something a fuckin' sight worse to her!" He always carried his head on one side as if listening for something. He did a lot of this with his frequent, "Just carry on, nip, I have some union business to attend to." This, I suspected, had something to do with his motoring expertise. He revelled in the name-dropping of Labour Party bigwigs with whom he would consort on their occasional visits.

It was a time that payment on the basis of piecework was being negotiated by management and union, prices for particular jobs being allocated on the basis of time required. This Jimmy worked out on a basis of maximizing personal income while being allowed ample time for his equally personal projects using yard materials, his own, and if necessary, others' skills. There was no doubt that he was an excellent craftsman, well worth having if you could elicit sufficient of his interest on your behalf. These projects included, over a six-month period, a three-foot diameter French polished hardwood coffee table, a large hardwood tool box with multiple drawers, two aluminum saucepans, two aluminum dustpans, two hardwood reading lamps with extendible monel metal stands, a tea pot stand, and complete reconditioning of a motor bike which was sold for high profit.

There is no doubt that the highest standards of skilled craftsmanship abounded in the yard, as well. Nothing escaped the eagle eyes of the Admiralty inspectors. This also applied to the boat shop where they built the lifeboats for the Royal National Lifeboat Institution. These were strategically located around the coast to assist in saving life at sea. Each was a masterpiece of the highest workmanship, elegance of finish and design. On the other hand, there appeared no limit to the ingenuity of private manufacture and pilfering of resources. On one occasion Jimmy asked me to pick up some wood for him at the boat shop. Unsuspectingly, I did as he asked only to find out later that I had been chased by, but had been accidentally lost by, a suspicious foreman. Had I been caught I had no doubt as to who would have been left to face the consequences!

However, if the works manager could have his car reconditioned in the works, I suppose one might expect emulation by the workforce. Presumably this was tacitly understood by all as part of the perquisites.

Later I was transferred to Bill, one of the other fitters. He was much given to expressing himself in homely metaphors, thus, on finishing his smoke: "This won't buy the baby a new dress!" More commonly, when viewing some further evidence of my ineptitude with file or hack saw: "Well, a man on a galloping horse wouldn't notice it!"

As the months progressed, I became increasingly aware of what seemed to be a general sense of hostility. On occasion, I was shocked to find out I had been blamed for blunders by others on work that I had nothing to do with – explanations that were readily accepted by charge hands and foremen. I once asked one of the other apprentices, for whom I was able to perform a small favour, for the reason. His response was enlightening: "It's just because you are a college boy and when anything goes wrong they want to take it out of you."

The worst of them was a small group for whom a few inchoate shibboleths of Communist jargon provided complete justification for their natural propensities for mindless violence. There were endless jibes about priests and nuns but I refused to be drawn. On the other hand, I have always seemed to possess an inner resource of determination with a limit that would not be crossed. I would keep a large double-ended spanner near me on the workbench with the full intention that, if attacked, one of them would be taken away on a stretcher. In retrospect, that is perhaps why the eventuality never arose. I suspect it is the sense of imposing fear that encourages the bully.

We had occasional "patients" from the invasion fleet alongside the fitting out berth. A large Landing Ship Tank, with its huge bow doors, had engine problems and had to be explored from stem to stern. A smaller Landing Craft Tank with its bow ramp and back problems had to have railway line welded along its deck for strengthening. In this latter case, one of the apprentices stole the ammunition from the magazines of the sten guns on the bridge because they fitted a pistol he had acquired. I pointed out that this was a terrible thing to do since the lives of the crew could depend on them. He said that he had never thought of it like that and returned the ammunition. Later he told me not to be so silly because he had to steal it again!

Very occasionally, I would be assigned a job on my own such as: "Fit B.M. 526." I would look for the boiler mounting in question in the heap of drawings on the drafting table in the charge-hand's office. I would draw the necessary parts and equipment from stores: the air drain-cock itself, four mounting studs and nuts, stud-box, half-inch compressed air drill and drilling post, appropriate drill, and taps to cut the thread in the holes drilled in the steel pad already part of the big eight-inch bend atop the steam drum of the boiler. If the studs were not exactly level with the tops of the nuts when the cock was mounted, I would have to remove the offending stud and drill again. I had to be very careful, for one could easily drill through into the steam space of the bend itself and scrap the whole fitting. Nevertheless, there was the satisfaction of having completed some small contribution on my own. The more independent I could be in carrying out a task, the more satisfying the work was.

Work on *H.M.S. Cavalier* neared completion with a test firing of the after-mounted deck torpedo tube. It was exciting to watch the torpedo, with its dummy warhead attached to a coiled recovery line, propelled by its cordite charge to ensure adequate clearance of the deck. A homely pie plate holding a cone of soft mud was used to show the clearance. Tugs nudged another hull alongside the fitting-out berth. For some time the shipyard no longer echoed to the staccato thunder of riveting hammers on steel plate, as rumour had it that this was the first all-welded destroyer to be built in Britain.

It was further thought to be the first "corrugated" ship ever to be built in the world! Many problems were encountered with buckled plates. Attempted straightening involved welding rackets to hold "strong-backs" into position and driving wedges. While watching this performance one day I saw a welder working on a seam behind a labourer, caught up in some reflective reverie over his drooping fag, and whose steel boot heel protectors proved irresistible to a deft touch with the electrode. The reverie continued – that is until he tried to move and found himself welded solidly to the deck!

Such moments of levity were few and far between, however, and I dearly longed to escape from the place. The only way to do that, in light of continuing conscription, was to successfully complete the First Year Engineering Examinations. I fitted up the little table in my garret with a length of cable and a solitary electric bulb. For the next several months I kept up an average of two and a half hours of study every night, according to my little diary. There is also a record of the jobs I worked on such as super heater headers, a water level regulator, soot blowers, pull rods, black smoke fitting, water testing, spot facing, air cock mounting, and so on. More eloquently are the increasingly common testaments to my predicament such as: "another bloody awful day!" I had come to detest it all with an unrelenting intensity.

The close to my day would be a final solitary walk past the Royal Yacht Club and along the sea front. As the days lengthened with approach of summer, that time of evening when the setting sun tinges the world with wonder, there would be an urgent longing for some break in my own inner storm-clouded horizon. An old letter home records one occasion, when the horizon appeared as a: "mauve-pencilled fresco topped by the crimson glow of the sunset. The masthead lights of the anchored ships gleam through the gathering twilight to the solemn tolling of a distant bell buoy. A hospital ship glides seaward, a clear-cut silhouette, her red crosses dimly discernible while up aloft her running lights burn clear. There is an occasional glow from a dead light that has not been properly secured. At last, as she vanishes round the point, the stirring of the wind in the trees reminds that the hour is late and I must return." Thus would this longing begin to raise a new urgency, a new question. Would life ever afford me the opportunity of setting forth upon the sea, bound upon some great adventure? Somehow I had to get away from the yard and its oppressive environment. Somehow I had to secure for myself what lay over that distant horizon and beckoned with such insistence. Perhaps a transfer might be made possible on educational grounds.

I could anticipate little sympathy at J. S. White's so I sought advice in the local employment office. A friendly official suggested how it might be done within the framework of the *Essential Services Act*. I applied for employment as an apprentice at Harland and Wolff's repair works in Southampton Docks. This would enable me to attend evening courses at University College Southampton.

My last meeting with the manager of the engine works at J. S. White's was to request a statement testifying to the satisfactory completion of a year as an apprentice fitter. Outmaneuvered, but true to form, his response was: "I will do absolutely nothing to help you!" In retrospect I can imagine the burden that rested on his shoulders, one that I would not wish to carry. Still, I heard that his children were attending university. All too often one assumes that one's superiors in any hierarchy of power are well disposed to what seems to be a reasonable and honourable intention. In those early vulnerable years, one of the hardest lessons I would have to learn was to accept such encounters as part of a much greater journey, without becoming subject to some enduring attitude of cynicism and discouragement.

If my year at King's College had afforded something of a transition from the closeted confines of my Catholic boarding school, I was totally unprepared for the sustained ethos of my new surroundings in J.S. White's even if, at last, I found myself in an environment that had consistently beckoned through out my boyhood days: the sea, the ships that sailed upon it, and the engines that empowered them. There was an increasing perception of becoming trapped in my own earlier formation without any preparatory knowledge of, or perspective on, the realities of life outside Roman Catholicism, its religious orders or institutions. Yet I could only assume that they continued to have some real answers to the problems of life and its role in the universe. Somehow I had to accept and put up with what seemed to be the intrinsic wickedness of the world in which I lived and worked.

UNIVERSITY COLLEGE SOUTHAMPTON
AND THE ADMIRALTY SHIPYARDS, HAMPSHIRE (1945)

On the 5th July 1945 I finally left J.S. White's, ending a thoroughly disagreeable association with an immense sense of relief. I returned to visit the family in London, and my old friends at the convent in Twickenham and at Presentation College in Reading. On the 16th July 1945, I started work at Harland and Wolff's repair works in Southampton Docks. Life here was very different, and the company had a genuine concern for the training of their apprentices. One day a week was allowed for attendance at courses and, with the others, I found we could always bring our concerns to our genial supervisor, Mr. M. Humphreys. I also enrolled in night classes, five a week, at University College Southampton.

We were issued with heavy canvas bib and brace overalls and collarless canvas jackets. These would be scrubbed regularly with a broom, detergent and steam hose on a concrete slab. The net result was not unlike a suit of armour with the joints welded solid! I was issued with a tool bag, a half dozen spanners, hammer and chisel, file and scraper. If they ever found an adjustable spanner or Stilson, it would immediately go into the sea: "Spanners are for nuts and if you have a problem, the blacksmith will tighten it up for you!"

The daily round became established, catching the morning tram, grinding and clanking its way down towards the docks, thick with tobacco smoke and expectoration that called for watching where I stepped. The large high-roofed, corrugated-iron repair shop, dominated inside by its overhead crane running the length of the shop on its tracks, lay beside No. 6 dry dock. The work was varied and vastly more interesting than at J. S. White's. Initially, however, I was concerned with re-tubing oil coolers, then "breaking free" the huge diesel cylinder liners from their tightly fitting cooling water jackets, using massive "strong-backs" screw jacks and a forty-pound sledge hammer.

On the 16th October I was assigned to work "outside," that is, to work on ships lying at various berths throughout the extensive dock area. It became important to make sure one got to the gangway in the morning promptly on time before the time checker returned to the main works. The work was varied and, as winter drew on, I came to appreciate the warmth of ship's engine rooms more and more. For example, when assisting in the removal of the turbine rotor from the starboard main steam alternator in the troop ship *Queen of Bermuda*, or those of the diesel Union Castle ships, heated by steam radiators and powerful blowers, I came to particularly appreciate these latter when I had a prolonged bout of neuralgia. By the time I got to the ship my face would be aching and throbbing. I would climb up to the blast of hot air and the heat would speedily remove the pain. After the trip in an open truck to the works canteen, and back, I would repeat the performance.

At the opposite end of that spectrum was the time I removed an array of 4-inch fuel oil lines located below the boiler room floor plates in the *Ulster Monarch*, once in regular service across the Irish Sea, then converted to the role of a commando transport, and now being reconverted back to her original purpose. The ship was in dry dock and the sides of the boiler room had been removed for re-plating. The wind-driven snow was blowing straight across the boiler room. As I loosened the flange bolts that were embedded in soot, surreptitiously discarded by her wartime stokers, I was covered up to the elbows in a freezing mixture of soot and thick bunker crude!

The basin next to No. 6 dry dock was always interesting because it was here that one could find the vast grey bulk of the *R.M.S. Queen Mary* or the *R.M.S. Queen Elizabeth*. Once, in my inflexible canvas uniform, I walked past seven different guards, ship's police, military police and soldiers and did a tour of the *R.M.S. Queen Mary*.

Most of our work was on the Union Castle passenger liners. I have always thought them among the most beautiful ships ever built, with their graceful lines, lavender hulls and white superstructure. The large Harland and Wolff diesel engines were double acting, that is, the fuel explosions occurred both above and below the piston. This made for dramatic complications in intake and exhaust valve arrangements, the science of which would only be resolved for me by a beautiful sectioned model in the Science Museum in South Kensington.

My second practical lesson in trade union practice came when I was working on a pipeline under the floor plates between the main engines in one of these Union Castle liners. Looking up, I became aware of a pair of shiny black boots just level with my eyes, and then the owner, the scowling visage of one of our foremen in the classic garb of heavy blue serge suit and bowler hat: "Did you lift that plate?" I said that I had. "Can't you see there are holes drilled in it?" I pointed out that there were no bolts in them. "Put it back and go and get the boilermaker to lift it!"

I eventually found the boilermaker in one of the first class cabins with a billycan of tea, spectacles on the end of his nose, deep in a newspaper. He responded to my request with an: "I'll be right down, nip" (the local jargon for apprentice!), and returned to his paper. I spent two days waiting, occasionally visiting on the boat deck watching the heartbreaking sight of families seeing off passengers who were already boarding, for she was loading war brides bound for Australia. Perhaps a small greengrocers van would pull up at the end of the gangway and Dad would look up at the ship while Mum and a young woman with a baby would try to prolong their parting. Eventually I was able to finish the job that I had almost completed when ordered to stop by the foreman.

If there was little improvement with respect to safety, as seemed common in heavy industry in those days, at least the problem was recognized. A full-time first aid assistant with his equipment and stretcher must be installed on board before any of the work crew could start. There seemed to be ample opportunity for clients! On the 6th December 1945, I was assigned the task of tightening up the banjo gear in the slippery black oily confines of the crankcase. The 8-inch piston and its rod had to be oil-cooled through a telescopic pipe attached to the rod just above the crosshead by an appropriately described "banjo gear." I was standing on the huge crank throw when it seemed that everything around me started moving; the throw, piston rod, banjo gear, crosshead, connecting rod, exhaust eccentric straps. Fortunately, I managed to throw myself out through the open crankcase door on to the plates between the two main engines. Apparently a foreman had started to turn the engine over without bothering to find out if anybody was inside!

A more concrete realization of this aspect of the work was brought home to me in the course of my activities in the engine room of a large Dutch passenger liner, now a troop ship, the *Johan van Oldenbarenvelt* (*JvO*). Her main propulsion was provided by two large Burmeister and Wain diesel engines each of which was surmounted by an elaborate array of cam gear for opening and closing the valves to the cylinders. They were preparing to start the engine and I rushed up several steel ladders to watch the fascinating display of mechanical gear on the engine tops. As soon as I appeared, however, two Dutch oilers, lined up in the shelter of the huge exhaust trunking in the middle of the engine, and one of the ship's engineers down on his hands and knees behind the cooling pipes, started shouting volubly in Dutch and waving their arms, the meaning clearly being that I should take myself off elsewhere. The reason came later when one of the oilers showed me an ignition housing whose predecessor had recently exploded under the high pressure starting air. He pointed to the scars around the upper casement caused by the shattered fragments from the failed housing. He was a kindly man for he then brought me along to the galley to purloin some delicious savoury pastries the likes of which were unheard of in my wartime England. This may have assisted a psychological shift in my allegiance from mechanical engineering to the application of science to engineering. The *JvO* was, however, far from finished with me yet! The symbolic lesson would be well and truly driven home!

I had been working on the large for'ard diesel generator in the wide bay between the port main engine and the ship's side. The engineer started the generator. I was standing in the narrow alleyway when a big end bolt sheared and a massive nut, about the size of two large fists, smashed through the side of the engine, gouged the steel in a column of the main engine, and hurtled past me down the alleyway. It was necessary to restart the after generator. This time I made sure I was well clear and watched from a catwalk on the main engine looking down on the bay. I watched him push the starting lever from air onto fuel when there was a tremendous explosion and I was suffocated and blinded by hot gas for a few moments. I shot out of the engine room like a scalded cat, then realized that there were people down there and I must go back. To my surprise, except for a lot of smoke, everything seemed to be running normally. I returned to my earlier vantage point to see what had happened. Just in front of where I was standing was a large spring-loaded relief plate in the exhaust trunking from the generator. The engineer had forgotten to reopen the large butterfly valve to the funnel and the relief plate had opened and discharged the exhaust from the first cylinder firings into my interested countenance!

The *JvO* would again come to my attention through a developing friendship with Alard Ages with whom I would share many voyages and conversations through our work with The Institute of Ocean Sciences near Victoria B.C. Al was a junior deck officer on the *JvO* in 1945. It was through Al that I would learn that in 1963, this venerable vessel had caught on fire and floundered in the Atlantic with the loss of one hundred and twenty-eight passengers and crew. In 2007, Al would himself publish his memoirs, *Guarded By Angels: Memoir of a Dutch Youth in WWII*, an account which I would find most moving.

Around the docks, roads and quays were generally shared with railway tracks and it was always important to watch out for something imponderable to shoot round a corner. Usually there was ample warning unless, as happened to a reflective colleague, he got caught by a buffer square in the chest, but was fortunately thrown clear!

One ship in which I was working required my crossing a large bank of railway sidings, formerly associated with the transatlantic passenger liner traffic, for lunch. One last siding, near No. 6 dry dock, at the end of which was the works canteen and my much favoured corned beef patty, chips and gravy, was separated from the rest of the stacks of railway sleepers which greatly limited one's range of view. For the previous week a string of goods wagons had been standing there, and I acquired the ill-advised habit of ducking underneath between the wheels. On this occasion, as I put my hand on the buffer beam and bent down, I noticed that it was the last car in the string and decided I might as well walk round the end. As I straightened up the cars jerked into motion down the line providing me with one of the biggest scares of my life. Only the night before, I had seen a film in which the most dramatic scene had been the horror of a victim regaining consciousness after both legs had been amputated in much the same situation. Such a combination of symbols can have an immensely powerful dispositional effect in terms of caution around tracks and trains.

Symbols play a major role in the generation of feelings that urge to action in some direction. The excitement of working with great heat engines became replaced by a sense of boredom with the presently familiar. I wanted to know more about the explanatory background, about design criteria and measurement of performance. On a more immediate practical level, here also could lie the way to a welcome independence from the harsh authority of fitters, charge hands and foremen! Apparently there were persisting ongoing problems with corrosion in the main bearings of the starboard engine. Two scientists arrived in white coats with sophisticated apparatus connected to electrical leads from strategic locations within the engine. Ever since, I have always had a secret reverence for the flickering trace against the pale green glow emitted by the screen of what I came to know as a cathode ray oscilloscope. What did its visual representation of minute electrical signals tell to those who had the requisite knowledge and skill in application?

It seems to me that throughout life there can often occur associations with someone having something held in common, something from our own pasts. As mentioned, one of the junior ship's officers aboard the *Johan* would many years later become a friend and colleague in an extensive oceanographic survey program in the coastal waters of southern British Columbia. A shipyard manager from Cape Town, sitting next to me on a Trans Atlantic flight, turned out to have joined J.S. White's shortly before myself and had to enter submarine service in the Royal Navy. Someone sitting next to me on a bus in South Africa had worked with my father during the war. A retired policeman from Liverpool, whom I met in Vancouver some twenty-five years later, turned out to be the same constable who had called to inquire about me when I became a doctoral student at the University of Liverpool, stating that my name and address had been found under suspicious circumstances in a car in Chester. Since he had turned in his notebooks on retirement, we could not clear up the mystery.

A somewhat less alarming, but very embarrassing situation later would occur on another of those ships. I had been asked to trace a pipeline that ran through a large air ventilation trunking. It was coated inside with a thick fur of black oily fuzz, much of which readily transferred to my person as I crawled along on all fours in total darkness and growing sense of alarm. Firstly I would miss the truck that would take me back to the works canteen for my lunchtime favourite. Secondly, the previous week, one of the people working on a ship out in the Solent had been decapitated in identical circumstances. Unwarned, he had been in exactly the wrong position when they carried out a practice closing of all watertight doors. At last, however, I encountered fresh air and discovered a vertical shaft above my head with a glimmer of daylight at the top and rungs that enabled a climb towards that beautiful daylight. To my intense relief, there was a small steel door shut fast by dogs. Loosening the dogs I at last managed to tumble out into bright light once again.

I found myself the object of appalled fascination on the part of a group many echelons above myself on the ladder of marine importance. Tables were arranged on three sides of a square enclosed by four oval cross-sectioned bright orange pillars, from one of which there suddenly emerged an indescribably filthy demonic apparition from the depths, i.e., me! Seated at this ceremonial handing-over luncheon were senior officials from the Union Castle Line and Harland's, their be-jewelled ladies in elegant attire, officers resplendent in gold braid. In pristine white monkey jacket and immaculately creased black trouser one such stepped over my bag of half-scattered tools with infinite disdain. In retrospect I can afford to laugh, but at the time I felt nothing but terrible humiliation. Somehow I had to find a way up to better things. I had to complete my engineering courses and find a better way of life.

I had written to my old friend Brother Canice at Presentation College. His reply reveals, perhaps, another glimpse of forming character conditioned by such events, but of which I was totally unaware at the time. "It's a good man that knows what he wants and bends every energy to it and pulls it off, especially true where hard work is concerned. You know, Pat, there were plenty of people you have surprised in this quest of yours for experience, experience got the tough way. Many did not expect you would stick it, but evidently yours was more than a boyhood enthusiasm for ships. I know you won't disappoint those who believe in you." Looking back over the years, there is no one more surprised than myself.

I asked to see the works manager, Mr. Allen, and requested a leave of absence to sit the External First Year Engineering examinations.

A pair of shrewd blue eyes watched me from across the desk: "What would you like to be?"

I said that I would like to be a university lecturer.

"I think that is a very laudable ambition."

Full of hope I took off with my leave granted. However, if by the end of the year I knew the work inside out, anxiety and a steady toll of fifteen-hour working days took its own toll. Though I knew I had done badly, I still had hopes. When the results were posted in the glass-covered notice boards outside Imperial College in South Kensington, there was a deluge of rain so heavy that it even flooded part of Tube system. I had to deflect the water flowing down the glass so I could read the successful candidates' examination numbers. There was a break in the sequence, 4447 then 4449; my number 4448 was omitted and I knew that my worst fears had been realized. Were prayer and hard work all meaningless in the divine ordination of events, an ordering power that remained absolutely oblivious of our innermost longings and yearnings? Were my parents and Packy, Maurus and the rest of the Roman Catholic community the victims of some sort of cosmic confidence trick? There seemed to be a terrible inevitability in the lines of G. K. Chesterton:

I tell you naught for your comfort,
Yea naught for your desire,
Save that the sky grows darker yet
And the sea rises higher.

It was true enough insofar as that paralysis of mind and failure in every subject that occurred amid the gloomy formality of the examination halls of the University of London was to much enhance the painful uncertainty as to whether I was capable of doing the work and an unquenchable fear of the examination process. Thus there arose an intrinsic conviction with respect to my natural ability as being inferior to that which was required to meet the tasks in life that beckoned so insistently. In some such manner can we acquire those scars from the past that carry their own destructive dynamism into some future performance. Religious faith was reduced to a sort of insurance policy because there was no alternative and there might be just some tiny element of truth underlying the customary incantations and rituals. In the sensitivity of my early days, such vulnerability can be much accentuated by some offhand personal criticism. All too clearly I recall, for example, the contemptuous comment of the chemistry lecturer on learning, not only of my lack of any science background, but also my innocence of any prior military training in the school corps (we didn't have one!): "You don't seem to have done very much of anything, have you, Crean?" Our lives can turn on such moments of humiliation before the listening class.

I was strongly advised to take a recuperative holiday on medical grounds. I joined the family who had arranged to stay in a boarding house in Howth. The high promontory of Howth Head curving round from its narrow isthmus forms the northern boundary of Dublin Bay. One could rent a rowing boat in Howth Harbour from Mr. McLaughlin who let me have a boat for a full morning for half a crown. I loved to row round Ireland's Eye. Rounding the Stack,

I could row into the long cave where the water lapped the foot of its northern face. The restless swell slopped and gurgled in the depths of the cave while I rested on the oars and looked back at the world of light outside the entrance, trying not to think of the future. Though I had done everything I could to actively participate in the war at sea, all that seemed to remain was conscription and a couple of years as a soldier in the Army of the Rhine!

PART TWO

A YOUNG MAN'S EXPLORATIONS

CHAPTER IV

DUBLIN, IRELAND

BACHELOR OF SCIENCE DEGREE
AND DIPLOMA IN CHEMICAL TECHNOLOGY,
UNIVERSITY COLLEGE DUBLIN (1945–1950)

I managed to obtain belated entry into the Faculty of Science in University College, Dublin. Walking down the quays with a battered family suitcase, for a moment, I felt I was entering a totally foreign country, only to be swept away by a tremendous sense of coming home to where I really belonged. Kitty had arranged for me to stay with an old friend, Lilian, who lived in a semi-detached house in a large council housing estate out in Drimnagh. Access to and from the city was provided by the large double-decker buses which threaded their way through one of the poorest areas of Dublin, the Coombe. Near the corner where we turned round past Keefe's the knackers, the stench called for clasped nose and a suspension of breathing for as long as could reasonably be managed.

Taken in a Dublin suburb in the back garden of Lillian Leake's home – Kitty's long time friend. We were waiting to hear if my application to University College Dublin had been accepted. It was the summer of 1946.

Lilian worked for the telephone company but was at heart, I think, a musician for the little living room was largely occupied by a grand piano. She had a long-term relationship with Tom that never blossomed into marriage though there was no dearth of possible reasons in the Dublin of those days. Many years later he would find her lying dead before the grand piano.

When I first entered the entrance hall of University College Dublin on Earlsford Terrace, I asked a chap warming himself on a radiator (heat was very scarce in Dublin then) where I might find the Applied Mathematics lecture: "I'm going there myself, and I'll show you." That was over sixty-five years ago and Mick Torpey from County Clare, his wife Kitty, and their family, have remained amongst my closest friends ever since. During that first year at U.C.D. we would become inseparable companions, the tall dark, slow-spoken countryman, and the unsophisticated Londoner. I was always fascinated and perhaps a little awed, by the depths of Mick's insights into people and human nature in general. Many an expedition on weekends found us out on our bicycles, perhaps to the Hill of Howth or Bray Head or perhaps the Wicklow Mountains. Mick was staying with his brother Jack and his wife Mary who always saw us generously supplied with sandwiches for our outings.

It was utterly delightful living in the ambience of a Catholic country, of having friends who shared those convictions so well established by my parents and friends at the other end of Pope's Grotto – Packy, Maurus and Brendan and all the rest of the kitchen sisters. One night a month there was a Sodality night for students and Newman's University Church on St. Stephen's Green would be packed with young people with extra chairs on the altar and in the aisles. Somehow it didn't seem to matter that the inspirational genius of Newman had long since departed from that place and the lack luster, perfunctory homilies from either of the two university chaplains amounted to nothing more, as I would later realize, than wet cardboard cut outs of truth!

It was already apparent that for true spiritual counseling, something that went beyond the legalism of static generalities into the realm of understanding and compassion, one had to "shop around." So it was that I came to know Father Canice at St. Teresa's Clarendon Street, of the Discalced Carmelite Order. By and large, it seemed to me that the priests of the religious orders were apt to be more in touch with the real world than the hierarchical rank and file disciplinarians.

For myself, the call for closer involvement in student life around the university led to my moving to a tall Georgian house in Pembroke Street. By and large the Dublin landladies of those days seemed to resemble regimental sergeant majors. Rules were rules. If you were a few minutes late for a meal, you were out of luck! The summons for meals employed an ancient voice pipe and whistle mounted on a landing halfway up to the top floor. On one occasion, when no response was heard for the whistle above, a lungful was gathered for another mighty puff, abruptly terminated by a discharge of filthy water from the pipe, supplied by someone with a watering can at the other end with which he had replaced the whistle.

There was only one bathroom and toilet and when the latter had been irretrievably blocked and I was confined to bed with flu, in desperation minor requirements of nature could only be met by commandeering the sink, while major requirements could only be met by dressing and heading for the facilities in the college. Clearly an alternative had to be found.

The house on Pembroke Street formed a long facade of similar houses with half basements and a flight of outside steps leading up to a small terrace onto which opened the paired front doors of adjoining houses. The houses were removed well back from the road with a paved path separating the two lawns. In fact, I discovered if you got out through the skylight on the roof you could walk the whole length of the block. The lodger's dining room was on the first floor separated from the private dining room by folding wooden doors through which everything could be heard. We were chronically hungry and the landlady was known to us as Squeers. When one of the maids who served us gave someone a second biscuit (a single biscuit constituted dessert), she was threatened with instant dismissal if the offence occurred again. Squeers was much given to entertaining local priests and nuns, clearly audible through the partition. Rationing was still in force and we had little doubt where the largesse was coming from.

A particular source of annoyance was the boyfriend of the girl who lived in the house next door, and who, in the early hours, would drive her home, revving the noisy engine and exchanging loud and louder endearments as she proceeded up to the front door. One night he was asked in and Lenahan, returning from the pub, seized the opportunity. Rousing the rest of us, we carried the car up the front steps and left it outside the front door ready for him. Instead, a large policeman on the beat observed the situation for a while and then, returning with three stalwarts of like magnitude wheeled the car out of sight up the road.

I never came across any mixed lodging houses as women students seemed to be largely housed in religious houses run by the nuns such as Dominican Hall on Stephen's Green. A strict surveillance and enforced curfew had to be observed.

Finally, a friend of mine, a dental student, got me into the place where he was staying in Grove Park. Old McCann was a treasure and treated us as if we were her own family, which I suppose, in a way we became. Our living and dining area was the front room, the usual basement type with its window looking onto a small walled declivity below ground level. The mantle piece above the fireplace was adorned with two female statues in black marble known affectionately to our largely medical clientele as U-reen and U-rine. On Sundays we would get a treat baked by McCann herself which we knew as "soot cakes" but which were appreciated and enjoyed nonetheless. The maid, Sheila, slaved away in the kitchen or the dark little scullery where she could often be heard singing away like a little bird. She always seemed to be in good spirits. Looking back, I hope that life brought them, each in their own way, the just reward that their courage and hard work deserved.

I shared the top front room with a physics student called Tom Ryan. We would lull ourselves off to sleep inventing technical Limericks, sometimes about one of the professors that we disliked. Thus:

> *Doc Nevin had a cyclatron that he would fill with cream*
> *Best quality country butter, came out along the beam!*

or,

> *Doc Nevin had an etalon through which the light did pass*
> *One day he sat upon it – got interference on his ass!*

On one occasion when Mick and myself were on an outing with our bicycles, at the foot of the high waterfall the Powerscourt Demesne, I slipped and landed with bent knee on a pointed rock. Mick's impatience with the leisurely progress back to Dublin eventually led me to roll up my trouser leg and, to my justification and Mick's consternation, found a liberal stream of blood now beginning to soak my sock. I had to get it stitched up at St. Vincent's hospital and spent the next month with a completely inflexible knee getting about on the bicycle to lectures peddling with one foot and with the disabled other dangling.

These were the days of the Howth Tram that climbed laboriously up to the head to the summit. We would go walking through the gorse and the heather around the golf course that filled the highest part of the headland overlooked by prominences something after the manner of the crown of a molar. We would return then around and down again to Sutton on the narrow isthmus leading out to the headland. From a seat on the open upper deck, with the straining cadences of its whining motor and its swaying to the sound of the trolley singing on the wire overhead, we would enjoy the view over the great sweep of

A weekend cycling trip to fellow student Susan Boyle's family's farm in County Wicklow.

Dublin Bay down to Bray Head, the Sugarloaf and the Wicklow mountains in the background while in the foreground on the other shore, the long north and south granite piers each ending with its own lighthouse reaching out into the bay. Within the harbour were the mail boat piers with their regular sailings across the Irish Sea to Holyhead.

Time moved on and the work piled up. Pure and applied maths, also the physics lectures and laboratory practicals were held in the austere surroundings of University College on Earlsfort Terrace. This latter formed the fourth side of an irregular quadrangle of streets enclosing Iveagh Gardens. Through the gardens you could walk to the students' building with its basement cafeteria and common rooms at 86 Stephen's Green, next to University Church, looking across to the gardens with the trees, flower beds, and ornamental lakes, the little humpbacked bridge that provided the shortest walk to Grafton Street and the rest of the city. At the College of Science on Merrion Street on the other side of Stephen's Green, we attended to chemistry, both lectures and practicals.

The Royal College of Science had been the last great classical building, with its pediment Ionic columns and lead dome, to be erected by the English administration in Dublin. As one ascended the steps leading to the entrance hall, one was under stony observation by a statue of Robert Boyle to the left and by Sir William Rowan Hamilton on the right. It would be fifty years before I glimpsed something of the immense spiritual implications of the contribution to thermodynamics by the former, or the principle of least action by the latter. Subsequently I was able to erect, for myself, a convincing conceptual model based on energy and information that located the accumulative process of collective human consciousness in an evolutionary universe. It would bring a profound sense of meaning and anticipation as to what can come for each human consciousness up the "evolutionary turnpike." For the moment, though, work had to be done on a seemingly endless flow of required learning though what really mattered was what would turn up on the examination questions.

When those first year examinations were over, amid our shared gloomy forebodings of the likely outcome on a pensive cycle ride up the valley of the River Liffey, Mick and myself came across a large yellow aeroplane in a field and a local aeronaut offering rides for a few shillings. We debated at length the remedial possibilities in terms of mental uplift against the considerable expense and finally decided in favour of our first experience of powered flight. As the countryside with its fields and houses, farms and woodlands unfolded below us, there was a fascination which now, after many hundreds of thousands of air miles, still remains as vivid and exciting. Later I would recognize such an overview as symbolic of what can occur with respect to one's own conscious record which can be revisited, again and again, in the light of an ever more mature appropriation of the norms of one's own conscious procedures. In some such manner, we can become privy to the emotions occasioned by profoundly wonderful past experiences, but without the original tensions that had accompanied them.

The conclusion of that first year saw me squeak through the examinations, but being admitted to second year was really all that mattered. "I am very disappointed in you, Crean," said Dr. Nevin. Mick however was less fortunate and decided to return to his native county where he would conquer other fields more to his taste and formidable talents. I would miss him and our weekend rambles.

I joined the St. Vincent de Paul Society that would distribute food vouchers to the poor in Dublin. I would find that one had only to go through some archway into a tenement area behind the well-lit prosperous shop fronts to find a terrible and soul-destroying depth of utter poverty. I loved my Catholic Dublin with its great well-attended churches and common faith, but there was a side to it that I could not understand.

Completing second year with my usual required minimal achievement, I got started on the third year. One of the most interesting guest lecture speakers I would hear was Erwin Schrodinger of the Dublin Institute of Advanced Studies. The subject matter was far over my head though this was something I was well accustomed to. Nonetheless, there was an indelible imprint left by the man who entered from the door beside the blackboard and, with his fingers resting on the long black demonstration bench of the large physics lecture theatre, slowly sidled down to where a small raised stand for his notes stood half way along. All the while, he beamed vaguely at the assembled silent audience, eyes swimming behind the large spectacles. Reaching the offending stand, he concentrated his gaze on someone in the front row who removed it. Apparently

Erwin Schrodinger, one of the greatest of a small group of physicists who have completely revolutionalized human understanding of the physical universe that constitutes our home, did not need notes, less still, the wherewithal to prop them up! On reading a published version of the lecture some decades later, I felt immensely privileged to have been present for its original delivery. The slow, but accumulative progression of affectively laden meaning over the course of life admits of the integration of earlier parts through those more lately acquired.

I would spend every night of the week with my books studying in the National Library. Each little desk had its own green-shaded light adding to the general atmosphere that was wonderfully conducive to concentration. When the library closed at 9 p.m., there would be coffee and conversation. I had one acquaintance advanced in Honours Mathematical Physics who lived near me in Grove Park. I would bombard him with questions as we stood overlooking the parapet of Portobello Bridge over the Grand Canal watching the reflected streetlights in the still water. Close by the canal bank was a private nursing home and when we saw bright lights burning on the top floor at the far end we knew that some emergency surgery was in progress and said a silent prayer that all would go well.

As my courses progressed I became increasingly fascinated by the implications of the many-faceted and ongoing growth in scientific understanding of the universe, of an intelligible reality that reaches far beyond any capacity of sense. It was profoundly moving to me, for example, to determine the wavelengths of light, using a diffraction grating or Fresnel's biprism in the physics laboratory, achieving accurate reproducible measurements from which one could determine magnitudes of order one ten millionth of a millimetre, of the way in which the power of mind can gain quantitative access and some predictive capability with respect to the incredibly minute entities of its own physical ground. On the other hand there were basic questions that remained insistent. The most fundamental and all-embracing concept at the heart of science is that of energy. I was told that energy is only knowable by its effects. No matter what the achievements of science, if we don't know what knowing is, then we don't know what we are talking about!

My first lecture on statistics started out with the comment that there was no satisfactory way of logically defining probability. This would seem to be another fundamental concept that became completely elusive in terms of knowing. Another problem concerned the square root of minus one and the role of "imaginary numbers" in the physical universe. What did such terms as "energy," "probability," and "complex number" really mean? How did the concept "meaning" fit into the great scheme of the universe? What did "meaning" itself mean? Thus would the imponderables of such immensities, as have pushed human thought over time to its limits, constitute a conviction that what really only mattered was what could be of practical use and thus subject to both personal and collective verification. I would later take heart from the assertion in a history of technology that the engineers and their steam engines ultimately contributed more to the science of thermodynamics than did the scientists of their own time!

Two good friendships I formed at that time seemed to share my own allergy to examinations: Sylvester O'Farrell and Joseph Plunkett. Sylvester had started ahead of me yet would acquire his degree some time later at St. Mary's University, Halifax. Years later, he would score in the top half percent in the Graduate Record examinations screening applicants for the leading graduate schools in North America. Joe's fascination was with geology but the degree eluded him also. Nonetheless, he proved so successful in exploration that he was able to sell out his interests leaving, so I gathered, his wife and child financially independent on his early and untimely death.

Sylvester's family had a large house in its own grounds outside the city in the fashionable area of Rathgar. A small gate lodge guarded the entrance to the short driveway that led past the broad sweep of lawn and tennis court to a large two-and-a-half-storey house. Adjoining the latter was a walled-in little court-yard, off which opened outhouses, which formerly I supposed to have been stables. A broad flight of stone steps led up to the first floor. The O'Farrell's pharmaceutical supply company and the stockrooms were located on the first floor. On entering the broad front hall, one was greeted by the faintly distinc-tive, though not unpleasant, odour from the stacked boxes of adhesive surgical dressings in the storerooms. Stairs led up to the large second floor living quar-ters. There was a framed photograph of a signals regiment from the First World War on the wall of the upper landing which often gave me pause to ponder. Sylvester's father was one of only half a dozen of those serried ranks of young men who had survived the carnage after being invalided out as victim of a poi-son gas attack. Sylvester's parents were extraordinarily kind to me. Food was still short, particularly in student lodgings, and his father's standard refrain when I appeared round the corner, was: "Here's Pat, hide the bread!"

Sylvester had the use of the firm's van that gave us a marvelous freedom of Dublin's fascinating hinterland. Later Sylvester himself acquired "Don Giovanni," a tiny cream-painted baby Austin, of early 1920s vintage. It was a sort of large pram with a tiny, but incredibly noisy little engine sticking out under its dainty diminutive bonnet in front of the straight up and down glass (potential death trap) windscreen. It had little doors with latches, if you both-ered to use them, and a gate gear box that required double-declutching. In the middle of the steering wheel were little heavily chromed levers for advancing or retarding the spark or adjusting the mixture. Mostly I found it easier to leave the art of gear changing to Syl. We used an empty Castro Oil tin for a muffler, though usually it remained on the back seat so we could show any inquisitive

Garda officer that our muffler had just fallen off! This was indeed the very stuff of real classic motoring. We loved it! Stalling at traffic lights was a problem but I would simply jump out and push from the back until we were started again. On one occasion, the driver of a huge cement truck, watching the procedure, was totally drowned out by our seven-horsepower fire cracker propulsion and could hardly get his own monster going for the laughter. Somehow the population of Dublin seemed to tolerate us well, if not actually enjoy our antics.

Sylvester had a small private chemical laboratory on the lowest floor of their family home. Explosives exerted an irresistible experimental fascination. Once he tried an electrolytic method of preparing the highly unstable and explosive lead picrate that didn't seem to work. He wandered off but omitted to switch the apparatus off. When he came back he had enough of the stuff to blow the end off the house. Fortunately it was in the sink so he discretely turned on the water, committed it to the Dublin sewage system, and hastily took off.

When the student Chemical Society decided to hold a seminar on explosives, Sylvester was the natural choice, with myself as his assistant. Our trial practice would take place in his own lab, one of a series of rooms opening off on either side of a single broad corridor. The first experimental demonstration was of black gunpowder using an antique horse pistol that, in Sylvester's opinion, I would be really good at pulling the trigger. Taking the precaution of standing in one of the rooms and poking the pistol round the corner through the open door. I duly pulled the trigger and produced an enormous explosion with clouds of smoke. This was followed by a dead silence broken only by the sound of falling plaster. The two of us watched in horror as the opposite wall developed a large gaping crack at the top, while the falling plaster was pouring out a similar crack at the bottom. Everybody was out at the time and Sylvester thought perhaps the wall needed some attention anyhow.

As it happened, the lecture was an immense success. Sylvester droned on with loads of technical data and equations, and the audience, well aware of his capabilities, was becoming rather bored and restless. Finally he droned on to my key warning: "Mr. Crean will now demonstrate this effect."

I was high up in the darkness of the large tiered chemistry theatre and pulled the trigger on cue, as practiced. An enormous belch of flame, smoke and particles roared out over the backs of the assembled heads below. Sylvester had not, indeed, let them down!

My good friend Joe came of a very distinguished Irish family. The grisly head of one of them, Blessed Oliver, remains on public display in a church in Drogheda, while his uncle, one of the signatories of the proclamation of Irish Independence, was executed after the rising in Easter 1916. I gathered that Joe was a Papal Count, but also that it would have been the height of indiscretion to mention the matter. Sadly, he would die as a young man in an accidental fall in his garage. Joe and myself shared an immense affection for the Irish countryside, particularly the Wicklow Mountains. One of the high moments of our years of friendship, when I returned from one of my later whaling voyages, would be to take off down the old military road in his battered Mercedes, amid landscapes that remain fondest of all in my memories.

In my second year, an event occurred which would have a profound effect on the rest of my life. It was at a "hop" in the "Aula Max" beside 86 Stephens Green that I met May, and we were going to meet for coffee in Bewley's on Grafton Street the following day. That night as I made my way home, down Harcourt Street, then crossing the humpbacked bridge over the Grand Canal to my nearby digs in Grove Park, a totally new aura had enveloped the familiar lamp-lit grey pavements, the Georgian doorways, fronts of closed shops looming in the darkness. Everything was suffused throughout with an enormous sense of exciting purpose. I remembered the deep sense of spiritual peace in the

Dressed up for a dance at University College Dublin in 1949. L to R: Tom Ryan, Sylvester O'Farrell; and myself.

presence of my old friend in Shalbourne, the presence of the feminine. But this was even further charged with a youthful purpose, of bringing forth new life on a shared journey that would take on the turbulent challenges of existence. It had, of course, nothing whatever to do with the catechetically enjoined ideals of love of God and love of neighbour, attitudes of mind that could only be brought by rigid intellectual control of all spontaneities of emotion.

Thus it was that May would become the centre of my hopes and affections for many years. Falling in love brings about a deep reorientation of one's conscious living which is then directed to someone other than oneself. If it offers an enormous incentive to new dimensions of shared spiritual growing, it can also take the form of a desire to possess, or at least give that impression. In authenticity of distinction, patience would seem to play a crucial role. I suspect the lines of W. B. Yeats may have been all too appropriate:

> *She bade me take life easy, as the leaves grow on the tree*
> *But I, being young and foolish, with her would not agree.*

Just before the final examinations the following year, May received a grant to continue her French studies in Paris and ended our relationship. Somehow I had known that my own enthusiasm was not reciprocated, though still, the news was devastating. Over the period of the examinations, I would lie awake at night listening to the Rathmines Town Hall clock chiming the quarters and the hours, so registering the sleep lost and intensifying wakefulness in the effort to sleep.

I could hardly believe the news that I had passed the primary degree in mathematics, physics and chemistry. But as I entered a fourth year for a Diploma in Chemical Technology, following my attraction to Applied Science, I knew that life would never be quite the same again. Again Yeats, who had undergone much the same experience with Maud Gonne, comes to mind:

She bade me take life easy, as the grass grows on the weirs
But I was young and foolish, and now am full of tears.

Sometimes some dramatization catches the prevailing mood of those days in 1949, such was true of Carol Reed's film dramatization of Graham Greene's *The Third Man* then showing in Dublin. The closing scene, where the girl walks away in silence down the long avenue of trees that leads from the graveyard to the tram stop, caught the moment perfectly. You try to do the right thing, but all the effort, all the commitment drifts off into silence and you are left alone with the futility of what might have been.

So it was that I sought respite in my beloved Wicklow Mountains. It was a particularly great joy to be able to undertake weekends of walking with good friends, later of rock-climbing with the Irish Mountaineering Club, and eventually the unforgettable experience of an expedition to that high world of ice and rock in the Swiss Alps. My companions on those adventures, those that have survived the attrition of the years, remain so to this day. In real friendship there is mediated much that transcends the normal process of the days.

These essentially happy and modestly successful four years ultimately came to an end, even though formal courses always seemed to leave one with so many unanswered questions. It was not all unwarranted however, for some decades later I was able to bring together enough understanding of the fundamental ideas to be overcome by the overwhelming sense of the magnificence of the universe which is truly our proper home. I had come to love Dublin and on occasion, walking home on a summer night watching the foliage of the trees around Stephen's Green hanging motionless in the lamplight, there would be a hastily smothered pang of my having to leave it all. Employment prospects were poor in Ireland, particularly without some very special skills or appropriate influential connections.

One of the last outings in the summer of 1950 with Aleck Creighton and

UCD Graduation Day, 1950! A Bachelor of Science Degree and a Diploma in Chemical Technology. My father's response to my excited phone call home: "Wait a minute now! You're telling me you've got your degree?"

his brother-in-law Mike Brachi was to our favourite climbing location, where the screes and cliffs of Luggala rose steeply above the dark waters of the Lough Dan below. Michael was a whaling chemist and, sitting on a rocky ledge looking out over that unforgettable panorama, I became fascinated with the account of his Antarctic voyages. On expressing my interest, he suggested that I write to Chris Ash at their head office in London. Though an initial response indicated no vacancies it was followed almost immediately by an offer of employment. Apparently Michael himself was required to carry out a special project at Food

Manufacturers Research Laboratory in England and I happened to apply to exactly the right place at exactly the right time. By such occasions the directions taken by our lives are determined. At this remove, such moves are not matters of pure chance but would seem properly occasioned by one's positively responding to a constructive eclecticism, wherein is formed the enduring pattern of each life.

A week later, watching the lights of Dun Laoghaire fall astern of the Holyhead mail boat, I was swept by a torrent of conflicting emotions. On the one hand was the prospect I had so longed for – a great sea adventure. On the other, part of me knew that I was somehow, like so many before me, leaving Ireland for good, leaving the country of my family roots where I had come to feel so at home.

CHAPTER V

WHALING YEARS

LIFE ABOARD *S.S. BALAENA* (1950–1951)

In the hungry years following the Second World War interest in Europe turned towards the rich stocks of oil and protein to be found on the whaling grounds off Antarctica. Of the pelagic expeditions that were equipped and set forth, one of the most successful was that of the Anglo Norwegian whale factory ship *Balaena*, launched from a Harland and Wolff, Belfast, slipway in 1946. My appointment as assistant chemist to *Balaena* constituted a remarkable stroke of exciting good fortune, presaging an experience that remains just as vivid and alive some sixty years later.

On the 25th September 1950, nudged by tugs into the stream from our fitting-out berth at Palmer's at Hebburn-On-Tyne, with a first tremor of engines, *Balaena* began to gather way down the Tyne, past moored ships, cranes, gantries and lofting assembly sheds, the grey morning punctuated by the occasional flash of a welder's arc or staccato burst of a riveting hammer. Then, open horizon ahead, engine beat and speed increased. The bow lifted to a first North

Sea swell. The bell buoy marking the channel entrance, obeisant to *Balaena*'s wake, bade clangorous farewell to a setting forth upon such great business. At last we are off!

The passage to Oslo Fjord and a sheltered anchorage near Husvik is short but there was ample time to explore my new surroundings: a varied flotilla of small boats, ferries, whaling gear, stores and crew from the nearby major Norwegian whaling centre of Tonsberg. Everything seems to have been thought out by someone, from a spare propeller shaft for a whale catcher to the latest antibiotics for the ship's hospital. Anchor weighed, *Balaena* was flanked down the inlet by launches and fishing boats, carrying families and well-wishers, until, to stentorian blast of steam whistle echoing from wooded hillsides, our remaining escorts fell astern as course was altered into the broad sweep of the Skaggerak. Rounding the north of Scotland, our last sight of the British Isles through misting rain was the high dark-grey outline of the rocky island of St. Kilda. We became accustomed to the sights, sounds and motions of a vessel under way, always sensitive to the vagaries of sea and weather.

There was a variety of preparatory work for the whaling season. More southerly latitudes of the North Atlantic and moderating conditions occasioned much deck activity. We welcome the easy tropic passage, the constantly refreshing breeze from the ship's way. During the day, a great assortment of wire cables and strops were cut and spliced for use in flensing and lemming operations. Later, after darkness fell, there were movies on deck. High above our heads the after running light weaved a gentle pattern against a brilliant canopy of stars. There was the occasional streak of a meteorite or lightning flash on a distant horizon.

Some of the crew would bring up their bedding and sleep on the cooler deck spaces by the stern rail of the ship. I could not have done it for there was always something disturbing about that part of the ship. Looking out from the bow towards where we were going, towards new horizons was always exhilarating. In contrast, looking back from the stern, towards where we had been, always made me feel uneasy. Looking to the future seemed to be the proper emphasis. Many years later I would find an echo of such feelings in the reflections of T. S. Eliot, himself watching the ship's wake by night from the deck of an Atlantic passenger liner:

> Fare forward, O voyagers, O seamen
> You who came to port, and you whose bodies
> Will suffer the trial and judgment of the sea,
> Or whatever event, this is your real destination.

But in those younger days of high excitement and prospect of adventure, such prescience lay far beyond my own horizon. Later I would grasp the demanding symbolism of the sea.

On the 14th October the low barren sun-baked outline of Sombrero Island heralded our entrance into the Caribbean. On the 16th October we secured alongside a finger pier at the Esso refinery, Lago, Aruba in the Netherlands West Indies and commenced filling our thirty-six tanks, each of five hundred ton capacity, with heavy fuel oil. The more fortunate lunched on the awninged patio of the Esso refinery club by the beach. Now, accustomed to the heat, we were shocked by the air-conditioned chill of the company offices when we collected mail.

In view of our deep draught, loading was completed at anchor outside the reef from one of the smaller refinery tankers, commonly referred to as the Maracaibo "mosquito fleet." We watched the lazily swimming sharks through still clear blue translucent water and then the spinning propeller of the tanker as she cast off.

Balaena *moored in Oslo Fjord near Tonsberg, Norway.*

An early photo of Balaena, *found for me by the librarian at the Maritime Museum in Vancouver B.C., showing the original flight deck and hanger for a Walrus aircraft, initially used for spotting whale. When I came onboard in 1950 for my first whaling season, the aircraft were no longer being used and the hanger had become a storage area and "slop-chest" for crew purchases such as boots, clothing, tobacco and liquor.*

Balaena *at anchor off Cape Town, South Africa, with Tabletop Mountain in the background. Explosives could not be transferred to the catchers in the docks so* Balaena *had to lie at anchor outside.*

Weighing anchor on the 17th October, we passed occasional islands thick with jungle and through the great muddy plume of the Amazon until, with Trinidad on the starboard beam, course was set for Cape Town. The cheap pine whaling deck, receptive to the steel-spiked heels of the flensers, lemmers and labourers, was laid over our main oak deck. With a total complement of some five hundred, there was no shortage of labour. Flush steel plates were positioned over the heavy pivoted, dogged and bolted covers to the large pressurized boilers and digesters immediately below on the main factory deck.

From afar off, on the 5th November, forewarned by a solitary cloud on the horizon in bright morning sunshine, *Balaena* approached the magnificent smoky-blue outline of Table Mountain, the immediate towering backdrop to beaches, people, all the buildings and bustle of Cape Town. We joined our catchers, buoy and expedition boats already secured alongside in Duncan Dock.

I had been given the address of an old acquaintance from Dublin who was now teaching in the botanical department of the University of Cape Town. I started out on foot, in my social innocence, to see some more of the place. Apparently, much of my route lay through parts of the city where the only Europeans entering were parties of well-armed police! I finished up in the dark at a gate lodge of the South African Survey establishment. On the concrete floor sat an African in a blanket before a heap of glowing embers while at a small table with a telephone by one wall was an enormous coloured man watching me. I explained my predicament, that the ship would sail tomorrow and my search for an old friend. I couldn't have had a more friendly or helpful reception. After some phone enquiries, he told me that my friend would be home at ten and how to find him. Having some time in hand we started chatting. When he told me that I shouldn't be talking to him, I started to laugh, but he was quite serious. The notion of "apartheid" seemed so absurd, that is, of course, until I glimpsed the horror of the thing in action.

We parted on the best of racial terms and I was waiting for Karl when he arrived home. It was the first time I had seen a literal enactment of the classic expression, "his jaw dropped!" After a delightful reunion, he drove me back to the ship with a stack of Dublin social magazines and a copy of Jacques Maritain's *Introduction to Philosophy*. This latter would, apparently, acquaint me with the rudiments of the vast philosophical and theological foundations of my Roman Catholicism.

On the 6th November, lying off in the bay in accord with legal requirement, we ammunitioned the catchers and set a southerly course. Here the narrow, warm south-flowing Agulhas Current from the Indian Ocean rounds the southern tip of Africa and meets the cold east-flowing Antarctic Circumpolar Current. As air and water temperatures dropped rapidly, we bade reluctant farewell to the balmy subtropics. Soon the assembled fleet were rolling and pitching in that violence of the sea occasioned by the great westerly winds of the notorious Roaring Forties, largely uninhibited in fetch over the immense expanse of the Southern Ocean.

It was now that the skill and workmanship of *Balaena's* designers and builders, seamen and engineers, was tested. As the wind screamed around the superstructure, mast and funnel guys, great cresting seas would break over the bulwarks and slash across the wide expanse of heeling open deck. The ship became a well-loved living thing, one's loyal champion parrying and thrusting against the onslaught of the storm.

All loose objects were secured or stowed amongst clothing in the cabin drawers. Meals became exciting. Thus, for example, on one occasion three of us landed on our backs, under the evening smorgasbord. Some one had omitted to re-secure our mess room chairs to the deck after cleaning. The cream cheese was eventually recovered from my right slipper but was charitably pronounced none the worse! On the 10th November, the first pack ice is sighted, and with it, moderating weather. We had arrived on the whaling grounds. There now began the steady routine of fleet operations that would continue for upward of some three months of intense activity.

Divided into two twelve-hour watches, a daily pattern of events is established which continued for seven days a week, broken only by exigencies of weather and two hours for Christmas dinner. The latter will be the sole occasion for our hairy complement to appear incongruously dressed in best attire! The fleet consists of ten whale catchers, both the newer Setter and older Terje boats; two buoy boats, ex-corvettes, used to return catch to *Balaena*; two expedition boats used to scout for whale and to ferry supplies or transfer bags of meat meal to the storage and supply ship *Thule*; also to carry cargo nets of meat to the refrigerator ship *Bransfield*.

Balaena was the heart of the operation supplying fuel, food, stores, spares, explosives, also workshop and medical services. To aid in directing operations, there was a large steel plate, marked by concentric range rings, on the bridge. This was constantly updated to provide a running plot. On it, labeled magnets indicated the relative positions of the ships, also whale that have been killed, inflated for positive buoyancy, and flagged. Positions were determined by radio direction finder and electronic ranging system, developed on board. This operated over greater distances than conventional radar.

Some eighteen fleets were operating on the whaling grounds. By international agreement there was a strict limitation on catch, monitored by inspectors, to conserve stocks. These included baleen Blue, Fin, Humpback and Sei whales, also the toothed Sperm whale. Whatever the combined fleet's success or failure, when the quota is reached, all whaling must cease. Competition was intense but *Balaena* had always been amongst the top few performers, if not first or second. We had unbounded confidence in Captain Virik, commander of the fleet, and his seemingly constant and formidable presence on the bridge, resplendent in his favoured cloth cap and riding breeches.

In this regard we all had our own fancies. Mine was for a war-surplus Air Raid Warden's black battledress and, from the ship's slop chest, leather bedroom slippers, secured with fishing twine, for use in the lab and factory! This was supplemented by an old duffle coat, cadged off the freezer foreman, and heavy leather sea boots for occasions when sample material from the whaling deck was required.

Balaena was a large tanker, its tween decks consisting of a tank deck with very limited headroom supporting the much higher factory deck, immediately below the topside flensing and lemming decks. Aft of these were the boiler and engine rooms, crew accommodation, ship's hospital and slop chest where one could buy toiletries, clothing, boots, etc. Here also was the laboratory, crowded with instruments and glassware, where I worked, and below it two smaller

A fellow whaler's composite impression of Balaena *in full operation on the Antarctic whaling grounds. Both flensing and lemming decks are busy removing blubber and dismembering a carcass. A whale catcher is refueling at the bunker port in her starboard side amidships. In the foreground another catcher is leaving after delivering a whale to the group moored astern of the factory ship. An ex-corvette acting as a towing vessel is approaching the after quarter of the factory ship to deliver another whale. In the upper right centre of the picture one of the ex-catchers that is used as an expedition boat or for local transport with her distinctive cargo boom delivering sacks of meat meal to our storage ship,* Thule. *On the horizon is one of our fuel oil tankers while another catcher is shown skirting an iceberg.*

laboratories, one of which includes a photographic darkroom. Occasionally we developed films for some of the crew. Invariably, each will include a shot of some worthy posing beside an enormous limp whale's penis!

Furthest aft was the steering flat with its great-toothed quadrant bolted to the rudder stock and servomotor. Close by was the ship's explosives magazine, which we hoped was well respected by vessels close manoeuvring to position tail flukes at the foot of the slipway. This latter sloped steeply upward through the after superstructure, to the main flensing and lemming decks.

Amidships there was a superstructure, always known as the Marble Arch, bearing two fifty-ton winches. These were attached by heavy cables to the two arms of the massive scissors grab used to haul whale tail first up the slipway onto the main deck. A single whale may be up to one hundred feet in length and weigh as much as one hundred tons. The open space below the winches afforded space for the carcass to be drawn forward by another winch, from the flensing deck, where the blubber was removed, onto the lemming deck where final dismemberment occurred. Forward of the main deck was the bridge superstructure, radio and instrument rooms, accommodation for senior officers, galley, provision and mess rooms, the hold and freezing plant, and the bo's'ns locker with its unique blended aroma of tar, paint, solvent and cordage.

On the 12th November, the first whale was hauled on deck. The blubber was swiftly cut and winches used to peel back the great strips much the way one might peel a banana. These were fed down into a hogger and then pumped into one of the ten twenty-ton pressure boilers below. The carcass was drawn forward onto the lemming deck and the great back fillets of meat were removed. A massive hook-shaped knife, pulled by a powerful winch, was used to sever the ribs. Further reduction involved the large steam-powered bone saws. Tougher whale parts and internal organs were fed down into the rotating cage of one of the eight twenty-two-ton Kvaerner pressure digesters with their attendant slowly stirred pressurized settling tanks. Oil was skimmed off and the remaining slurry fed to centrifuges for separation of solids, fines and water.

Depending on quality, meat from the great back muscles was cut up and frozen in sixty-pound blocks or transferred in cargo nets to the refrigerator ship *Bransfield*. Alternatively, it was put through one of two large Fauth screw cookers. Solids were separated out by vibrating screens and screw presses and then diverted to fall from tray to tray in the flame-fired Buell dryers. This process yielded a ninety-five percent protein high quality meat meal. Liquids, after

The two fifty-ton winches housed on "Marble Arch", the bridge over the junction between the lemming and the flensing decks, for hauling whales up the slipway. Shown is the planking used to protect Balaena's *main deck from the spiked boots of the flensers and lemmers. It was installed steaming southward through the tropics at the beginning of each season, and dumped overboard on the homeward bound.*

The lower jawbone of a whale on the after lemming deck. Also shown is a sheet of blubber awaiting dismemberment and being fed into the hogger below the main deck where it would be pumped into the cookers.

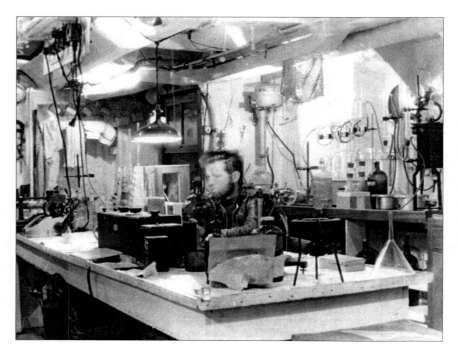

The chemistry lab where I worked the night shift as junior chemist during three off-shore whaling seasons 1950 to 1953. During the summer season of 1952, I worked at the shore station at Donkergat, South Africa before re-joining the fleet for the off-shore 1952-1953 expedition.

various stages of centrifugal separation, desludgers, clarifiers, purifiers, then fil-tering through plate and frame presses, went to double effect evaporators. Final concentration under the more gentle vacuum finishers yielded a clear concen-trate of delicious meat extract.

My job, in this connection, was to determine the final moisture, creatine and creatinine contents of the sample, usually enjoying some of it licked off the end of a standard glass rod. This often occurred while waiting for a moment when the ship's motion will allow the laboratory balance to stop its antics and permit a weighing. After a while, when the meat extract foreman's patience begins to run out, I must do the best I can!

Bone went down into one of the twenty-two, twelve-ton pressure boilers where it was under steam for six hours, the oil being skimmed off using sight glasses. The residue was dumped out onto a conveyor belt and returned over the side to nature. Whale liver, rich in Vitamin A, was hogged, and fed through steam heated rollers to the solvent extraction plant to provide a high potency oil. This was used for vitaminizing the margarine later to be produced ashore from our whale oil. The residual flakes were bagged for meal rich in Vitamin B2. In assaying the oil potency, after a breakage resulting from an unfortunate and unexpected ship movement, I had to remember not to leave the very expensive optical cells on top of the Beckman Spectrophotometer!

I soon became accustomed to the routine of the whaling grounds. After a coffee in the mess, I read the notes in the laboratory logbook from the senior chemist and scheduled the night's work, usually involving analyses for product quality, or of raw materials, pertinent to plant present, or possible future, operation. This was my only contact with the dayshift. I worked alone and tended to get out of touch. Once, for example, surprised by finding an area of smoke-blackened twisted steelwork on the factory deck, I discovered that a serious fire had occurred two weeks earlier! My Norwegian colleagues were more interested in coaching me to address another of their number with some selection of highly offensive expletives, evoking great hilarity, rather than in my grasping any of their own conversations. Thus, I became dextrous at being extremely rude in Norwegian while the laboratory tended to become my hermitage!

Off watch, I had a go at the Dublin social magazines given to me by Karl in Cape Town. Somehow, in contrast to the busy and purposeful round of our activities on the whaling grounds, these seemed so trivial and boring that they soon went over the side. Whatever my love for the Dublin of my student days,

I felt a sense of pride in what we were doing and the omnipresent challenge of the sea and ice where we earned our living.

I then turned to Maritain for some authentic spiritual enlightenment. However, after my second reading, the only genuine conviction that I was left with was that I hadn't the faintest idea of what the book was about! My fascination was with practical matters, measurements that could be made, practical applications that would both employ and verify the merit of the outcome. Could such an erudite muddle of words have any practical and verifiable application in meeting the demands of human living?

Perhaps largely from habit, before turning in, I would spend a little time in prayer and reflection kneeling on the short settee and looking out through the steel-encircled disc of heavy glass, secured by massive wing-nuts, towards the rim of grey horizon broken only by an occasional table berg, lustreless and flat by the light of our usually overcast Antarctic summer. Were the words of my prayers just meaningless patter? A sort of insurance policy in case there was something out there listening? Could there really be some master plan of meaning to it all, even though it far transcended the limits of merely human thought?

One aspect of the work was severely taxing. My fortitude in the presence of biological dismemberment, and even worse, the odours apt to be attendant upon it, was very limited. There was a program involving analyses of intestines that proved very demanding. The sheer magnitude of the organs doesn't seem to help. Much nicety in timing between judgment of wind direction, asphyxia and throwing up is called for!

Returning to the lab with my ghastly sample with its wriggling complement of intestinal parasites in its large porcelain dish, I would deposit it on the bench at the far end of the laboratory, retiring rapidly to the other to take a deep breath before running down with forceps and scissor to cut it all up. The next step was to smother it in sodium sulphate to absorb the moisture. After that it became a matter of chemistry rather than biology and I could resume normal breathing! There is something quite intransigent in such matter of spontaneities of feeling and attitude. I have never been able to bridge the gap between the two disciplines, occasioned by such grave visceral displeasure. Others, such as my friend Mike Brachi, never seemed more fulfilled than when rummaging about with a huge knife in a heap of something on deck that I found horrific!

Breakfast was accompanied by a mimeographed news sheet, typed up by our whale inspector, from the B.B.C. overseas service. Knowing this, one of our radio operators once put out an old taped broadcast, from an earlier voyage, on the ship's radio that the inspector, amazed at the quality of reception, dutifully recorded and distributed. None of us noticed anything unusual! We became, I suppose, so thoroughly engrossed in the immediate business at hand that the outside world assumed an air of unreality.

On the 25th November, we got an unexpected opportunity to mail a letter home. One of the whale catchers had lost a propeller blade in the ice and steamed north to Fremantle for repairs. Though its absence mid-season was a significant handicap to the fleet, we knew that the company would try to get some airmail back to us if timing allowed.

Voice radio communications among the ships of the fleet were of the greatest interest to our competitors. Accordingly, our transmitters were fitted with scramblers that required matching receivers to permit intelligible conversation. We were much entertained when we heard a catcher belonging to another fleet reporting that the Japanese were in the vicinity!

The big steel door of the bunker port in *Balaena's* side usually remained open and was the scene of much traffic as the smaller vessels came alongside, using a whale as fender, to refuel and take on stores and explosives. It was also an opportunity to exchange gossip about the latest of the gunners' idiosyncrasies.

These star performers in our little community tended to be highly superstitious and unpredictable with respect to anything that might be thought to prejudice their performance!

Sometimes I had to make a rather dodgy leap onto a bulwark, while grabbing the shrouds of a catcher, as it rose and fell beside the bunker port. I didn't much like this for the seawater below me was one and a half degrees below freezing. I had found by experiment that, when dipped in it, my hand immediately went numb, thus precluding any sensation of cold! The reason for such an unwelcome excursion was usually to draw boiler water samples for analysis when contamination by condenser leakage of cooling seawater was suspected.

Twice a week, I was night shift film projectionist. My projection booth was a provision room next to one of the big whalers' messes, a suitable hinged flap being cut in the bulkhead. This also provided a shelf for the projector. I developed a taste for dried smoked mackerel, numerous bundles of which hung from the deck head. In bad weather I had to hold the projector in place. An unfortunate mishap once occurred while I was groping in the dark for another mackerel. I did not want to incur again the grave displeasure of an unusually tough and outspoken audience!

Our accustomed seascape usually included drifting pack ice and icebergs under seemingly perennial grey skies. Some of the bergs were enormous, one being of the order of eighty miles on one side. Occasionally there was bright sunshine, excellent visibility, good catching, exquisite shades of blue in sea and ice. High good humour prevailed throughout the ship's complement. We were at full cook. Sometimes, however, the visibility closed in. A film of pristine white snow covered our usually bloody deck and there were no whale. The plant fell silent. All conversation was kept to a perfunctory careful minimum. It was not for this that we came down here.

Thus, for example, on one such occasion as I passed an old Scottish winch-man disconsolately viewing the empty deck, I remarked, "Not much of a day, Jock!"

The answer spat back at me was vitriolic: "Whut dae ye expect in the Antarrrctic!"

Before her christening and launching from a Harland and Wolff slipway, *Balaena*'s official designation was Hull No. 1327. On the 21st September, *Balaena* shared an experience with an earlier predecessor, Hull No. 401. I had come up on deck for some fresh air and was watching the loose pack ice swiftly thumping and grinding down the side of the ship. There was a sudden impact, the ship staggered, heeled to port, recovered, and resumed her passage. As I watched, a high wall of ice carrying much antifouling paint and marine growth from below our water line, reared up on end above our starboard main deck bulwarks. I was little concerned because I knew of the massive strengthening of our forefoot and bow plates for such a contingency. Later I would be much reminded of the experience of Quartermaster George Rowe on the afterdeck of *Titanic*!

At coffee in the mess shortly afterwards, there was a different story. The forefoot had been broken through and the flooded forward compartment bulkhead was in need of being heavily shored up by the crew. I set out to take a look but was warned that the skipper was on the bridge and did not take kindly to sightseers! I would later choose my timing to look down at the buckled plates as white water poured back and forth, with every rise and fall of the waves. As with *Titanic*'s forepeak tank, so we became accustomed to noisy blasts in and out of the vents. It seemed, however, that we could still continue the whaling season.

A third of the way through the season excitement mounted with the prospect of mail, picked up at Aruba, as our tanker *M.V. Biscoe*, loaded with oil fuel, had come through Panama to exchange fuel oil for our whale oil. When

Clearly evident is the damage sustained in the forefoot of Balaena *as a result of a collision with a large ice flow in the Antarctic on the 21st September, 1950.* Balaena *is seen here lying in dry dock at Hebburn on the Tyne, August 1951.*

weather permitted, she secured alongside using four whales as fenders. There was work here for the chemists to ensure that tanks have been properly cleaned, samples drawn and analyzed for insurance purposes, before she started on the long voyage homeward.

Two thirds of the way through the season this was repeated with our tanker *M.V. Powell.* This event was rendered all the more remarkable for Captain Cornwell was accompanied by his wife, as usual. When she first appeared on the bridge wing looking down on our gory main deck operations, everything stopped and all eyes were fixed on the solitary woman to visit our community! For those of us who were a little tired of the ship's Norwegian cuisine she prepared a very English and very robust, veal and ham pie. When, somewhat disapprovingly, the mess steward served me a great slab, honour required that I finish it off, though it took almost the rest of the watch to manage it!

Most of the summer in these latitudes there were twenty-four hours of daylight. But then a perceptible interval of twilight was soon followed by rapidly lengthening hours of darkness. Now, work on deck required floodlights, and in the steam-clouded gloom, one must be vigilant for a suddenly taut steel cable by your feet and some many-ton mass of meat and bone lunging suddenly out of the darkness, all the while dodging open manhole covers to the digesters below.

The production figures were growing and looked good. For every 2,000 barrels of oil, a rum tot was issued to all hands. A sweepstake was started on what would be our total oil production for the season. In the final days, the non-participating chemists, responsible for the production figures, had to be discrete as to what the final figure for the season would be – not that much advice wasn't sought!

On the 5th March, as the long terrible night of the Antarctic winter was coming upon us, the radio signal, *STOP FANGST*, announced the end of the season. Now, all the smaller vessels had to be bunkered and provisioned. But then, in the vicinity of Peter the First Island, as the weather broke, we found ourselves in a blizzard of blinding snow and the short range on the bridge radar showed some two hundred bergs in our immediate vicinity. Following a screen formed by three of our highly manoeuvrable catchers in line ahead, the fleet followed in sequence on a generally northerly course at full speed. They were good at this, though it much disturbed our whale inspector, a retired naval officer.

With clearing weather the fleet went its various ways, some to over-winter in Cape Town. For the next month *Balaena* followed a great circle course to the Irish Sea and the South Stack Light. The temporary wooden whaling deck now worn, splintered and riddled with deadly bacteria, was ripped up and thrown over the side. The engines settled down to their long uninterrupted task. The swift glittering steely dance of the great crossheads and connecting rods, the spinning of the massive crankthrows to the hiss of steam through the valve chests, the muted roar of fan and furnace, the rhythmic clack of feed pump shuttle valve united in some swelling diapason of power that would not be stayed. As the days turned into weeks, the great grey rolling swells of the Southern Ocean gave way to a deep, tropical, translucent blue foam sparkling along steel flanks. So the crude oil in our bunkers, from deep in the ground of South America, turned into steam by our roaring furnaces and fed to the exquisitely informed and skilfully fashioned poetry of our great engines, would advance the horizons of each human consciousness amid our complement to new and untried dimensions of our living.

Everything that was accessible topside or in the factory was scrubbed with caustic soda and readied for painting. Lying in my bunk in the early morning, the bright sunlight streaming through the wide open cabin ports, flickering reflections on the cabin deck head, the hiss of foam along the ship's side, the pulse of engines, all endowed with great delight those first waking moments. We'd done our job and were homeward bound!

But then, in April we received a distress call from one of our refrigerator ships, the *S.S. Ketos*. She had not accompanied us to the Antarctic but had been chartered to carry a cargo of cement from Denmark to Brazil. The steam jacket of an evaporator used to distill fresh water from seawater had exploded, punching a hole through the hull in the engine room which rapidly flooded. She was not that far distant from us. While careful watch was kept on our own damaged bulkhead, *Balaena* speeded up to full engine revolutions and one could sense that slight but characteristic 'whip' to the hull. We were informed that an Italian passenger liner was standing by but she failed to answer our radio signals. It turned out that she had attempted to take *Ketos* in tow but, with a collapsing bulkhead, the crew were removed as she started to founder. We were able to slacken off our engine revolutions and ease the strain on our own bulkhead.

This scene yielded to the grey windswept vastness of the North Atlantic. Again I reached for the duffle coat, swaying on the back of the cabin door, before going out on deck. Soon, however, instead of an unbroken horizon, we occasionally sighted another vessel, then seabirds and fishing boats. The last of the walkways on the factory deck were finished off with their coat of dark green paint. Excitement mounted throughout the ship as we entered the Irish Sea. There appeared to port the Wicklow, and to starboard the Welsh Mountains. With the South Stack lighthouse on the starboard beam we altered course for Liverpool Bay. One of the launches dropped from the Trinity House vessel standing to in Liverpool Bay sped towards us. The pilot boarded over the main deck bulwark and was escorted by the mate to the bridge.

Balaena, entering the channel to a clangorous welcome from the bell buoy, made her way, between the channel markers, to anchor in the Mersey on the 15th April 1951. Around us now were the cranes and warehouses, the masts and funnels of ships behind dock caissons. A busy passenger ferry from Birkenhead, bound for the Liverpool Stage, slewed against the fast flowing tidal stream. All were watched over by the great green patinated birds, each atop one of the twin towers of the waterfront Liver Building. For many years, including two world wars, they had seen the coming and going of merchantmen, many of them never to return. Now, coming in from sea, I felt the unseen presence of a distinguished company – seafarers who, whatever the odds, got on with the job, among them my Uncle Edmund and my Uncle Harry.

The lighters appeared from Lever Brothers' plant, further up river, to load oil, but our preoccupation was with the paying-off tender, lying alongside the bunker port, to ferry us ashore. Taking the London Underground from Euston Station to Waterloo, tanned, bearded and clutching a huge sea bag, I watched my fellow passengers, pale, expressionless and seemingly trapped in some long-accustomed routine. I felt myself to be extraordinarily fortunate. Soon I turned the key in the lock of number 6 Orford Gardens, Strawberry Hill – my loud inquiry from the hall elicited a delighted response. The voyage was done. I had sailed round the world. Not only that! I had a small monthly retainer that would be quite adequate to meet my needs for a summer of glorious freedom.

My next visit was to see my old friend in Shalbourne. All the magic of my earlier experience remained as vivid as ever, the old manor and stables, the dogs and horses, all watched over by the nearby downs from which I had seen the Nazi bomber. It seemed an absolutely appropriate sort of place to return to and recount my great adventures on the high seas. Well did my old scout leader know it, for I think what she really enjoyed was my own enjoyment of it all. This time I had two magnificent whale teeth to present as a memento of the voyage that, for many years, would sit on the broad windowsill in the dining room.

It was the time of the Festival of Britain. The old high shot tower that I used to pass on my way over Waterloo Bridge was gone and replaced by the pageantry of the Festival, including the great new Concert Hall. I spent a day there but became so exhausted by such a profusion of exhibits that I spent most of the afternoon asleep in a deck chair overlooking the river.

My old friend from the hostel on Saint George's Square had graduated in medicine and was now an anesthetist in St. George's Hospital at Hyde Park Corner. With some of his fellow doctors and nurses we had a wild evening on the rides and attractions at the Festival Pleasure Gardens at Battersea. I had great fun in the ghost train with a nurse companion by swiftly dangling my fingers over her face in the dark eliciting screams of consternation until she realized the attentions were not spectral. On emerging with a great cry to her friends, "Do you know what he did?" – I was greeted by the icy glare of the long queue, all of whom thought they could only too well imagine!

Then it was off for the remainder of the summer to Ireland. My first ambition was a visit with my old friend Joe Plunkett and a drive in his old Mercedes down to Wicklow. Where the old military road curves upward at the head of the valley there is a commanding and unforgettable view of Glencree. I was seized with an enormous longing and affection. This was the country of my own roots and it was the friendships of the Torpeys and the O'Farrells, the Plunketts and the Crichtons with whom I wished to share my life.

There followed wonderful climbing expeditions with Aleck Crichton to the cliffs above Lough Dan. And later, there would be a visit to one of my most favourite places in my most favourite country, the undulating landscape of the sheep farm on the shores of Ballysadare Bay, the Crichton family home. Here the great surf of the Atlantic beats upon the shallow sandbars at its mouth, below the steep slopes and imposing profile of Knocknarea.

SECOND EXPEDITION TO THE ANTARCTIC (1951–1952)

All too soon the summer was over and another season at sea was at hand. *Balaena* celebrated my twenty-fifth birthday on the 14th August by docking at Palmers Yard for refit. I travelled over to Newcastle on Tyne and joined the ship in dry dock. I was impressed by the amount of damage done to the forefoot by that collision with ice. The major problem about living on a ship in dry dock, however, is that one cannot use the sanitary facilities. If needs must, this meant getting up in the middle of the night, dressing, and heading down the gangway and along the dock to a sort of unlit communal, and appallingly smelly, brick outhouse.

It was thus, that on the 28th August, as soon I finished the work I promptly left for Newcastle Central and the train for Liverpool. Such impromptu trips off the main rail routes took, as I discovered, all night and several changes before I was finally able to get a flight to Dublin to visit friends and family.

Returning a week or so later to London and meetings at the company offices on Grosvenor Square, I again found myself heading back to Newcastle to rejoin *Balaena*. Delivered once again by taxi under the night glare of mercury arc lights high up on the steel work of dockside cranes, I found our refrigerator ship *Bransfield* secured alongside the dock, while *Balaena* and then a large naval fleet oiler were rafted alongside. Shouldering my gear over *Bransfield's* main deck, I collected my cabin key from the mate, settled in, and fell into a deep sleep.

A couple of hours later I was blinking confusedly into a bright flashlight as a guttural voice urgently enjoined me to: "Get up, get up. *Bransfield* is on fire!"

With a shock I realized that the cabin was filled with a dull red light and shot over to the porthole to see a large ship's ventilator mere feet away glowing cherry red and spouting a great jet of flame. There were seven fire appliances on the quay and a fire float in the river pouring water into *Bransfield* that was now listing heavily, her starboard bridge wing leaning on *Balaena's* main deck bulwarks. Her masts, derricks and aerials leaned awkwardly over us. Work staging and heavy equipment toppled, oxy-acetylene gas bottles rolled and crashed as they broke free.

Eventually, hastily summoned tugs moved the fleet oiler and then our selves from the burning ship. Later we heard that the firemen were ordered off *Bransfield*, when *Balaena* was moved, because it appeared that *Bransfield* might capsize at the dock. As it happened, the fire was successfully dealt with and *Bransfield* joined us later in the Antarctic for that season.

For the last of our stay, we lay at anchor downstream, being ferried back and forth by one of the ship's motor lifeboats. One night, returning from town, this would provide me with another unpleasant encounter with trains. The dock gate that I thought was convenient for *Balaena* proved to be on the wrong side of a great unlit bank of coal sidings at the other side of which, beyond the towering coal staithes, I could see the lights of *Balaena*. Tripping over unseen tracks and ankle deep in coal dust, I was half way across when I heard the unmistakable rumble of coal wagons approaching in the darkness. Frantically, I floundered towards the staithes and with enormous relief, heard the wagons rumble and clank in the darkness behind me.

On the 22nd September the clank of the anchor winch of the fo'c'sle was followed by the first engine movements as we set forth upon another great adventure, out through the buoyed channel and into the North Sea. Soon we were secured by anchor and shore lines to the rocks at Husvik in Oslo Fjord. Again we became the scene of immense loading activity as small boats loaded whaling gear and supplies from Tonsberg.

Having some time to spare, Chris Ash, Mike Brachi and myself took off by train to Drammen and then to Kongsberg, magnificent in autumn foliage, where they made the guns for the whale catchers, and from thence up the long valley into the mountains where we transferred to rail car and passenger ferry. This would bring us up to Rjukan, the site of the great hydroelectric power scheme. As we pulled in to the little town it seemed that every room in every building was ablaze with light. During the war, the Nazis had used the power to produce heavy water intended for research into nuclear weapons. After the failure of the R.A.F. to bomb the generating station deep in the narrow valley, the courageous action of a small group of Norwegian forces, trained in Britain and parachuted into the neighbouring mountains, successfully incapacitated the plant and even managed to sink the rail ferry, with its precious tank cars of heavy water, in the immense depth of Lake Tinssjo.

We proceeded by bus up the steep head of the valley, past the great penstocks, to spend the night in a little hotel on the shores of Mosvatn. The following day we climbed to the top of Gausta where there is a manned weather station. Apparently light refreshment was normally available, but the sole occupant seemed suspicious and taciturn in the extreme. Mike looked around the little room and, noticing a plate in the wall peeked through a small hole, only to step back smartly with a cry of "My God – another eye!"

On the 5th October we slipped our moorings and headed toward the open sea amid a flotilla of small boats, returning to the North Sea and around the north of Scotland to the Atlantic. Four days later, radioed warnings of a strong storm in our area were soon followed by rapidly deteriorating weather. On the 11th October, a broken tooth in the great steering quadrant which was mounted on the rudder stem and operated by a gear and servomotor from the bridge, left us adrift and violently plunging and rolling while trying to keep the bow into the seas by engine movements.

It was impressive to watch the huge seas that night with their foam-torn crests as they swept out of the darkness into the ship's lights and as speedily vanished. Securing the quadrant, a segment of teeth was replaced and course resumed. We were thankful for the skilled efforts of our engineers in the cramped and dangerous conditions of the violently moving steering flat. By daybreak, the work was done and, to our relief, we resumed course at much reduced speed. There is something deeply disturbing about being adrift in storm conditions, so symbolic, as it well is, of those inner storms of the mind that can vitiate conscious control of one's affairs.

On the 16th October the weather started to moderate and soon we were able to move the little projection hut into position on the meat deck, behind the after superstructure, and watch movies displayed on the back of the structure housing our bi winches over Marble Arch – amid that wondrous tropical magic of a vast canopy of brilliant stars. Shortly before midnight on the 20th October, passing the Sombrero light flashing atop its tower close by on the starboard beam, we entered the Caribbean. Now it was time to write letters to be mailed home from Aruba where we were soon loading fuel oil alongside the finger pier at the Esso Refinery, taking the time for a swim in the warm waters of the lagoon, followed by lunch at the club.

Crossing the South Atlantic we secured alongside in Cape Town on the 12th November. Travelling more circumspectly this time by the suburban rail line, I received a great welcome from Karl and his friends the Heustons at Rondebosch. The punctuation of sea voyaging by such wonderful moments, the pacing of life's events by periods of ship-born routine, enlightened by such anticipations and adventure, was enormously fulfilling. The tyranny of commuting back and forth to a stuffy office seemed remote. I had escaped and was truly glad of it.

On the 14th November we slipped Duncan Dock and set course for the ice and the whaling grounds. Two days later we passed *William Barendz*, one of our competitors, and were soon rolling heavily in huge seas, the decks impassable and chaos in the mess. On the 19th November the first whale was shot and the first ice sighted. And so we turned to the routine of the whaling grounds.

My New Year's resolution for 1952 was that I would keep a brief summary of events for the remainder of the voyage in my little pocket diary. However laconic the comments, they serve to vividly recreate the salient incidents, attitudes and concerns over the remainder of the season. My friend Gulickson, the third mate, promised to supply me with the ship's noon positions, making it possible for me to record our progress on a large South Polar Chart secured on the ship's bulkhead in my cabin. An added advantage was that a small nut dangling from a pin through the South Pole enabled me to watch the ship's roll measured by the degrees of longitude covered. The first entry noted was the

Photograph of myself taken by Chris Ash, senior chemist/day shift, during my third whaling season 1952-1953.

brevity of our greeting to the New Year owed to Gulickson managing to blow our powerful ship's siren apart and pulling the lanyard off the ship's bell! Other sample jottings convey something of that life on the whaling grounds:

3rd January, S.68 degrees, 21 minutes, E.172 degrees, 38 minutes. 6 Blue, 1 Fin. Mix-up in the forward separator room and meat extract plant filled up with whale oil, glue water and meat extract – solidified meat extract blocked the pipes, necessitating dismantling – weather rough and foggy – M.V. Powell hove to 50 miles off – some big bergs around. I found 16% oil in glue water from CV19 separators! – ascorbic acid work had been dropped because of problems with pentoses and uranic acid – concentrate on spleen analyses

9th January, S.70 degrees, 06 minutes, E.168 degrees, 45 minutes. 5 Blue, 6 Fin, 3 Sperm. Busy night with liver and meat extract analyses – peculiar creatine readings – repair gauge cock on flasher but it still seems to be leaking – very hot drilling in the factory – think I can get a good buff from the electrician – weather foggy and very cold

10th January, S.70 degrees, 12 minutes, E.168 degrees, 55 minutes. 6 Blue, 15 Fin. Extremely busy night again – feeling very tired – do another series of tests on separators – also meat extract batch – manage small fire in the fume cupboard but put it out with wet towel – lot of ice crashed down off the radar – dangerous if you are out on the bridge

12th January, S.68 degrees, 28 minutes, W.174 degrees, 06 minutes. 1 Blue, 21 Fin. Go over to M.V. Powell – left dangling in bo's'ns chair between two ships which rolled apart taughtening the rope immediately in front of my eyes like a steel bar, only rapid intervention by the mate on the tanker saving me from a swift descent through the offal between the two ships into the freezing waters below, due to bloody fool on the foreplan securing the line – drink with second mate (on tanker) – meat extract and liver oil (analysis)

13th January, S.68 degrees, 02 minutes, W.173 degrees, 48 minutes. 2

Blue, 40 Fin. Show (film) "Birds and Bees" – sentimental nonsense – more salt problems (boiler water) meat extract and liver oil (analyses) – weather cold calm clear but cloudy – sea like glass and many bergs around – spend most enjoyable few minutes on fo'c'sle absorbing tranquility of scene compared to the plans (flensing and lemming) and factory

18th January, S.69 degrees, 52 minutes, W.177 degrees, 07 minutes. 17 Blue. Hurray some sunshine – Syd Brown (biologist and whale inspector) has a revolting foetus in the lower lab which he keeps injecting with a hypodermic of appalling dimensions – very pleasant party with Eilertson (3rd engineer) and three hour argument on religion

21st January, S.70 degrees, 19 minutes, W.174 degrees, 13 minutes. 25 Blue, 8 Fin, 4 Sperm. Weather fine – take sample on deck of liver from 66 foot Fin with 9 foot foetus – spent much of night writing home – whales too burnt (putrefied) for meat extract – deserter from catcher found on board after 14 days – now working on Belsen (meat meal dryers) – M.V. Biscoe (tanker) should be here in early March – visit from Johann (bunker port bos'n) – "don't go in that strop there, come to Tvedestrand" (obtaining boiler water samples for analyses often involved boarding a whale catcher rising and falling alongside the open bunker port in the side of Balaena, putting one leg through a rope strop, and being lowered to grab a shroud and land on the catcher bulwark. On my first attempt, I banged my head on the unnoticed steel block rigged outboard of the ship's side but was fortunately grabbed by the watchful Johann)

23rd January, S.70 degrees, 24 minutes, W.171 degrees, 57 minutes. 12 Blue, 27 Fin. 50,000 barrels up – 66 foot Fin shot with Wetlesen gas harpoon hauled up – take sample of liver – invited by 2nd mate for a drink -very pleasant chat – he had a whole selection of battered binoculars from catchers – I think one must have been dropped from the crow's nest

27th January, S.69 degrees, 42 minutes, W.172 degrees, 10 minutes. 1 Blue, 64 Fin. Show "Captain Boycott" – what will the Norwegians think of England after "Eureka Stockade" – enjoyed it very much myself – M.V. Powell came alongside – notice order hard a port as she draws level stopping her stern from colliding with us as happened last time

28th January, S.69 degrees, 16 minutes, W.171 degrees, 56 minutes. 13 Blue, 36 Fin. M.V. Powell alongside – go over to do tanks (measure ullages and draw samples) drink with chief engineer and then the Captain – went over in the basket (large and padded slung between two derricks) – much more comfortable – woken during the day by collision as she was leaving due to sudden heavy swell

30th January, S.64 degrees 54 minutes, W.171 degrees, 01 minutes. 18 Blue, 5 Fin. Sight two Japanese factory ships – 1 tanker and 1 transport – see them clearly through large mounted bridge binoculars – get hold of duffel coat at last and present bottle to big bos'n – Paddy Linden did some fine repairs on the coat

7th February, S.71 degrees, 02 minutes, W.174 degrees, 07 minutes. 8 Blue, 2 Fin, 1 Sperm. M.V. Biscoe arrives and takes some photographs – very nearly a collision as she cut across our bow – we had to go full astern with wheel hard over – she got stuck in ice – liver oil and meat extract (analyses) – fix Soxhlets (apparatus for extracting oil from solid samples, placed in thimbles and washed by refluxed ether) – many gulls around

18th February, S.70 degrees, 14 minutes, W.173 degrees, 11 minutes. 3 Blue, 39 Fin. M.V. Biscoe left at 23.00 – four hours pumping would have finished her cargo – storm came up very suddenly – screaming wind, blinding snow and pitch dark – she was lucky to get clear without damage – manage to get prints (I had made in our darkroom) over to Brian (Mullen, 3rd mate)

21st February, S.70 degrees, 13 minutes, W.172 degrees, 14 minutes. 2

Blue, 16 Fin. Usual routine and typing repair list – do some rum distilling in lower laboratory, a very pleasant occupation – somehow the steward managed to get salt water in it (every 2,000 barrels of whale oil production a tot of rum was issued to all hands. On this occasion the steward had inadvertently diluted the cask with seawater and approached Chris Ash as to whether something could be done about it. Chris regretted that little could be done about such a terrible blunder but that we would do the best we could. From then on, the large still in the lower laboratory was kept busy until we had a large number of bottles of pure rum. A couple of these were returned to the steward as representing, more or less, our best professional intentions!!!)

4th March, S.71 degrees, 13 minutes, W.171 degrees, 14 minutes. 11 Blue, 21 Fin. Steaming slowly through pack ice and many floes – ship shuddering heavily when she hits them – snowing – heavy swell and shifting ice – intensely cold

5th March, S.71 degrees, 44 minutes, W.171 degrees, 53 minutes. STOP FANGST – ice forming everywhere and bitterly cold – strong wind and snowing hard – start bunkering catchers (for voyage home)

7th March, S.70 degrees, 12 minutes, W.166 degrees, 53 minutes. Continue clearing up lab – steaming at 8 knots with catcher screen ahead – three boats over thirty miles (due to the very poor visibility near Peter the First Island, the fleet altered course to northward to get clear of bad weather, navigating by radar and in line ahead formation. The radar screen displayed an area of about 200 square miles and included approximately 200 large ice bergs at the time. It was fascinating to watch the line of ships on the radar screen, snaking their way among the bergs)

17th March (St Patrick's Day), S.62 degrees, 08 minutes, W.87 degrees, 04 minutes. Great celebration – manage to squeeze ten into cabin

18th March, S.59 degrees, 14 minutes, W.72 degrees, 32 minutes. Pass

close off Cape Horn – see the Horn itself through bridge glasses – a black
mountain ascending to jagged peak flanked with whitish precipices

On the 1st April the captain passed out the Rotterdam telegram. Apparently the gunners from the *Abraham Larsen* fleet had flown home from Cape Town. When coming in to land at Schiphol, a private plane had suddenly appeared and the landing was aborted. Unfortunately two of the engines had already been put in reverse and the plane crashed killing all on board.

On the 9th April, we passed the *Abraham Larsen* herself, homeward bound. I sent a telegram accepting the post, offered the previous day, as chemist at the Saldhana Bay Whaling Station in South Africa. At 23.00 hours the light on Cape Finisterre was abeam.

On the 12th April, as we were heading up the buoyed channel towards Liverpool, the ship's siren started blowing and the vessel herself slewed round in the channel. One of the cabin boys had jumped off the stern. The Trinity House pilot tender immediately realized what was happening and headed for us, dropping her launches as she came. Through the glasses I could just make out his head in the water before he vanished; his body was never recovered. I hardly knew him, but Paddy Linden, in tears and watching beside me on deck, told me that he had tried to calm the young man and got him to go below. Now at the end of the voyage and unable to face whatever problems lay ahead, he had chosen to end his own life.

How little it is that we can know of the extremities and turmoil of mind that can be hidden behind some mask of normalcy. One of the most surly, taciturn and evil-looking characters in *Balaena*, who had been a stowaway, proved such a good worker that he was welcomed back. Once I met him hurrying along from the radio room carrying a radiogram when he snapped: "I've no glasses, read it."

It said: "Operation successful, all my love, Mary."

Hearing that, without a word, he vanished back into his own silence and down the alleyway.

We secured alongside in Canada dock at noon and the voyage was done. The moment I had been looking forward to for so long had arrived but now, standing at the head of the gangway looking down at the dock, there is a profound reluctance to face up to a massive change in the accustomed shared routine of life. This may have been not all that unusual. I have since read about survivors of the terrible wartime prison camps in the Far East who, on returning to England, lived together in small groups unable to face the prospect of returning to their old lives. Nevertheless, fare forward I must!

Returning to a big welcome at Orford Gardens it was time to catch up on all that had happened in my absence. However one item took precedence over all the rest. I was saddened to hear that the old friend of my pre-war childhood days in Pope's Lodge across from the Sisters of Mercy Convent, Sister Patrick, was gravely ill in hospital.

The following day, as I entered the ward, I was greeted by the welcome in those kindly eyes, set off in the little weather-beaten face in its familiar white coif and black veil. It was the same old Packy. I prattled on about my great adventures but the words seemed all wrong for the occasion. Then I realized that what she was enjoying was my own enjoyment in telling all my stories! Her small gnarled brown hands rested on the pristine white coverlet – these were the hands that picked me up when I slithered off my bike and split my ear on a metal pole and rescued the football which I had kicked into the river when the senior girls in the school wouldn't let us play. When it was time to go I didn't know what to do or say. Awkwardly I raised her hand and kissed it. As I made my way out of the ward, I looked back once more to that most gentle of smiles. She was so much wiser than I. The most important things of all reach far beyond mere words.

During the voyage we had received a request for scapular and tracheal whale cartilage for use in plastic surgery. The following day, carrying two large glass jars of preserved cartilage, I took the train down to East Grinstead where the hospital was located. It had originally been founded to deal with the terrible burn injuries sustained by air crew during the war. The delight with which our material was received became clear when I saw them stowed away in the cartilage bank, a domestic fridge in the matron's office containing a solitary little jar with a specimen no larger than my little finger. After a splendid lunch, the surgeon, Mr. Schofield, insisted on showing me the photographic records of their work. As large colour plate after colour plate passed before my eyes, showing the most appalling injuries and remedial procedures undertaken, I was ready to collapse. Eventually he invited me to be present when they used the material – but I hurriedly assured him that, regrettably, I would be away for the summer!

After receiving the necessary injections at the Hospital for Tropical Diseases in London, there was time for a glorious week in Dublin before leaving for South Africa. It was wonderful to see my old friends, the O'Farrells, the Plunketts, the Torpeys and the Crichtons. There was, however, a particular project that I had in mind. I knew that it was one of Kitty's fondest longings that the family would own some small piece of property in Ireland. My mother had heard about a cottage on Howth Summit from the lady we used to stay with on our visits to Howth and which was now for sale. I was delighted to be able to put my savings from the two whaling seasons into the price of it. Though I repeatedly asked them to take full ownership, my parents were adamant that it remain in my name. They would come there for their summer holidays. But in a way I would only later come to understand, it was "Pat's cottage" they were looking after with the hope, so avidly shared by myself, that one day it would become my home.

SALDHANA BAY WHALING STATION,
SOUTH AFRICA & THIRD WHALING VOYAGE (1952–1953)

The company wanted the chemist, me, at the Saldhana Bay Whaling Station in South Africa as soon as was practical for starting up the plant. Accordingly, I flew to Copenhagen on the 25th April and from there, where one of our engines failed on take off, to Oslo. On reporting to our office, I was fortunately redirected at the last moment from my original charter flight that crashed on a mountainside killing all on board.

As it happened, the flight I took was not all that uneventful. After being struck by lightning over Greece, putting the radio out of action, we arrived at night at Heraklion in Crete unannounced and in darkness with no sign of any airport and fuel low. After circling the town and firing flares from the cockpit, cans of petrol were ignited along the runway and we landed. I didn't realize how close a call the whole venture was until I saw the pilot coming down the cabin aisle, white as a sheet and his shirt and uniform jacket collar soaked in sweat. There were several more stops along the way before we arrived at the Bloemfontein Airport in South Africa where the whaling crew and myself were met and driven to the whaling station.

The whaling station was located some forty miles from the nearest village, a place where the sand and thorn scrub reach out to the wave-worn rocky shore of the South Atlantic. We lived in a large bungalow, with a wide stoep, overlooking the plant and the broad sweep of the bay. It was all novel and exciting, yet Africa awoke for me a sense of some haunting presence, of an immense spiritual antiquity.

A daily routine soon established itself. After breakfast I would make my way to the little laboratory that stood slightly apart from the plant buildings. Here I would check the samples drawn from the "batch pots" of the previous 24 hours' oil production for colour and free fatty acid to determine to which

The Dondergat shore station where I spent the summer of 1952 as the resident chemist.

of our storage tanks they should be pumped. Then it was up to the tank farm to measure the ullages of the tanks that were being filled. Then there were the various routine lab tasks and calculations, boiler water samples to be tested, standard solutions to be made up and calibrated, official samples for oil consignments to be shipped to our buyers on the Randt. These would be carried by barge to Saldhana and transferred to tank cars waiting on the dock.

Filling the cars required some care for we had complaints from South African Railway about overfilling the tank cars when any expansion due to temperature changes could lead to spillage. Understandably, the last thing needed by the driving wheels of locomotives straining to haul freight from the low-lying coastal plane up onto the 6000-foot-high great plateau of southern Africa was us lubricating the track for them!

Then we had complaints about shipping short weight. The buyers weighed the tank cars before and after loading. I had to use tables supplied for the tank car and measured ullage from the lid. Prior to loading, two Africans cleaned out the inside of the tank car and I decided to get into the car myself and see what was happening – much to the disgust of the Afrikaaner foreman. Sure enough, the cleaning was impeccable over that part of the car that could be seen from the hatch, the rest was covered with a thick accumulation of solidified oil coatings. This could readily account for our discrepancies. After appropriate exhortation to remedy the matter, the two Africans pushed me up into the hatch opening where, to my consternation, I became immovably wedged. The foreman, now livid, and his assistant, standing on the little catwalk, pulled on either arm from above while the Africans, now convulsed with laughter, continued their exertions from below. I was aghast at what appeared to be the only feasible solution – removing my trousers, when I realized that there were two tabs of metal supporting the lid of the tank car holding me firmly by the hips. All that was needed was a rotation through 90 degrees. Overwhelmed with relief at my release, I stuck my head through the hatch to join in the merriment below. For the foreman, however, my "loss of racial face" was irretrievable. Superior persons of the right colour do not get stuck in tank car hatches.

Despite extensive drilling, it had proved impossible to find any source of fresh water and supplies had to be brought for Saldhana by the water boat. This was a large ex-naval diesel launch in which the whole boat was flooded with fresh water except for the engine room. This seemed to provide sufficient buoyancy for it to carry out its purpose. I became great friends with the skipper, a Cape coloured who dried strips of whale meat biltong wherever they could be dangled about the boat. I would have occasional outings with him to Saldhana and he eventually let me steer the boat. The steering wheel was in the little open-backed wheelhouse atop the engine room casing and was connected by chains to a cumbersome yoke on the rudder. Consequently, it required great patience before any alteration of course might be anticipated. I learnt this, to my friend's consternation, by doing a complete figure eight in the harbour at Saldhana, mercifully without hitting anybody or anything else.

Eventually, he would let me take the boat back while he would settle down in a snug corner of the warm engine room. Coming back at night I had to keep two leading lights, that is one mounted behind the other, in line, one above the other, so as to avoid the sunken wreck of an old hospital ship that could only be seen at low water, then alter course to starboard for the whaling station. The first time I tried this was a blowy night and we plunged along with the spray flying, glowing red or green respectively as it was lit up by the port and starboard navigation lights. I found it wonderfully exhilarating and was thoroughly in my element until he made his sleepy way up on deck, only to give a startled cry, grab the helm, and put her hard over. He had apparently omitted to tell me that the lights were mounted well back from the sea on a hillside. I was about to drive the boat hard up onto the rocky foreshore in the pitch dark!

The only way of getting off the station for a break was along some forty miles of dirt road to the nearest highway and from thence another forty miles to Cape Town. We had three vehicles: a comfortable Studebaker saloon car, a bouncy Fargo pick-up, and a bulky Chevrolet van with minimal provision for the driver to see anything other than more of its interior. The only problem was I didn't know how to drive. I had, however, an Irish driving license which, when I got it, could be purchased for ten shillings. Whether a person had actually ever seen a motor car or not was irrelevant, nevertheless I used it to get a visitor's driving permit.

On my first foray I was stuck with the Chevrolet but consoled myself with the thought that the friends I wished to visit lived outside the city. I would be spared trying to master control of the direction and motion of the vehicle through complicated traffic. Then, at the last minute, I was asked to pick somebody up at the Adderly Street Station in the middle of the city. That I managed to do so without killing myself or any one else remains a mystery. Then I had to master the Fargo. On the level it was straightforward enough, but on a hill it took a long time for me to avoid a sort of syncopated lurching progress as I bounced up and down in the cab involuntarily clutching and de-clutching. Fortunately for me this manner of progress failed to catch the eye of management.

The most remarkable character on the station was James, my African assist-ant in the laboratory. He was extraordinarily adept in picking up the routine skills required and had an arithmetical prowess an order of magnitude beyond my own.

For some reason or another, the station chemist was thought to be the immediate source of medical assistance. In the case of myself, such confidence could hardly have been more firmly misplaced. There was also present, how-ever, a restlessness, a need to attend to other aspects of life not present in my technical world. Often, after dinner in the mess, I would walk along the shore, past the explosives magazine and around the point to where there opened up the long deserted expanse of the lagoon, its shores unmarked by any human habitation. Some distance up from the beach, there was a small clearing in the thorn scrub, and a tiny neglected cemetery of seamen whose ships had once lain in the anchorage. The youngest was a seventeen-year-old from *H.M.S. Boadicea* who, according to the faded inscription, died falling from aloft in 1882. There, with the remains of those for whom life's voyage had ended in that desolate place, away from the clattering winches and noise of the plant, poised between the dark obsidian of the lagoon and the rim of hills hard and black against the fading light, the plumage of the flamingos massed on a sandbank would some-times blaze with fire in the last rays of a setting African sun. In the stillness and

James Benson, the laboratory assistant at Donkergat, and his 'brother' (on his right). James was a delightful companion in the lab and quite outshone myself in his arithmetical abilities.

loneliness of the place there was an insistent urging that somehow its haunting beauty was meant to be shared – some longing would not be stilled.

Once, while delivering oil by lighter to the railhead some two hours steaming across the bay from the whaling station, I delivered a letter to the wife of one of our catcher captains. Standing in the doorway, in my old leather sea boots and dark blue battledress, waiting for a reply, I was intensely aware of something compelling and mysterious, of a fascination I did not understand, the presence of the feminine. I recalled that sense of deep fulfilment, of some mystically evocative sharing that could enchant those evenings in Shalbourne, then so far away. Perhaps it was time to seek a new direction in life.

Joining the ship in Cape Town on the 9th December 1952, I set forth on my third Antarctic whaling voyage. It turned out that fourteen of the crew were missing, including my cabin mate Michael Brachi and also Paddy Linden. They were being picked up by one of our whale catchers that had not yet left.

According to Mike he had brought a charming young cousin up to the top of Table Mountain on the cableway to view *Balaena* lying far below secured alongside in Duncan Dock. It was something of a shock when he beheld the berth to be vacant, his home and livelihood having departed for the Southern Ocean. He insisted that he had been told the wrong day. An alternative hypothesis explained the oversight as being due to a strong distracting affection inspired by his delightful young companion!

What had happened to Paddy Linden and his shipmate Mike McGurk was very different, and provided an insight into the disgusting and squalid nature of the apartheid regime in South Africa. Looking for the Merchant Navy Club, they got lost and asked the way from some girls passing them in the street. A watching policeman appeared and arrested all of them. Despite their protestations about their intentions and *Balaena's* imminent departure, they were told to plead guilty in court for soliciting sex from coloured women and pay the fine or they could forget the next whaling season!

There is an outcome to the voyage that can be readily found in the chemist's report. Typical production tonnages might include whale oil 25,000, sperm oil

Christmas of 1952 being celebrated in the festively adorned officer's lounge. Proceeding from front clockwise: Mike Brachi, assistant chemist; myself, assistant chemist; Ian Lewis, assistant fridge engineer; "Shep" Shepherd, instruments; Hugh Symons, biologist; Bill Mitchell, fridge engineer.

2,000, frozen meat 4,000, meat meal 4,000, grax meal 1,000, meat extract 130, liver meal 200, and liver oil 30. Most of the whale oil will be turned into margarine, a product that resulted from the early efforts by chemists to produce butter from animal fat. Numerous other items will also be delivered, a whale brain for Charing Cross Hospital, scapular and tracheal cartilage for the plastic surgeons at East Grinstead Hospital, a whale's eye for a New York hospital, pituitary and adrenal glands for pharmaceutical companies. Someone estimates that there will be a year's supply of margarine for about six million people and, given all our other products, that there will be few in the British Isles that remain untouched by our endeavours in one way or another.

I took this photo at the end of the 1953 season: "Shep" Shepherd, Ian Lewis, Mike Brachi, Hugh Symons and Chris Ash.

For each of us there is an individual and deeper outcome. For some it will be a return to a summer of farming or fishing before setting forth on the next season. For some it will be other ships. For some it will be a holiday and preparation for the next season. For myself there will be graduate studies in Toronto. For many of us, there are memories of an accomplishment much needed for our time, some clear-cut milestone reached and passed on the journey of each life. Certainly for myself those surely remain.

In a few short years, other cheaper and more readily available sources of edible oil will be found. The days of the great whaling fleets will largely end. In 1962 *Balaena* will be sold to Japanese interests. These will centre primarily on whale meat for human consumption. As I concluded my final voyage there was, as has now become evident, a somewhat naïve sense that the whale stocks would replenish amid those krill-abundant and far distant, cold southern waters.

It still remains, however, only a step in the right direction. There remains a further consideration, that which seeks the well being of the global community. In this regard, the operations of *Balaena* accorded with an international agreement to regulate catching in order to conserve whale stocks. It was also agreed to respect the zone of the Southern Ocean between 70 and 160 degrees west longitude as a whale preserve. There were others who did not do so. Thus, for example, there is a reference in *The History of Modern Whaling* to Aristotle Onassis as the "whaling pirate" and to the fact that his "floating factory the *Olympic Challenger* will take its place in the history of whaling as one of its blackest chapters."

Another example I happened on by chance at the Donkergat whaling station. I was admiring a beautiful little steam engine that drove the paddle in a large mixing tank, apparently for whale oil. One of the Africans told me that it used to be running all the time before United Whalers had taken over the station. The quality of the oil is judged by the amount of free acid it contains. After death the fat in the body of the whale begins to break down into glycerol and fatty acids. Thus the amount of free fatty acid is a measure of the lack of freshness of the processed whale material and its commercial value. I could only suppose that the illicit stirring of some neutralizing reagent into the oil would have produced a spurious increase in value!

The dramatic decrease in the Blue whale population was, however, only too evident in our own catch records. Now, some fifty years later, it has been estimated that there has been a ninety percent depletion of the fish stocks of the ocean mostly through extremely efficient factory ship operations not unlike our own. There is much to be said for the intriguing Gaia hypothesis in which the planet can be seen as a holistic self-regulating system in which the activities of the biosphere are closely connected with the complex processes of geology, climatology, atmospheric and ocean physics. In the long-term global good ordering of the planet, competition is an inefficient means of stimulating human striving, a poor second to cooperation.

New problems require new solutions, ideas that tend to spring most readily into minds, stilled by some reflective process of becoming personally present to the vast diversification and complexification of evolutionary world process, and openness to whatever individual role one is called. I suspect that such an endeavour can lead to a spontaneity of peace and satisfaction that lies beyond our direct command. What is evolving is information and we each become an indestructible part of it, destined for some role beyond our present event horizon.

Times have moved on but my three *Balaena* voyages in 1950 to 1953 as an assistant chemist continue to furnish an allegory of hope, of a company that brought together the requisite skills, quality of workmanship and personal consideration. Though no ship is impregnable to the worst the sea can offer, prevalent not more so anywhere than in the stormy reaches of the Southern Ocean, a high level of organization and preparedness in undertaking such expeditions for the vital purpose of providing foodstuffs for a Britain still under rationing after the Second World War provided an allegory of service which seemed to me of far reaching significance in our world today. It constituted a significant contribution to some emerging global good of order insofar as it enabled, at least in principle, the possibility of further social collaboration in bringing about higher levels of order and freedom from suffering. In that there was an enduring sense of satisfaction, rooted in some such depth of meaning, though that would only become explicit after many years of reflection on the experiences of others.

Fare forward, O voyagers, O seamen,

for, as incomparably, and very properly, expressed by Chesterton:

There is good news yet to hear, and fine things to be seen,
Before we go to paradise, by way of Kensal Green!

CHAPTER VI

STOP FANGST!

A REFLECTION

With the lengthening perspective of the passing years, my experiences of life aboard *Balaena* would become rounded out as but a particular part of a vastly greater enterprise, of its relation to the emergent role of human conscious life on planet Earth. It would seem to be increasingly clear that the decreasing net availability of cosmic energy to initiate change, to bring about and sustain self-organizing systems, occurs in parallel with the emergence of higher levels of order, complexity, functioning. In the very forefront of this process there has come about the most extraordinary evolutionary development of all, an accumulative and over all net progression in meaning, the collective product of responsible human minds over millennia.

On the 9th September 2001, at the Stratton House Hotel in Cirencester, Gloucestershire, I attended a dinner of 'alumni' who sailed in *Balaena*. It marked for myself a delightful reunion with some of my old shipmates including my friend Hugh Symons, once a whaling inspector. We had bid our adieus to each other fifty years prior on Adderly Street in Capetown. *Balaena* had become something very special, shared by all of us and still vividly alive for each of us, each in our own individual way. We had once known her as home and workplace and an ordering source of focus and intention concerned with the supply of nutrient fats and protein to a hungry Europe.

A few days later, on the 11th September, while visiting my niece and her family in Swansea, Wales, there would occur the unbelievable horror of deliberately planned mass murder in the violent demolition of the twin towers of the World Trade Centre in New York. In the wake of this horror, I would be reminded of the fictionalized account of another whaling voyage, published just one hundred years before my own, which was based by Herman Melville on his own experience of a whaling voyage ten years earlier. It became a classic study of the role of evil and hate, of obsession with hate and lust for revenge that would destroy not only Captain Ahab, but also the vessel and its crew, save only for the narrator of the story.

The significance of my earlier voyages in *Balaena* stood in a long-term contrast, filled with hope as I reflected on the extraordinary level of collaborative effort in the organizing, equipping, financing, recruiting and the requisite skilled personnel. There are many such enterprises, institutions mobilizing particular groups to fulfil communal needs whether on a local or world scale. Thus can individual needs be met, more and more effectively, as human consciousness is progressively freed from anxieties associated with earning a living and survival. There opens up newer exciting perspectives as the promise of its yet unrealized evolutionary potential becomes increasingly apparent through the role of questioning in its own essential attentive, intelligent, reasonable and responsible questioning, and the progressive and accumulative nature of the individual and collective consciousness contents that results. One cannot coherently question that one questions. Nor can one set any limit to the meaning that results for one can always ask: "Is this the last question?"

The drama of those days accomplished something that needed to be made explicit, something that needed to be lived, appropriated, integrated as part of oneself. Sometimes, when the wind screamed around the after superstructure, through the mast and funnel guys, great cresting seas would break over the bulwarks, slashing across a wide expanse of heeling open deck. I would once again reach for the duffle coat, swaying on the back of my cabin door, in preparation for going out on deck and, wedging myself in some sheltered vantage point, I would watch it all and feel a sense of exultation at the challenge and the meeting of it. The ship became a well-loved living thing, my loyal champion, parrying and thrusting against the onslaught of the storm.

On the 8th March 1952, with the onset of the Antarctic winter, it was bitterly cold and a raging blizzard brought about zero visibility. The short range on the radar disclosed over a hundred bergs in our vicinity. A catcher screen was deployed ahead of *Balaena* and while the rest of the fleet followed in line ahead, we threaded our way northward by radar at a steady speed of eight knots. Commander Buckle was distraught at such un-seaman-like bravado but I had faith in the well-honed skills of our Norwegian shipmasters. It was fascinating to watch the 'snake' of ships on the large radar scan threading their way among the bergs.

At the completion of my third voyage, and with no small reluctance, I bade farewell to *Balaena*. The powerful symbolism of sailing the sea would become a metaphor for life itself. I began to understand the origin of the feelings when I came across T. S. Eliot's lines, inspired by his own experience on another deck in the course of an ocean passage:

> *Watching the furrow that widens behind you,*
> *You shall not think 'the past is finished'*

Or 'the future is before us'.
At nightfall, in the rigging and the aerial,
In a voice descanting, (though not to the ear)
The murmuring shell of time, (and not in any language)
'Fare forward, you who think you are voyaging;
You are not those who saw the harbour
Receding, or those who will disembark
Here between the hither and the farther shore
While time is withdrawn, consider the future
And the past with an equal mind.
At the moment which is not action or inaction
You can receive this: "on whatever sphere of being
The mind of man may be intent
At the time of death" – that is the one action
(And the time of death is every moment)
Which shall fructify in the lives of others:
And do not think of the fruit of action.
Fare forward.

There had been a real sense of satisfaction in the work, of worthwhile accomplishment. It seemed to be an exercise which symbolized for me the fundamental values that bring about some overall good of order that not only makes community function, but also contributes to helping make possible new advances that can enrich human living and reduce human suffering. In contributing to the vital needs of others through the cargoes we brought home, the many skills cooperating to bring about our successful operations on passage and on the whaling grounds, the fleet exemplified a high level of social organization. Bringing together the necessary available expertise in such a way, it became an invaluable example for me of the way in which response to the various levels of vital, social, and cultural values can fructify in the lives of all. My experience of the company marked that quality which contributed so much to that success, the personal value of each who trusted our lives to a well-found ship with the best that the latest technology could supply in terms of well-being and comfort. However, to fare forward for myself, involved opening up new horizons – horizons that now beckoned on my own life's voyage. The meaning of the word "research" held an ineluctable fascination, even if my examination record was hardly conducive to such exalted ambition.

For the moment however, there remained the delightful prospect of a summer in Ireland and the renewal of old friendships. Though I had informed the whaling company of my intention to attend the Chemical Engineering Department of the University of Toronto for graduate studies in the coming September, they generously continued to pay me my monthly retainer until the time of my departure for Canada.

Now I could take up residence in my beloved cottage up on Howth Summit. I would set off on the glorious old Howth tram, with its stunning view of Dublin Bay, as it clattered importantly down to where I could catch the bus into town. In the evenings I would return and Kitty would have something hot in the oven for me and we would sit and discuss the day's events. Often we would go to visit some of her old friends from her own childhood days in Dublin. On one occasion Sylvester drove Kitty and myself out to an old estate she had known as a child.

Kitty was full of stories about such places. Noting the massive front door she said that visiting it many years ago she had herself once commented on the door. The old lady who lived there said that there was a story about the door told to her by her mother who, as a child herself, had been looked after by an aged family retainer who remembered the occasion when the door was being hung. It was a beautiful summer day in July without a cloud in the sky. They were, however, all puzzled by the sound of a distant thunderstorm. It turned out to be the guns of the Battle of the Boyne in 1690!

On the 24th May 1953, there occurred an event that left an indelible and very moving impression. I visited Sylvester's home out in Rathgar and had a delightful and convivial lunch with the family, responding happily to all the queries about my recent sea adventures. After lunch, the others were occupied elsewhere and so I seated myself in the comfortable armchair from which I could look out over the lawn and tennis court to where a row of trees flanked the property wall along the road. I was contentedly smoking my pipe when I glimpsed a figure that seemed to be familiar walking along the road. I was watching the next gap between the trees to see if I was right when a precise string of words exploded into consciousness with an incisiveness that literally stood the hair on the back of my neck on end: "Mr. O'Farrell is going to die!" I whipped round but was alone in the room with the door shut. Though much perplexed, I eventually dismissed the matter as some "trick of the mind" and of no consequence, as certainly he had been in such good form over lunch.

I made my way back into town to meet my old friend, Mick Torpey, who was in Dublin from County Clare and planned to stay with me at the cottage on Howth Summit overnight. That evening, as we sat by the turf fire smoking and talking, I told Mick of my experience while making light of there being any substance to it.

Mick was silent for a while, looking reflectively into the glowing turf. Then he said, "I'm afraid that you will be right."

I dismissed it all, however, as being merely some sort of mental aberration.

The following day I saw him off into town and returned later that evening to the cottage. On the table in the living room was the old typewriter I had rescued from the dump at the whaling station and in it was a note from Sylvester who had a key to the cottage. It said that his father had died in the early hours of the morning.

If such matters do not fit into some publicly verifiable overall scheme involving the realm of what is usually referred to as the human spirit, it remained for me an indestructible datum concerned with something that still remained over that then present evolutionary horizon.

PART THREE

CAREER & FAMILY

CHAPTER VII

CANADA

MASTER OF SCIENCE DEGREE IN CHEMICAL ENGINEERING, UNIVERSITY OF TORONTO & COAL HARBOUR WHALING STATION, VANCOUVER ISLAND, B.C. (1953–1955)

On the 28th August 1953 I again sailed out of Liverpool, but this time aboard an Italian emigrant passenger liner, the *S.S. Sydney*. Judging by the extremes of some of my fellow passengers in rough weather, I was glad that I had well and truly found my sea legs in *Balaena*. Following a seven-day passage we docked at Wolf's Cove, Quebec. Descending the gangway into the lofty customs shed I had a quite extraordinary déjà vu experience – the certainty that in some sense I had been there before though it was my first visit to North America. Does there exist some pattern of conscious events to which our future will conform? Canada would provide trials leading to the very edge of sanity and limits of my human circle, yet it would also provide the means for eventual recovery and return.

I knew nothing about the country except from my schoolboy geography classes – of the transcontinental railways, of fisheries, forestry, mining and farming. The things that really excited me about Canada in those long ago years were pictures of a steam locomotive emerging from the figure-eight tunnel of Kicking Horse Pass in the Rocky Mountains and Grey Owl's books I discovered in the library at Shalbourne Manor as an adventurous and curious boy scout. I had also read a book at school about the hardy lives and deep faith of "les habitants" who lived along the shores of the St. Lawrence River, and thought it would be good to see such things and meet such people.

We had some hours to wait for the train and a kindly Quebecer, spotting us for what we were, stopped his car and brought us for a quick tour to see the Château Frontenac and the Plains of Abraham. Leaving in mid-afternoon it was an overnight trip to Toronto. It was a memorable trip for its discomfort as the air conditioning failed and the heat was oppressive. At Smiths Falls, I alighted in the company of a fellow traveller, a professor from a university in California who made a comment that has always stuck in my mind; "North America is full of small towns like this where young people grow up with no other ambition than to own a motor car."

Toronto reminded me of Johannesburg – a large metropolis devoted exclusively to making money. I found accommodation at a student cooperative, sharing a room with a cheerful English geologist who also had experience in Africa. His liking for opening the window at night would rapidly succumb to our first experience of Canadian winter!

The big advantage in coming to Toronto was that I could support myself on income earned as a part-time demonstrator in one of the first year chemical laboratories to a rambunctious crowd of engineering students. The afternoon started with a short introduction to the work to be carried out. Long an inveterate pipe smoker, I managed to start off one afternoon by setting myself on fire from a too hastily pocketed pipe that was still alight. This manifested itself, to my horror, as a wisp of violet smoke and foul smell emerging from my coat pocket. Fortunately no one else noticed. I ruffled through my notes for something and then rushed out into the corridor to extinguish the fire, then pulling an envelope out of my pocket, returned nonchalantly without having made a spectacle of myself.

I started work on my thesis on mass and heat transfer studies in gas-liquid contacting under the supervision of a professor of English origin whom I well liked and respected. I built my experimental apparatus on the spacious balcony floor that overlooked the main Chemical Engineering Laboratory down below. It involved a large domestic type sheet metal storage tank, with a weight-loaded safety valve attached to a powerful air compressor and a bubble-cap test column. The compressor and tank were so noisy that I had to enclose the assembly in plywood lined with fibreglass.

On one occasion, I had to make some adjustment that required disconnecting the air compressor. Since it employed a high voltage, we were not allowed to do this task ourselves and I had to get the electrician. He reconnected the motor when I was finished and I started the compressor up. Everything was fine until the powerful tone of the compressor deepened, the outlet pipe from the tank started to cant over, the plywood casing burst open as there was a tremendous bang that echoed throughout the building. The electrician had reversed the connections on the compressor that had become a very powerful vacuum pump. With the safety valve shut, the tank had collapsed under the weight of atmospheric pressure.

"What do I do now?" says the electrician.

Horrified at the thought of having to rebuild everything when I was nearly finished my experiments: "You blow it back out again," said I!

There was another enormous bang as the tank more or less regained its original shape. Then a crowd appeared, led by the Dean, to see what had happened.

"Just getting things straightened out a bit," I said casually in response to his obvious alarm!

Living in the co-op we all had allocated tasks. My job was cleaning toilets, the disagreeable nature of which meant the task had the advantage of not being overly time-consuming. I also encountered peanut butter and jam sandwiches for the first time in the social centre of our house which was the kitchen. One chap had a guitar and we decided, for a joke, to enter the American Barber Shop Quartet Contest being held in Toronto. To our amazement we won the competition. They wanted an encore but we only knew the one song!

In the innocence and enthusiasm of my early years I was apt to invest the academic world of learning with high ideals of personal integrity and performance. If, indeed, that is often the case, that world is just as apt to be riven by human failings as any other walk of life. In fact, after my final oral examination, my supervisor, a man of high competence and integrity, observed that the oral had amounted to a personal attack upon both himself and myself by another faculty member. Hearing that I had passed and would be awarded a Master's Degree in Applied Science, I left Toronto much disgusted with my own performance. It would be some years before I discovered, on receiving a transcript of the results, that I had achieved an honours grade on my research project.

My fondest ambition was to eventually find permanent employment in the processing side of the fisheries industry in Ireland. I had been approached by the chief engineer with the Irish Sea Fisheries Board who had heard of my experience as a factory ship chemist with experience pertinent to the proposed operation of a fish processing plant on the west coast. He arranged an interview with the president of the board who suggested getting more experience of fisheries technology pending the eventual completion of the plant and negotiations for fleet operation, then some years in the future. Thus, towards the end of my studies in Toronto, I was interviewed by Dr. Neal Carter, who was the director of the Fisheries Research Board of Canada's Technological Laboratory in Vancouver. He soon commanded both my liking and respect. I was offered a post at the laboratory to commence in January 1955.

Following the successful defense of my thesis in the fall of 1954 I returned for a holiday with my family in London. On visiting the offices of the whaling company, I was asked to undertake a special research project involving trials of a new experimental meat meal plant which employed a gas turbine for both power for size reduction of biological materials and hot gas exhaust for drying. I wrote to Dr. Carter suggesting that this work could be of subsequent significance to fish processing on the Canadian west coast, but was asked to conform with our original starting date.

On leaving London for Vancouver via Shannon Airport, I stopped off in Dublin with a particular purpose in mind. My affection for May had, if anything, grown with time. I proposed marriage and she asked for more time. But I was torn by an enormous tension between honouring a commitment to Vancouver and the deepest yearnings of my heart. Attending mass at the Haddington Road Church on the Sunday immediately prior to my departure, there occurred a brief but intense psychosomatic paralysis, as if my chest had turned into a block of stone. But affairs of the mind must take precedence over any such aberrations of body and feeling.

I flew to Shannon only to find that my flight had been delayed and I must spend the night in residential quarters at the airport. These were located on the other side of the airport and in the darkness of that cold winter night I walked around the end of the main runway. All of a sudden there was a great whispering which grew to an explosive roar of engines, landing lights and flashing beacons as a huge Constellation hurtled over my head to land a short distance down the runway. Whenever we board an airplane we must have faith in the good intention, and high skills that reduce the probability of failure to acceptable proportions. In some instinctive way I knew this to also be true for the skills required for day-to-day living, however, such had not yet been acquired by myself. Thoughts of May pressed hard upon me until there was a flash of insight. My old friend Mick Torpey lived near the airport and he was so much wiser than myself in the concrete business of living. I called, but the phone rang and rang in an empty house. It was a pivotal moment in my life, a turning point. In the morning I boarded my flight to the other side of a continent on the other side of an ocean. I had with me May's curriculum vitae, with a view to her interest in finding employment, and was buoyed up by the hope that she would join me in Vancouver.

The next decade would bring to the full the consequences of that decision. I would eventually be forced to some sort of terrible spiritual confrontation with my own early formative years. There is a prescient quote from John Henry Newman in the entrance foyer of his University Church on Stephen's Green in Dublin: "It is the rule of God's providence that we succeed by failure." Succeed I would, but that I would know nothing about until many, many years later. Fail I would, imminent upon my arrival in Vancouver!

On arriving at the Fisheries Technological Laboratory in the old Coca Cola building on Richards Street, I was shown into Dr. Carter's office. He seemed surprised and asked me if I was here on holiday. I said "No, I've come to start work." It transpired, however, that, according to Kenneth Johnstone's history of the Fisheries Research Board of Canada, Dr. Carter had fallen out of favour with the local fishing industry, was declared to be an ineffective director and was being transferred to editorial duties in Ottawa. He was in the process of being replaced by Dr. H.L.A. Tarr who did not want another chemical engineer. I had flown from London to Vancouver to a job that had ceased to exist.

With the entrance of Newfoundland into Confederation there was strong political pressure to find senior posts in Ottawa for a number of people involved in fisheries. So it was that the Industrial Development Service was created and a Newfoundlander by the name of Lou Bradbury was put in charge. This meant that much of the responsibility for development was removed from the Fisheries Research Board, a course not favoured by the then deputy minister of Fisheries. I was assigned to take charge of the work of the Technological Unit at the Valleyfield Experimental Fisheries Plant located on Bonavista Bay on the east coat of Newfoundland. The location would have the blessings of the provincial premier and an Ottawa cabinet minister in whose riding it happened to be. It would not, however, enjoy the same by the F.R.B. Technological Unit in St. Johns, which both knew and served the local industry very well. They were simply ordered to do what they had been told by their political masters as, naively, did I.

In the meantime, I was asked to undertake a study at the Coal Harbour Whaling Station on the west coast of Vancouver Island on the use of antibiotics to retard post-mortem putrefaction in whales. If I had never managed to get out on any of *Balaena*'s fleet, I would get my fill of catcher life in the *M. V. Lavallee* which was operated by British Columbia Packers Ltd. The station was located on a long, roughly T-shaped inlet. There arose a problem in that the station, which was located on an old seaplane base near the intersection of the "T," could only be approached through narrows with swift-flowing tidal currents flooding or draining the cross bar of the "T." There often resulted considerable delays in getting the whale carcasses to the plant and much deterioration of the meat.

The work involved both inserting a linen-wrapped charge of chlortetracycline in the grenade which would be dispersed around the site of the explosion, and an aqueous solution of CTC that was included with the compressed air

May 1955. I spent a few months at Coal Harbour Whaling Station on the west coast of Vancouver Island, B.C. working on a research project concerning the use of antibiotics in retarding post-mortem putrefaction of whale. I took this photo from the Lavalee, *a whale catcher that was once a fish-packer.*

used to inflate the gut cavity through a perforated lance and which was re-quired to ensure positive buoyancy. Chemical analyses for volatile bases and bacterial counts on samples of tissue from both treated and untreated whales at comparable post mortem times provided convincing evidence of the success of the process.

The research process involved, of course, a number of trips out onto the whaling grounds. During the hours of darkness, leaving the required warning lights on, everybody turned in for the night leaving the boat to take care of itself. Unfortunately, the only spare bunk was in the wheelhouse, which, being quite high up could provide a pretty violent night's activity. On one occasion I was flung out completely traveling across the bridge on my back until brought up short by a bracketed fire extinguisher that came away from its post. I repeated

The rolling motion of the Lavalee *was exaggerated by the height of the bridge superstructure.*

the journey on a reciprocal course, only this time clutching a fire extinguisher to my chest. Hanging onto things in such weather conditions became second nature!

I had read accounts of the old-time harpooners hurling their lances into the flanks of the whale. Not me! Mighty men they must indeed have been if my attempts to insert the air lance into the gut cavity of a recently deceased whale secured alongside the catcher could constitute any gauge of the matter. Eventually I would leave the task to our, by now much entertained, large muscular gunner!

On my second trip, we received a tragic radio call from another of the catchers. One of the crew, who happened to be a brother-in-law of our own gunner, fell over the side and had been crushed between the whale and the catcher. The gunner dived in and tried to get him clear. He was, however, already unconscious and bleeding profusely from the mouth, and slipped away into the depths. There was nothing that we could do but continue our course for home with heavy hearts, trying to grasp what had happened with such suddenness and finality.

Later, on a downtown street in Vancouver waiting amongst a group of people for a bus, I suddenly realized that only one of them, from force of habit, was hanging on for dear life to the bus stop pole! I started to laugh and the rest of my prospective fellow passengers started edging imperceptibly away!

So it was that my involvement with the whaling industry drew to a close with a publication, with two colleagues, in the Progress Reports of the Pacific Coast Stations, Fisheries Research Board of Canada, No. 105, February 1956, of *Control of Post-Mortem Bacterial Spoilage of Whales with Chlortetracyclene*.

WEDLOCK, VANCOUVER, B.C. (1955–1959)

While still in Vancouver, it was an intense disappointment to learn that my long hoped for marriage to May, in Dublin, would not be realized. Further, the fisheries plans in Ireland failed. I became depressed and experienced a profound loss of any sense of meaningful direction. At about the same time, an Irish veterinarian of my acquaintance was moving out of his small apartment and suggested that I take it over. It was located over a funeral home. The landlady was a Mrs. T.J. Kearney who, with her daughter and two sons, lived in a larger adjoining apartment. One of the sons was physically and mentally handicapped. The nature of his affliction was never referred to though it seemed to have been due to falling out of his pram. I was given to understand that they had once been a wealthy Vancouver family who had, in some sense, been betrayed, and consequently impoverished by a one-time employee who had taken his knowledge and connections over to a rival company. This seemed to be such an active source of resentment that I assumed it to have been a fairly recent occurrence. Actually, as I found out many years later, it had occurred some thirteen years earlier.

I was made welcome and it seemed that I had found at least some minor respite from the storm! A friendship between the daughter and myself was warmly encouraged. Like James Joyce's Mrs. Mooney, the landlady in his insightful story, *The Boarding House*, Mrs. Kearney apparently decided to intervene. As nice as it was to feel comfortable with those of an Irish-Catholic background that I naively thought similar to my own, I was proving to be a reluctant suitor. Joyce's fictionalized ex-butcher landlady knew that moral problems, once established, could be settled with a catechetical "meat cleaver." Returning to my apartment from work on a Friday evening, Mrs. Kearney informed me that her daughter was waiting for me at a hotel over on Bowen Island where she had booked us in for the weekend. The prospect, however, of eternal damnation for sexual misadventures remained as vivid and terrible as ever in my mind. Being a "nice Catholic boy," it transpired that I was susceptible to a strong sense of pious duty and obligation, and overtime I would succumb to Mrs. Kearney's extant pressures without even being consciously aware of them.

Events seem to have then assumed a momentum of their own and in some such manner there arose an expectancy of marriage. It would be many years before I was able to recognize the circumstances in terms of the role of Prince Vasili's private agenda in the marriage of his daughter Helene to the unsuspecting Pierre, so eloquently dramatized in the B.B.C. production of Tolstoy's classic *War and Peace*. Pierre's soliloquy was unforgettable: "Of course I'm going to marry her, everyone expects it. But how did it happen?" So I would find confirmation in a dramatic re-enactment of my own feelings at the time.

Looking back over subsequent events there seems little doubt that Ellen was influenced even more by her mother's intentions than myself. A measure of my disengagement can be found in the fact that for many years I had no idea of the difference in our ages. Ellen was then thirty-nine years old to my twenty-nine. Was there, perhaps, a biological clock factor to Mrs. Kearney's determination that her daughter be married to this naïve and suggestible man sooner than later? Perhaps, as I would come to believe, at the heart of the matter it was not so much about her daughter being married and a new family's happiness, as it was about grandchildren and the longevity of the family funeral business.

In time I would read, and again find resonance in, others' literary works. Laurens van der Post had undergone the appalling experience of imprisonment during World War II in a Japanese prisoner-of-war camp, and came to understand that the real prisoners were the Japanese guards, subjected as they were to an imposed discipline of the psyche by a system demanding complete subservience. Whether an individual or a system, the result can be just as destructive to the human spirit that does not seek its own meaning, as indeed, did Victor Frankl make clear in the appalling circumstances of Auschwitz. It would be decades before I would begin to see how my own psychic disengagement in emotional matters were the quicksand to the inherent authoritarianism of power structures whether religious, academic, professional or individual. I had met my nemesis in Mrs. K., and through the intransigent influence of the power of her personality, my own consciousness would awaken and I would learn about self-appropriation and personal accountability – but that was eons away from these early susceptibilities of vulnerable personalities.

From early days, it was my habit to talk over personal decisions with some priest as friend and advisor. In this instance I talked to the parish priest, with whom, again, I thought I shared much of a common Irish background, about my misgivings. However, after watching a game on television, he merely noted that, of course, marriage was a good thing, stated that his housekeeper would be upset if he was late for his dinner and showed me the door. Presumably this devout Catholic family was fully cognizant of the responsibilities of marriage, as I, it would appear, was not.

A few months later, the 1st October 1955, in some awful moment of surrender to circumstances, I entered into a highly unsuitable and, to all intents and purposes, an *arranged* marriage, for which in truth both Ellen and myself were singularly ill prepared. On that occasion there was only one moment of lucidity for me when a solitary shaft of light momentarily pierced the ominous clouds of impotent awareness, only to vanish with the resumption of that ongoing obnubilation of intelligence, reason and responsibility. It took the form of the question: "My God, what am I doing?" only to be followed by the immediate response: "Things can't be any worse!" Such, however, would prove to be incorrect, and in terms of both personal and professional life, it set the scene for a long slow descent into the realm of neurosis – far from homeland, family and friends. In the years ahead, for all practical purposes, my sons' Uncle Frank would find himself in the role of being father to his young nephews.

My Aunt Rosalie, who was the Mother Superior of the Sacred Heart Convent near Ormskirk in Lancashire, had told my mother that she thought life would be difficult for me. I would eventually come to know what she meant and how, in the meeting and surmounting of challenge, I would emerge from the dark night of the soul into the illuminative anticipation of a universe magnificent beyond the wildest reaches of my imagination, that which has not yet occurred and for which, I believe, we are being prepared.

The great problem is, however, that we have to live life before we know how to do it, and it would be many years before I could grasp with clarity the nature of the agenda in which my own emotional unawareness had ensnared me. Having established such power over her own children, Mrs. Kearney had every reason to anticipate the extrapolation of her influence over my children and myself.

When, a couple of years later, the full destructive extent of my situation was becoming apparent, I again went to see the same parish priest, only, after hours of travel and waiting, to be turned away on the same grounds of inconveniencing his housekeeper! In the light of other similar experiences there was initiated a general distrust of the integrity of the institutional church, of a clerical bureaucracy that seemed to me to have become largely unhearing, uncaring and incapable of meeting the responsibilities it had appropriated for itself. Such distrust would grow steadily over the years as I watched the flourishing religious communities I had known as a child diminish radically in numbers or close down altogether.

I found myself alone, immersed in some intangible field of intransigent power that would set the slow downward locus of personal events for the next two decades. All too often, in that ignorance, naive misplacement of trust can exact a terrible price, to say nothing of the terrible price exacted when self-knowledge is at a minimum, if not almost altogether absent.

CHAPTER VIII

NEW BEGINNINGS

THE BIRTH OF TWO SONS & FISHERIES RESEARCH BOARD LABORATORIES, GRANDE-RIVIÈRE, P.Q, AND HALIFAX, N.S. (1955–1959)

The work I was to undertake involved a more systematic control of salting, desalting and drying of cod and thus improving the efficiency and productivity of an important industry in the Maritimes. The initial assignment was to the Fisheries Research Board Laboratory at Grande-Rivière, P.Q. Ellen and I drove across the continent from Vancouver and took up residence in a local hotel. A couple of weeks later we received a letter from Mrs. Kearney saying that her daughter was urgently needed at home and asking for her return to Vancouver until we could move into the new house that was being provided for us near the Valleyfield Experimental Fish Processing Plant in Newfoundland. The letter included an instruction that Ellen must not mention the request to her brother Francis (Frank). I said that she should use her own best judgment in making a decision.

I continued on a temporary basis at the Laboratory in Grande-Rivière, and in January 1956 I learned that Ellen was pregnant. After returning briefly to Valleyfield, it was agreed best for the baby to be born in Vancouver. The entire Valleyfield Project seemed plagued with uncertainties on all fronts. At the end of the year I was transferred to the Technological Laboratory in Halifax pending final transfer to Valleyfield that was supposedly due to become operational in 1957.

A singularly unpleasant aspect of the whole matter emerged when I was verbally offered a substantial promotion if I supported the dubious concerns of certain interested parties. I reported the matter to the Civil Service Commission but was told that this involved "cabinet level" intervention and they could do nothing about it. My contempt for life's institutions increased.

On the 23rd September 1956 our son Thomas Patrick was born. I returned to Vancouver and my mother came out from England for her first meeting with the family. In the course of the visit, I was shown a large house with a swimming pool overlooking the sea some distance south of Vancouver. It was proposed that this should become a joint extended family home. With all the finesse of the double-ended-spanner-defence of my apprenticeship days, I made it clear that this was entirely unacceptable to me. Shortly afterwards Mrs. Kearney ordered me to bring her for a drive in her usual peremptory manner reminiscent of my earlier military experience with drill sergeants, and I made it clear that such a command was just as unacceptable as the earlier plan of cohabitation. I was taken aback by the cold fury that greeted my refusal. I did not recognize the implacability of that resolve to bring me to heel or to find some means of driving me out and replacing me with her own son, nor did I recognize my own rough spirit in regard to unreasonable expectations of others over me.

As it would ultimately transpire I would begin to see that neither Ellen nor myself were truly independent human spirits. She was so "in tune" with her mother that they claimed a psychic bond, one that brooked no interference from anyone outside the tight Kearney circle, a circle of which I was clearly not a part. On the other hand, while world-travelled and of an adventurous spirit committed to an inquiry into first principles, my psyche was equally held in sway by an authoritarianism of a religious and deeply feared emotional kind. Our marriage appeared more and more not to be a match made in heaven. However, the success of the funeral business was strongly dependent on the im-peccability of moral standing in the Roman Catholic community in Vancouver including, of course, the irrevocability of marriage vows. Only years later, I would grasp the infinitely patient intricacies and machinations of power, the role of skilled myth-making that is the product of human intelligence in pur-suit of some obsessive personal purpose.

Unfortunately, the emergence of the enmity between my mother-in-law and myself would sadly impact my own mother's long awaited visit. Shortly after the incidents alluded to above, I received an urgent summons from Kitty saying that after a vicious attack upon myself by Ellen's mother, she felt she must leave the house immediately and catch the evening train east. We set off for the station but I was not allowed to see her off from the platform, so re-turned home. It turned out that the train was delayed overnight by blockage of the line in the Fraser Canyon. She phoned Mrs. Kearney and asked that she let me know of her changed circumstances. Kitty's message was not delivered. Instead, unbeknownst to myself, she was left to sit alone in the station over-night. The gauntlet had been well and truly laid.

One of the immense perplexities resulting from my fundamentalist and simplistic Roman Catholic formation concerned the unequivocal scriptural command to love my neighbour and even my enemies. After all, we were all du-tiful practicing Catholics. This called for unremitting effort in seeking to meet the needs of others. That terrible sense of entrapment in hopeless circumstances that had first appeared on a pre-war Twickenham railway platform now became a persistent presence. There was nothing to do but get on with what I saw as my duty – by sheer effort of will. I was certainly not the first to be impaled on the horns of such a dilemma and I often reflected on the famous epigram by Thomas Brown concerning Dr. Fell, Dean of Christ Church College, Oxford, in the late 17th century. I even paraphrased it for myself:

> *I do not love thee, Mrs. K.*
> *The reason why I cannot say*
> *But this I know, as well I may*
> *I do not love thee, Mrs. K.*

Returning to Quebec, I found myself in a flood of difficulty, both personal and professional. I was locked into a solitary pattern of the days, tangled in a web where the expedient agenda of others seemed to take precedence over any legitimate endeavour and, consequently, I became subject to a growing sense of disillusionment with life's institutions, whether professional or political, domestic or ecclesiastical. It was to challenge power but find no champion. My inner world fell into a darkness from which there seemed to be no escape, in which there seemed to be no meaning in such a futile passage of days.

There remained however the possibility of occasional respite in recourse to the world of the mind. I came across Eddington's *Nature of the Physical World*. It provided an enthralling overview of the physical universe, exquisitely coherent and assimilable, open to unimaginable wonders as yet to come. Whether in the guise of matter or radiation, surely energy was the nearest thing the human mind could grasp as the raw material of the universe.

In May 1957, work started at the Experimental Fish Processing Plant. It turned out to have been built at a central location in the riding of a provincial prime minister and a federal cabinet minister, presumably with a view to showing what they could do for the local community if re-elected. There was even a tremendous opening planned which involved flying the diplomatic corps to Gander from Ottawa, and from thence by helicopter to Valleyfield. Before the grand opening could be realized, the then Liberal Government fell from power. The plant manager had some of the lavish invitations but refused to let me have one as a political souvenir! It proved to be an entirely impractical location and operations were transferred in January 1958 to the Fisheries Technological Laboratory in Halifax, N.S.

I was immensely fortunate in the technical assistant who was appointed to the project, George Henri Imbeault, who had been recruited in Valleyfield with promises of accommodation for himself and his family at the Valleyfield site. George could turn his hand to anything in the practical line of work, fixing things, whether mechanical or electrical, and was even an accomplished blacksmith. In reality, he was very badly served by the Department of Fisheries in the matter. When the deputy minister paid a visit to the site I told him in no uncertain terms what I thought of the departmental behaviour in this regard. As soon as he returned to Ottawa, he terminated my employment and promoted George Henri to what seemed a quite unsuitable office job in Ottawa. Fortunately, the assistant chairman of the Fisheries Research Board for whom I had a genuine respect (it was reputed that he had refused to participate in the Valleyfield opening extravaganza!), transferred me to the Technological Station in Halifax, Nova Scotia to continue the salt fish work.

A later newspaper article on evidence given by the then MP for Queens-Lunenburg before the Commons Committee on Marine and Fisheries described the $800,000 experimental plant at Valleyfield as a "duplication of effort" at an "inaccessible location." Eventually the plant was bought from the Federal Government by a commercial interest in Newfoundland. I was beginning to learn something about the disturbing implications of politics in the context of research programs, supposedly undertaken to benefit the national community that was paying for it.

Ellen, who was again pregnant, returned with Tom to Vancouver at her mother's *request* while I proceeded alone to Halifax. Later, I was transferred to the Marine Oil Section to design and build a small recovery apparatus for solvents. Matters between the director and the head of the Marine Oils Section, a scientist of high professional standing, were becoming more and more tense. Later the director would transfer to UNESCO on grounds of being unable to "maintain discipline" in the larger station. The newly appointed director of the Halifax Fisheries Technological Laboratory had originally been director of the Grande-Rivière Laboratory and my supervisor. Lacking confidence in his abilities, I became increasingly concerned about the direction of our future program.

On the 3rd May 1958, my second son, Michael Kevin, was born in Vancouver. Unfortunately, in view of my professional and personal situation, the growth of our family felt, at the time, like an immense increase in personal responsibility in what was fast becoming a more and more arid world of religiously imposed duties and obligations. Ellen was again living with her mother and brothers in Vancouver and, though ostensibly only for her confinement, she appeared uninterested in returning with our young sons to create a family circle of our own. Given my own difficulties and the lack of loving affection between us, this was not an unpredictable outcome.

It had become increasingly obvious that the prospects of a satisfying career with the Fisheries Research Board of Canada were slim. I wrote to the professor under whom I had studied in Toronto inquiring about further employment with an opportunity to submit the work for an external Ph.D. from the University of London. He had since been appointed director of a new chemical engineering laboratory at Stevenage in England. He told me that several posts would be opening up in the following year, when they would move to a new facility, and that the work on distillation that I had been doing in Toronto would be included. He suggested that I apply for a post with them. I did, but unsuccessfully.

During this time in Halifax, on the basis of some tests carried out by an acquaintance who was both a psychologist and a priest, I embarked on almost two years of fortnightly psychiatric consultations. At Ellen's request, the psychiatrist wrote to a psychiatrist of her acquaintance in Vancouver stating that my defences were breaking down and there were many autistic tendencies though no evidence of schizophrenia. He also inferred a high intellectual ability that could only be satisfied by a correspondingly challenging Ph.D. He further concluded that I was responding to treatment but that Ellen's own relationship to her family should be investigated. This, however, was met with refusal. It was in fact becoming increasingly clear to me that Ellen would never leave her mother and that they now felt they had grounds to have Francis take over my role as father and let me fend for myself. The result was an inner darkness from which I could see no escape. At such a time, a momentous event with completely unforeseeable consequences may occur. And so indeed it did!

One evening, in August 1958, having nothing better to do, I sat in on a workshop being held in connection with a course of lectures given by a Canadian philosopher and theologian at St. Mary's University in Halifax, Nova Scotia. His name was Bernard Lonergan and, in growing fascination, I wondered if it would ever be possible to glimpse something of the universe as he saw it, a worldview which seemed to be some extraordinary synthesis of the secular and divine, something that soared above the usual trite paraphrasing of the scripture readings that constituted the Sunday homily. Perhaps there was a gleam of light at the end of my Roman Catholic tunnel, one that would not turn out to be another locomotive! Little did I suspect that it would eventually grow to blaze out upon the universe, the notion of a church that soars far beyond any mundane limitations of clerical bureaucracy, a fulfilling of the promise of Vatican Council II, a theological pluralism that would heal and unify, a church that would truly illumine the potential magnificence of that to which each one of us is given access by the gift of consciousness. I bought a copy of his masterwork, *Insight: A Study of Human Understanding*. At the beginning was the injunction; "Don't just take what I say, look at your own experience." It would be an experiment that would be performed, not publicly, but privately. Here, at last, there was a goal at which I could take aim. It would, however, take almost two decades before I had what I considered to be a practical "working model" – one that would then have to be tested. But, at the time, it was enough that at least a possibility existed.

If my childhood experience on a suburban railway platform led to a sense of hopelessness with respect to there being any meaning to life other than a dreary routine that ended in complete physical obliteration by death, two books by Sir Arthur Eddington, *The Nature of the Physical World* and *Space, Time and Gravitation*, suggested that there is more to it all than meets the eye. If the "really real" is that which can be tested out and verified by our senses, then the realm of meaning itself went far beyond the data of sense into the realm of that which is thought. This could be extended enormously by access to publicly verified thought produced in other human heads, whether past or present, from the equations of the physicist to the moving word pictures of literature. Could there be any link to the highly unconvincing pronouncements that characterized my own religious formation? I was deeply intrigued by the following quotation from the first of these two books: "We have to build the spiritual world out of symbols taken from our own personality, as we build the scientific world out of the metrical symbols of the mathematician. If not, it can only be left ungraspable – an environment dimly felt in moments of exaltation but lost to us in the sordid routine of life. To turn it into more continuous channels we must be able to approach World-Spirit in the midst of our cares and duties in that simpler relation of spirit to spirit in which all true religion finds expression."

Could I actually reason out the role of my own consciousness in this dispassionate universe that would lead to a genuine conviction as to the meaning of its own destiny, a hope and sense of purpose that was not based merely on fear?

UNIVERSITY OF OTTAWA, ONTARIO (1959–1961)

To sever the knot of my career frustrations I again turned to my interest in research work, and, in keeping with an insistent urge to understand more of the structure of the universe, I became a graduate student in Theoretical Chemical Physics, with a part-time teaching position, at the University of Ottawa. I was particularly fortunate in having a supervisor who excelled, not only in academic achievement, but also as a concerned and dedicated teacher. There would result a modest, but much valued, initiation into the esoteric and exciting realms of Quantum Mechanics and Statistical Thermodynamics. This led to successfully completing much of my graduate course requirements and research project: a normal mode analysis of a complex organic molecule. However, it was decided on the basis of a dreaded comprehensive oral (it started out with a contemptuous comment from the department head: "Now, if your nerves will stand it, Mr. Crean!"), that I should undertake extensive revision of organic chemistry courses.

Once again the ingrained fear resulting from that paralysis of mind in the examination halls of the University of London so many years earlier, had returned with foreseeable results. Intensely disappointed, having neither the financial resources nor any inclination towards that aspect of the field, I turned

Top: Following an unsuccessful doctorate attempt at the University of Ottawa, I returned to England for an extended rest. During that time I visited the Institute of Ocean Sciences at Godalming near Guildford. The director of the institute invited me to participate in an oceanographic cruise on the R.R.S. Discovery II *in January 1961.*

Bottom: I am shown here in the chains aboard R.R.S. Discovery II, *lowering a string of deep sea oceanographic sample bottles to determine salinity and oxygen.*

A family outing to the west coast of Vancouver Island with Ellen, Tom and Michael in the summer of 1961, having recently moved to Nanaimo, B.C.

again to my first love, the sea, and managed to obtain a position in physical oceanography with the Pacific Oceanographic Group on the West Coast commencing February 1961.

In the months prior to the start of this position, I returned to England for an extended family visit, unable as I was at the time to return to Vancouver and the increasing family discord and responsibilities awaiting me there. Towards the end of my stay in England, I visited the National Institute of Oceanography in Guildford, south of London. I was invited by the director to participate in a two-week long research cruise in January 1961 on the *R.R.S. Discovery II*. We sailed from Portsmouth to the Strait of Gibraltar where we conducted a standard oceanographic survey using a new type of deep-sea sampler developed at the Institute. With the need to find accommodation for the family in Nanaimo before the start of my employment, I then returned to Vancouver.

CHAPTER IX

LIFE CHALLENGES

THE PACIFIC OCEANOGRAPHIC GROUP, NANAIMO, B.C. (1961–1969)

The sixties saw the inception of manned flight beyond the terrestrial environment and into a "space" that contains it. Essentially a space provides some abstract ground for measurements that can bring concrete practical results. Genetic research in that decade also saw immense advances in knowledge of systems that can add information to themselves without outside help, provided an energy source was available. Could such notions be employed to provide a metaphor, a conceptual practical "working model" of that which lies at the forefront of such evolutionary developments, as far as we can presently know it – human consciousness? The most powerful space we can conceive of in that regard would seem to be all that is known together with all that remains to be known. Could each human consciousness, each entity that can think of itself as a "me," regard itself as a "craft" undergoing change in such a space, assembling itself in the course of a brief flash of incarnated consciousness in the more conventionally familiar space-time of the physicist? Could such a craft facilitate the process of adding information to itself? How could one test so ambitious a hypothesis?

In the summer of 1962, I came across Teilhard de Chardin's *Phenomenon of Man*. The notion of a world in evolutionary progress I found strongly appealing. This was characterized by a directed movement toward higher degrees of material complexity or organization, toward higher levels of consciousness or spirit. It received short shrift from the rigidly authoritarian and conservative Roman Catholic hierarchy. These latter were becoming less and less convincing. I was, however, fascinated by Teilhard's implications in the use of the concept "energy," of a "tangential" energy informing and controlling matter in its physico-chemical reactions and a radial energy by which matter is constituted as progressively higher forms of unity. Matter is in principle conscious matter, but it requires a high degree of organization before it can begin to manifest itself as consciousness. The cosmos can be considered in all its aspects including man, and both understood as a continuous process of evolution.

Another work that had a profound impact in 1965 was C.G. Jung's autobiographical work, *Memories, Dreams and Reflections*. This invited attention to the incredibly complex and swiftly changing flow of images and feelings accessible through the extraordinary capacity of human consciousness to reflect upon itself. I started making notes on dream materials that I recalled. These would, on later reflection, provide a remarkable symbolic illustration of psychic deterioration that had already occurred.

For example, the initial dreams following my marriage to Ellen could be typified by a hotel, which I associated with the conscious attitude of the psyche in relation to others, but which was characterized as being unreachable by the dream ego because of an insurmountable cliff, or where, when the dream ego was within, the interior was on fire. Later dreams emphasized the dream ego missing some vehicle, of being mysteriously held back from catching a plane, bus, train or ship. Though the matter of dreams never came up at the time of my consultations with the psychiatrist in Halifax, such material would seem to accord with the breakdown of psychic defences and the autistic tendency to withdraw into myself, that some development of attitude in adapting to the world was lacking. I hadn't the faintest idea of what the problem could be or from where it came. However, could the worldview developed by Bernard Lonergan provide any strategy for at least opening up a way for finding some sense of meaning in a life that had become devoid of meaning? In the meantime, I had to earn a living!

My work with the Pacific Oceanographic Group largely involved oceanographic surveys followed by prolonged periods of plotting up data by hand. Basically, if some pattern of oceanographic stations is occupied over an area and vertical profiles of salinity and temperature below the ship are available, a three-dimensional contoured density distribution can be determined with implications as to the motions probably associated with any "sloping" of such density surfaces. Water masses can also be characterized in terms of salinities and temperatures.

In September 1962 I was asked to undertake a detailed oceanographic survey of Dixon Entrance that was intended to confirm and elaborate data that had been obtained from a large fixed-bed hydraulic model of this major region of the northern waters of British Columbia. Such a model can prove to be a powerful tool in understanding the circulation of water in a particular region provided the forces dominating particular features in the model are those dominating that region of flow in nature. Though a large part of the Group's budget had been put into the model of the northern coastal waters of British Columbia, and despite a singular achievement by the engineer who built it with very limited resources, there would prove to exist at least one major design error. As a fixed bed model, it could not include the effects of the Earth's rotation. I would later find my misgivings amply confirmed on visiting Dutch and French laboratories where I could see for myself the effort required to simulate effects of the Earth's rotation.

The paper that I wrote using only those features that could be verified was repudiated by the officer-in-charge who threatened my salary and future career if I failed to make certain totally unjustified assertions which were quite at variance with my experimental findings. Further, he roundly criticized my use of the English language, pointing out that I used strange words and that foreigners might read the paper. It transpired from the secretary, however, that he made good use of his expanding vocabulary, once he had looked them up!

Authority that is loud and overbearing can often seem to derive much satisfaction from provoking concern and submission on the part of its victims. I eventually concluded that my respect for this authority in question was misplaced and on the occasion of the next outburst of loud dissatisfaction simply replied with a broad grin. There was no reoccurrence of these unpleasant scenes of emotional pique, and eventually the validity of my work was acknowledged. It was published as *Bulletin No. 156 of the Fisheries Research Board of Canada* in 1967.

In my first days at the Biological Station in Nanaimo, I had the pleasure of meeting Timothy Parsons, a biological oceanographer also employed by the Fisheries Research Board at the time. He and his family were in the process of moving and suggested we rent their newly vacated home on Waterfront Street.

The early sixties thus proved to be a time of much professional distress and tension. While our marriage was inherently troubled, it nevertheless made it doubly difficult to deal with the constant influence and interference of Mrs. Kearney in our affairs. It was a very difficult time for the family as Ellen and myself grew further apart. I very much enjoyed the few occasions when I had Tom and Michael to myself and we would go exploring. I would push my way up through the bush on the hillside above the house, Tom hanging onto my belt and Michael onto his until we found a clearing and shared out whatever snacks I had purloined from the kitchen. More frequently, at weekends, Ellen would take them over to stay with her Mother, Frank and Ed, who furnished the solitary connotation that the word "family" was allowed to signify in our affairs. Most of the time I was cast in the role of disciplinarian. In contrast, Frank lived the role of a loving and indulgent father. And so it was that the gap was patiently and steadily widened and the way paved with expensive gifts for the boys towards eventual immurement in the family business without the options offered by acquiring higher levels of education.

I eventually went over to Vancouver to again seek assistance from the Kearney's parish priest. This time I didn't even get in the door as I was met at the threshold with a sharp rebuff: "What can I do about it? My housekeeper gets upset if I'm late for my dinner," and he shut the door in my face. Later I tried other priests who simply referred me back to the scene of these earlier fiascos.

In July 1964 we purchased a quite delightful house in Deerborn Place, beautifully located on the mostly wooded hillside overlooking Departure Bay and within easy walking distance of the Pacific Biological Station. The high hallway included a half flight of stairs to the main floor, and another half flight that led down to a spacious half basement, its front windows opening onto the lawn on either side of the front door, its end windows looking onto the carport. The windows of the front living room commanded the impressive view of Departure Bay with its comings and goings of the mainland ferries and small boat traffic. In due course, I installed a washroom in the half basement which, with the large panelled living room, provided ideal guest accommodation. It

My parents with Tom and Michael in the carport of our home on Dearborn Place, Nanaimo B.C., during my father's his first trip to North America in 1965.

was appropriate that my parents could now visit our home on what would also be the occasion of my father's first visit to North America.

In May 1965, I met them at the Vancouver Airport and brought them over by car and ferry to our home in Nanaimo. The visit was immensely successful and I started to come to know my father in a way that had not occurred before. One of my most vivid memories was of him wading in the shallows with his trouser legs rolled up to the knees, his old black Homburg hat askew, declaiming passages from Shakespeare to the Strait of Georgia! I was discovering my father as a scholar.

By and large, the great majority of people live out their lives in the common sense realm of getting on with things, of solving the problems at hand

My father with Tom and Michael in front of Dearborn Place.

and then moving on to the next one. The emphasis is on relating, in terms of knowing and feeling, to the situation and the people around us. The scholar combines the common sense of his or her own time with that of other people at other times and places to understand the emergent meaning embodied in the thoughts and deeds of others.

Then came the time for our visit to the Kearneys on the mainland. We stayed at their beach house at Point Roberts. In due course Ellen drove my parents into Vancouver to meet Mrs. Kearney. When they returned, it became quickly apparent that something had clearly gone much amiss. Later that night, when I inquired about the visit, Ellen announced that my father had insulted her mother. On asking further as to what manner of insult was proffered, Ellen's

My father, mother, Michael, Tom and myself at Piper's Lagoon on Vancouver Island not far from Nanaimo.

angry response could be heard all too clearly throughout that darkened frame structure, "Go to hell!" Much later I would realize that the tragedy enacted by his own mother on the lives of his two sisters had too much in common with the imperiousness of Mrs. Kearney, particularly over those who had fallen under her power.

When the time came for their departure, I drove them down to the Victoria airport to catch the flight connecting with their London flight from Vancouver. As they climbed the boarding stairs and were about to enter the cabin of the Viscount, my father turned and waved to me. If I had always loved and respected him, it was never more so than now. Because his worldview was so far ahead of my own, I had previously found it difficult to communicate with him. Somehow his presence increased my own determination to find a

Tom and Michael.

worldview of my own that would prove satisfactory in terms appropriate to my own inner promptings and yearnings. So far it seemed to me that I had made a right mess of it.

For his own reading he had brought with him a copy of Alexander Kinglake's classic account of an expedition in 1835 to the Middle East, in the heyday of Victorian technological and imperial splendour. *Eothen* was admirably summarized by a local, and hospitable, Turkish military commander. "The armies of the English ride upon the vapours of boiling cauldrons, and their horses are flaming coals! whirr! whirr! all by wheels! whiz! whiz! all by steam!" The paragraphs my father wanted me to read dealt with Kinglake's reflections on setting up a camp at the end of a day's trek by camel on the journey through the desert from Gaza to Cairo: "There within my tent were heaps of luxuries

– dining rooms – dressing rooms – libraries – bedrooms – drawing rooms – oratories – all crowded into the space of a hearth-rug ... I feasted like a king – like four kings – like a boy in the fourth form." Could I ever achieve such an economy and maturity of spirit? It certainly did not seem like it at the time – but that time would come – much later on in the course of my own journey.

Just prior to his departure, Father said to me; "What chance have you when everything is decided by the committee in Vancouver? Whatever you do must be your own decision. Whatever that decision is, I will back you to the full."

Now there was a sense of being no longer so totally alone. On returning to Nanaimo I asked our family doctor, Dr. P. Gawthrop, for advice.

It was his opinion that there was nothing I could do about the complex and inordinately close ties between mother and daughter. A similar opinion was given to me by Dr. T. Cosgrove, a friend and retired doctor, who knew the Kearneys and ourselves. He advised me that Mrs. Kearney would try to destroy me if I opposed her and that she would destroy her own son Francis if he did likewise.

In 1967 Francis Kearney completed a degree in law at the University of British Columbia. Mrs. Kearney and himself were clearly delighted. As he said at his graduation party, in a voice heavy with emotion: "We did it together, Mother. We did it together!" An arguable rationalization, in terms of his mother's plans for her son, that emerged with the announcement of his appointment to the Marriage Tribunal of the Roman Catholic Archdiocese of Vancouver. As for his personal life, so far as I was aware, Frank's only association with a girl-friend had been terminated because, as Ellen pointed out, neither her mother nor herself considered the woman suitable. When I pointed out the possible unfairness to her brother, the peremptory response was; "Frank will do what I want!"

In the years following my parents' visit it appears in retrospect that a subtle change in the atmosphere of the house on Deerborne Place was emerging. There seemed to be more whispered conversations, an increased sense of my having interrupted confidential phone calls that were abruptly terminated, a sense of some hidden collaborative agenda. The common ground rules governing the situation, as proclaimed by a Roman Imperialism that proclaimed itself infallible and Catholic, were however unassailable. Doubtless matters would amend when eventually time would diminish the omnipotent influence of Mrs. Kearney over the lives and decisions of her children. Unassailable also, was the substantial dependence of the family business's success on continuing to maintain, at whatever cost, an impeccable stance in the eyes of Archdiocesan personnel and the scrupulous observation of the associated funeral rituals.

In spite of my own by now pretty well established misgivings of clerical efficacy in personal matters, I yet again confided in a priest, this time one who was a relation of the Kearneys. He promised to do what he could. I had little hope for I remember the only homily of his that I had heard contained the dubious theological insight that "heaven is like a golf course." I had heard that ecclesiastical preferment in The Archdiocese of Vancouver was apt to be heralded by an invitation to a round of golf with His Grace, the Archbishop! Perhaps the allusion was more Freudian in nature than a matter of spiritual inspiration! T.S. Eliot's reference seemed apposite:

> *Here were decent Godless people:*
> *Their only monument the asphalt road*
> *And a thousand lost golf balls*

In desperation, when on a subsequent visit to the Kearney beach house at Boundary Bay that year, I sought help from Ellen's brother, with whom I had always found communication difficult. He expressed his appreciation of my request and promised to do all he could. He returned to his mother's house in

Vancouver only to reappear some two hours later seething with anger at "my insolence."

In 1967, I again asked for advice from Dr. Paul Gawthrop. He suggested trying a marriage counsellor in Vancouver. Ellen agreed and after a couple of sessions, the counsellor told me that Ellen would become less dependent on her mother as the sessions proceeded. However, in Ellen's own words: "Mother feels that since we are the only two who really understand the situation, there would be no point in continuing!"

So the door was closed to any impartial intervention that might reach a viable solution. I had attempted to deal with my own problems, however unsuccessfully.

Turning again to Dr. Gawthrop, I was advised that the only glimmer of hope was to try and get Ellen, Tom, and Michael away from the unrelenting influence of "the family" in Vancouver. Such a solution would, however, take some time to evolve.

Matters at work were, in the meantime, undergoing a major improvement with the appointment in 1966 of a new Officer-in-Charge of the Pacific Oceanographic Group, Dr. Michael Waldichuk, a man whose integrity and work I much respected. He it was who gave me the opportunity to turn my career around. Some two decades later, shortly before his untimely death, I was able to present him with a text book and a Tidal Current Atlas that had resulted and thank him in person for having had the confidence in me that made it all possible.

It was Dr. Waldichuk who asked me to undertake a major study of the waters between Vancouver Island and the mainland coasts of British Columbia and the State of Washington. It seemed that a major priority was to avoid any extravagant blunders such as came to light with the Hecate Model which couldn't take into account the effects of the Earth's rotation. Rapid advances were being made in numerical modelling techniques at a number of different research institutes. Following a survey of this work, I proposed a series of visits to such institutes in the U. K., Holland, Germany, France and the United States in order to propose the best approach for our own local waters. The proposal was approved and the visits arranged for departure on the 28th September 1966. The first two of them to the Liverpool Tidal Institute and the University of Strathclyde could be carried out with my parents in the family Morris Minor. The prospect of renewing the growing closeness in the relation between my father and myself was enormously exciting.

Four days before my planned departure, on the 23rd September, I received a telegram with the devastating news that my father had died of a massive coronary thrombosis. I left immediately for London with a detour via Ottawa to collect a passport, my own having been sent for replacement by a diplomatic passport. I arrived in London after forty-eight sleepless hours and in a state of complete physical and emotional exhaustion. My mother insisted, however, that I should start on my planned trip to Glasgow and Liverpool, meeting a week later at the Sacred Heart Convent where her sister had been in charge throughout the war years.

I was grateful, under the circumstances, that my sister Kathleen, a trained nurse, and her husband Peter, a professional accountant, could decide on what should be done. (In September 1962, in response to a request from Kathleen, I granted permission for the deeds of the cottage in Howth to be deposited as security for a loan in connection with a partnership to be purchased for her husband.) They felt it was clearly best that my mother should go to live with them in Reading. Kathleen stated that my mother had once collapsed alone in the kitchen and could not live alone. The house could not be left unattended because of the likelihood of squatters or a break-in.

I drove up to Strathclyde for a week of consultations, then down to the

England, 1966, during the sad weeks following the sudden death of my father. I am in the garden of Ormskirk Convent with Kitty and her sister Rosalie, Mother Superior of the convent.

guesthouse of the Sacred Heart Convent at Ormskirk just north of Liverpool to meet Kitty. I was surprised when, on my arrival, I was immediately told to go to bed, but when I looked at my image in the mirror above the washbasin in my room, I was shocked to find myself looking at the grey weary wrinkled face of an old man! It was in these circumstances that Kitty lost ownership of her own home, funds from the sale of which were transferred to permit purchase of a larger house under the exclusive ownership of her daughter and son-in-law. I had profound misgivings though I could not articulate their precise nature to my own satisfaction. Letters from Kitty, now living with my sister and her family in Reading, if usually bringing me up to date on family doings, had begun to take on a slightly querulous note that seemed totally out of character.

My sister Kathleen and her husband Peter, at their home on Caversham Road near Reading, southwest of London, England.

Eventually these would culminate in the flat statement, "Nothing has gone right since I left my home in Strawberry Hill." I felt incapable of any action or response on Kitty's behalf.

From the point of view of work, the outcome of the trip was immensely successful in clearly indicating the complementary program of numerical modelling and extensive program of field observations which would best fulfil the task with which our group had been charged. With the acquisition of an I.B.M. computer by the Biological Station, and an arranged collaborative field program with our colleagues in the Tidal Branch of the Canadian Hydrographic Service in Victoria, a massive program covering the seasonal changes in water properties in waters between Vancouver Island and the mainland of coastal

On board the U.S.S. Stanton Island *of the American Navy during an expedition funded by the Canada Defence Research Board to the Arctic Ocean to investigate underwater, under-ice sound propagation.*

British Columbia was initiated. Little did I think that major cutbacks in research funding over the next twenty-five years would render these data uniquely and enduringly significant to assess potential changes that might result from possible climate change in the future. The future now looked very promising in terms of the research program and various expeditions to the Arctic Ocean; particularly so in contrast to life at the house on Deerborne.

One evening in July 1968, I returned from work to find the house deserted. Shortly afterwards, a taxi pulled up at the door and the driver handed me a letter which he said had been given him to deliver by a woman at the ferry terminal to the mainland. It declared Ellen's intention to return to live with her mother, on educational grounds, so that Tom and Michael could attend the Christian Brothers' College in Vancouver. A few days later I drove over

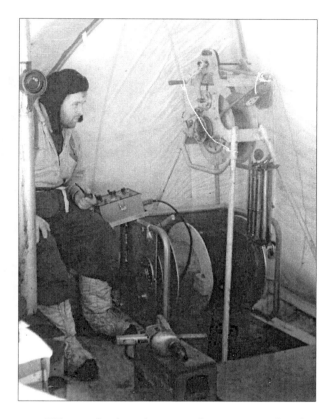

Lowering an STD recorder through a metre of ice to measure the salinity,
temperature and depth in the surrounding waters. The research tent is pitched on
the ice adjacent to where the crew enjoyed an ice-flow-cooled beer, the quaffing of
the latter being forbidden while on-board!

by car and ferry to Vancouver and was waiting in the Volkswagen, parked in
the lot behind the funeral home, when Ellen and her mother returned in the
Cadillac. For Mrs. Kearney the moment appeared to be an irresistible moment
of triumph: "Well now, Pat? Well now, Pat"?

Affirmed by my father's stated perspective and support, and my own experience, there was now no doubt remaining. There could have been many
spontaneities of response by Mrs. Kearney in that moment. I had once heard

Observing ice flows on the Wedell Sea on one of four expeditions to the Arctic on behalf of the Canadian Government.

her voice her intention that she wanted Tom to "grow up like Frank!" With Ellen's move to Vancouver, it would appear that she now felt assured that her plans would succeed. This would actually be brought about by ensuring that the boys would be adapted to a standard of living which, in the absence of any higher level of university education or professional training, would leave them with no alternative but her funeral business to sustain the standard of living to which they were being made accustomed. I was resolved to stand against her. However, as Shakespeare put it, "There's a divinity that shapes our ends/Rough hew them how we will!"

Reflecting on such events over the years I would eventually understand it thus. Whenever a human mind or spirit is under the control of hatred for anything that impedes getting what they want, the one responsible had better be prepared for the evil action that will probably follow. It seems to me that the fundamental injunction to the human intellect in the Garden of Eden, as described at the beginning of the Book of Genesis, pertained to the abuse of the ability to think, to question intelligently, and to understand rationally: *"You may eat indeed of all the trees in the garden, nevertheless of the tree of knowledge of good and evil you are not to eat; for on that day that you eat from it, you shall surely die."*

Good implies cooperative work in advancing order in the universe in whatever tiny context is given to each of us, with whatever abilities and in whatever circumstances fall to our lot. Evil involves the attempted avoidance of that work by using the very talents that make us human rather than animal in that evasion. The result is a regression to something below the primitive level of psyche. The further divine injunction at the beginning of the Book of Job, to Satan: *"All he has is in your power, but keep your hands off his person,"* symbolizes all the forces of physical and moral evils that challenge the human psyche. These, in turn, have to be overcome to bring about some abstract good of order, that which is concretely coming into being, both around us and within us.

Thus there is a fundamental freedom to use our mental abilities to expand each consciousness through solving problems in adapting to the demands of one's own time through acclimating to the collective field of meaning then extant. Nevertheless, we can never judge the absolute status of a person whose actions we perceive as evil for we are never privy to the complete collective psychic picture. There remains however, an essential freedom to responsibly inquire, intelligently question and rationally decide what is good for both our selves and others. Jewish psychiatrist Viktor Frankl found that even in the appalling confinements of Auschwitz, there were a very few, whether amongst guards, capos or prisoners, who could refuse approval of their state and still seek its meaning in some absolute overriding context.

Education is a matter of realizing some potential within one's own consciousness, with its extraordinary capacity to reflect back upon itself and grasp salient features of its own activities. It comes about through asking and answering questions that enable us to make better and better decisions in life. A person can set no limit to it for we can always ask, "Is this the last question?" Answers can be passed on from one human head to another down the eons of time to become individual contributions of meaning to a vast expanding field, all interconnected, all pointing to something that lies over our present event horizon for which we are being prepared and to which we will all belong. That the vast evolutionary momentum should come to a halt with the disintegration of our physical bodies is absurd. The funeral trade in Vancouver, however, would not have been my first choice for my sons as preparatory to coming abreast of the level of meaning that characterizes our own times. As for myself, I would come to realize that whether a life path is chosen by default or by intention, it is still chosen, and choose they would. The task of opening to the questions, to the said potential residing in this vast, expanding, interconnected field of meaning, would be theirs and theirs alone.

Over the better part of a decade, personal and professional problems had compounded to bring about an immense sense of personal isolation. My interest in Lonergan's work continued though I wondered if it would ever be possible to cull from such an immense and expanding volume of professional work in the realms of philosophy, theology and psychology any strategic group of insights which would afford useful practical guidance in terms of how it all worked and what one ought to do. I started reading introductory works dealing with Freud and Jung. Of particular interest was the autobiography of the latter, the graphic depiction of his growing awareness of the data of consciousness. I also became interested in the writings of Teilhard de Chardin and his major synthesis of the sacred and the profane. The emergence of human consciousness in an evolutionary context and implication of a spiritual destiny I found fascinating though perplexing. More and more the perfunctory paraphrasing of the readings in Sunday homilies appeared devoid of any significant meaning, having no conceivable relevance to my everyday habits of thought in a laboratory or with a computer. Regular attendance was an insurance policy, concerned with the possibility of some sort of life after death.

It seemed to be imperative that we be on our own as a family, even if only for a temporary period, if we were to survive as such. In the course of my overseas visits, both the person and the work of Norman Heaps at the Liverpool Tidal Observatory had particularly impressed me. The computational numerical scheme that he had developed for studies of North Sea tides and storm surges could be applied to the Canadian coastal waters of the west coast. I had already made a successful start on a simple multi-channel model using our own small computer at the Biological Station. I asked Dr. Rossiter, the director of the Observatory, if the work could form the basis of a doctoral thesis at the University of Liverpool with which the Observatory was associated. They asked me to deliver a seminar on my preliminary numerical model studies and accompanying program of field observations at the Institute. This provided a basis for assessing my application and led to my acceptance as a graduate student. While my proposal that such an educational and career opportunity be undertaken by the whole family met with enormous objections, Ellen eventually appeared to be persuaded of the possibilities of a new start. When my application was approved I applied for educational leave, pointing out the advantage of access to a much more powerful computer and the immediate availability of expert professional opinion. The application was granted and plans were laid to move the family to Liverpool in September 1969.

CHAPTER X

DOCTORAL DISSERTATION

TIDAL INSTITUTE AND

UNIVERSITY OF LIVERPOOL, U.K. (1969–1972)

The Tidal Observatory was situated on a high sandstone ridge that formed the backbone of the Wirral Peninsula on the south side of the Mersey River across from Liverpool with its miles of locks and dock basins. Founded originally to provide accurate time checks for the chronometers of sailing ships in the port of Liverpool, activities were extended to include studies of tides and tidal streams, a field in which it acquired a unique international reputation. From that location atop Bidston Hill, commanding a broad panorama of the Mersey, of the docks and seaward approaches, with its massive sandstone walls and twin domes housing the telescopes, the Observatory operated with the extraordinary competence, kindness and dedication of its staff. I loved every minute of the two years that I spent there. As well, the time in England offered a welcome opportunity to establish a meaningful relationship between ourselves, with my sister and her family, and time with Kitty.

Ellen, Tom and Michael in Birkenhead, across the River Mersey from Liverpool, where the family lived during my doctoral program.

The University of Liverpool physics department had acquired a large state-of-the-art I.B.M. computer. This was for their part in the European Atomic Energy program which involved analyses of tracks formed in particle detectors. Their primary concern at the time was setting up the required software and as a graduate student I was allowed access to it. Thus I spent much of my time shuttling back and forth through the Mersey Tunnel between the university and the Tidal Institute. I loved it all! It was also a remarkable advantage for my sponsoring employer, the Government of Canada, which fell heir to almost unlimited free computing time not to mention low tuition fees as a British-born subject!

Ellen and the boys on the path leading to the grotto in the gardens of what once was the residence of Alexander Pope in Twickenham, the home of my childhood and youth. The sleeping quarters of the Sisters of Mercy Convent are located in the building on the right.

On Sunday mornings the family, now residing in Birkenhead, would drive over to mass at the new Catholic Cathedral near the university. The building, with its high stained glass windows and side chapels is essentially cylindrical and surmounted by a high conical roof and spire. Seats are arranged in concentric rings about the central altar that lies below its spectacular suspended corona. The sacristy is below and the entrance hymn would swell in volume as the choir and celebrants would ascend the sloping ramp to the cathedral floor. Afterward we would have lunch in the cafeteria below and then go for a drive.

The Tidal Observatory was built in the 1800s to provide an accurate time check for ships using the Port of Liverpool and Birkenhead. The two domes are housings for the telescopes.

It might be, for example, Speke Hall with its magnificent 16th century half-timbering, out near the airport. There were many other places to visit in North Wales and Cheshire. More ambitious trips would take us to see York Cathedral and the nearby Railway Museum, with its extensive collection of superbly restored steam locomotives.

On one occasion, we stopped for a breather by the side of a small road, flanked by a narrow grass verge crossing a wide expanse of ploughed field. Suddenly we discovered to our amazement that Tom had vanished without the slightest suggestion as to how the completely impossible had occurred! Then a red face emerged out of the grass to reveal a deep culvert, totally grown over and concealed. Not only were we immensely grateful that Tom emerged none-the-worse-for-wear, but that we hadn't unwittingly parked in it!

A favourite place of immense symbolic significance, to myself at least, was the radio telescope at Jodrell Bank, its two-hundred-foot dish towering above the Cheshire plain. Thus was human thought reaching out into the very depths of the universe. Its designer and builder was Sir Bernard Lovell. He was a man of deep religious conviction and came to realize that the most exalted and demanding ideas of modern physics formed only a small part of a vastly greater picture. His biography would later refer to the fact that he had been teaching physics all his life without knowing what he had been talking about! Though I would never achieve the depth and breadth of his knowledge of physics, I would find out for myself that some of the most fundamental ideas gave rise to questions never addressed in my own physics courses, that there was indeed a magnificence and thrilling depths of meaning at the heart of things. This we are made privy by the gift of consciousness, if we make the effort that seems to be mandated by the spontaneity of questioning.

Often we would drive from the Wirral to visit my family in Reading. I found it difficult to set aside earlier feelings towards my sister affirmed as they had been years before by our old friend Sister Maurus who wisely observed how very different we were and how little we held in common. The visits were, however, important for family connections and Kitty obviously lived for our visits. Over time she made various oblique references to financial matters and eventually told me that she was being pressured for money by my sister. This seemed to me such incredible behaviour that, even when Kitty reported a request for two thousand pounds sterling, "in case something happened," I still did nothing about it. It seemed to me that my sister, particularly as a trained nurse, would be sensitive to such matters.

On her last visit to us in our apartment on the Wirral, it became obvious that Kitty had become seriously mentally disturbed, with references to the "gang" that was after her. I sought the advice of a geriatric psychiatrist who, after examining Kitty suggested hospitalization in Chester for one week for detailed assessment and evaluation of possible medication. The conclusion of the psychiatrist was that there were valid grounds for Kitty's condition and that I should look very carefully into her financial affairs. However, my sister and brother-in-law abruptly removed her back to Reading. A short time later Kitty died, on 18th November 1971.

One month later, Tom, Michael and Ellen returned to Vancouver for Christmas with her family, during which time Ellen and her mother made the decision that they would remain and the boys were re-enrolled at Vancouver College. I faced the monumental task of writing up the two years work and presenting the thesis as the basis for an oral examination. In accomplishing that task, I can never even begin to express the extraordinary kindness of our friends Stuart and Betty Walker, who worked with me evening after evening when Stuart would return from his work as a chemist with British Nuclear Fuels, Betty from her work at Beaufort Life Rafts. I would write text at the dining room table while Betty typed it in the living room, and Stuart would prepare dinner in the kitchen. And so it went on, over the weeks until the thing was done.

With the support of the Walkers and Norman Heaps, how could I fail? So many years of frustration and failure receded with, at long last, the successful completion of a doctoral dissertation in coastal fluid dynamics. Life can be worthwhile. Things can be different, if one is prepared to stay the course, in short, to get on with it. The field of battle lies within the deepest levels of oneself and that was far from over. The thought of returning to Vancouver filled me with dread but it had to be faced. While I had been offered a permanent position at the Tidal Institute, there was a gentleman's agreement that if supported on educational leave, one would work for at least an equivalent period of time with the Fisheries Research Board that had funded the leave. Abuse of that understanding could spoil someone else's chances.

My supervisor, Norman Heaps, and our association over the remaining years, up to the time of his premature death to cancer, was marked by a growth in both respect and affection. In his old cloth cap and raincoat, with battered brief case, he seemed to embody a level of technical accomplishment and integrity of quiet purpose that lay somewhere at the heart of England's achievements in science and industry.

There were many things to reflect upon as these two years came to an

Dr. Norman Heaps, an expert on tidal modeling, in his office at Bidston Observatory located on the Wirral peninsula near Liverpool. He is observing charts of the Irish Sea.

Dr. Norman Heaps accepted our invitation to visit the West Coast in the early 1970s and traveled with us on a road trip from the Calgary Airport to Vancouver.

end. It was sad that Kitty was not there to share that moment of success. She had worked for years as a shorthand typist to support my degree studies at University College Dublin. Using my savings from my three Antarctic voyages, I had purchased the cottage on Howth Head for my parents as a modest gesture of appreciation. Still, they had insisted it remain in my name. A closer relationship that I had hoped might develop between my sister and myself had not come to fruition, though the cousins established friendships that have grown with the years. I still had doubts as to whether we had collectively handled Kitty's last years in her best interest. Often, however, there is little that one can do about such matters that are accomplished before one has had time to assimilate the overall implications of what is being overtly done. For all of us, however, I have no doubt that nature in its own time exacts a measure of justice over our shortcomings.

CHAPTER XI

GESTATION OF A CONCEPTUAL MODEL

TRANSFORMATIVE DREAMS, VANCOUVER, B.C. (1972-1980)

Returning to Vancouver, I was able to continue work in a challenging and interesting field of research. In personal terms, however, there was again increasing frustration and again the all-too-familiar isolation from any sort of meaningful personal communal involvement. In September 1972 we purchased a house at 1419 Dogwood Street in Vancouver. The location was close to that of Mrs. Kearney but it now seemed pointless to try to resist a chain of events assuming their own inevitability.

In 1974, Jung's autobiography, *Memories, Dreams and Reflections*, was once again a catalyst in my reflections. Since my introduction to this work in the mid-sixties, I had gradually begun to see that the transformation and development of my own consciousness contents were something that could be objectified and worked with. A key element in this involved my old childhood fascination with dreams, which later became a fascination with the role of dreams that could be indicative of malfunction. I was also interested in the excitation of psychic processes as another manifestation of energy that is precisely analogous to that of other physical processes. Could it be related to the fundamental ordering process that brings about the evolutionary process in the universe? This seems to give rise to higher levels of diversification and complexity that can, in turn, be integrated in conscious process to bring about, individually and collectively, a vast and incredibly complex expanding field of meaning. I had, however, immense difficulty in trying to grasp Jung's analytical psychology as a practical working model. It seemed, however, that my childish fascination with "pictures on my pillow" had not been misplaced. Perhaps they could be interpreted as symbols in some manner that could shed light on the authenticity, or lack of it, in the course of one's own spiritual journey.

I was particularly intrigued by Jung's notion that conscious existence after death would have to continue on the level of consciousness attained by humanity, knowledge that has been brought to consciousness by other human beings. But what, then, was knowing? How was it empowered? Could there be any relation with the symbols of my own religious formation?

On a summer morning in 1975, we received a phone call from the Kearney seaside home on Boundary Bay that Frank had collapsed. We immediately drove out and, on pulling up at the front porch, we saw a figure, lying on a stretcher, shrouded in a blanket, feet still incongruously clad in a large pair of running shoes. As we hurried up the little path to the porch steps, a stentorian bellow came out from the open front door of the large living room in the familiar voice of Mrs. Kearney: "Where's my tea?" I remembered Dr. Cosgrove's remark several years before that nothing would be allowed to impede the mother's wishes, even if it destroyed her son. I knew that something had ended. With the death of the mother I could have seen a new lease on family life opening up, a new relationship with Frank. I had not thought that Frank would be the first to go. No, no, no! I knew that the fates of Ellen, Tom and Michael had slipped beyond my reach, that their completed incorporation into Mrs. Kearney's business and domestic arrangements was inevitable.

Indeed, it wasn't long before Ellen, Tom, and Michael went to live with her brother Edward, and their mother. It was clear that Ellen was completely dedicated to carrying out her mother's plans. On Christmas day, 1976, Mrs. Kearney, in my presence, informed a relative of her intended plans for Tom and Michael, now in their late teens, in her funeral business. I felt that the situation was so hopeless and resolved to have nothing else to do with the Kearneys. Where now could I turn?

Throughout the seventies there were occasional but insistent reminders, in terms of the spontaneities of dream symbolism, that was reminiscent of the slow psychic deterioration I had experienced earlier in Halifax. If the dream ego appears as a sort of "observer," other figures, particularly of strangers, tend to represent aspects of the dreamer's own psyche. A female figure personifies the unconscious feeling, or feminine side of a male dream ego. Thus, in one instance, a woman is looking out over a hillside when I see a crouching male figure with a rifle trained on her back. I tried to shout a warning but no sound emerges.

Another dream setting consisted of adjoining men's and women's washrooms, only the normally separating wall, over the washbasins between the two had been removed and the dream ego was looking at the profile of a woman of great beauty. Then, she turned to look at me and the other side of her face was hideously disfigured. Perhaps that disfigurement was at the root of my weariness and attendant inertia. It seemed that I must somehow recover the capacity to feel.

Yet another example brought in the context of religion. In this case, a woman was shouting nonsense from the altar of a small chapel to a listening congregation that included the dream ego. Behind the woman was a tall dark figure in expensive white brocade and wearing a golden headband that the dream ego knows to be evil. As the woman picks up a stone book from the altar, the dream ego stands up and shouts, "Why doesn't someone do something – by the power of the cross, depart from this woman." The figure vanishes and the woman falls back against the wall, silent, and looking up at me.

I could not remedy such matters by some effort of will. Somehow I knew I needed to seek the symbols that could bring about the authentic realization of that aspect of myself. I remembered some sense of benign cosmic presence encountered all those years ago in visits to the Benedictine Abbeys at Buckfast and Quarr in England, also at Roscrea in Ireland. Perhaps that was where to start.

In 1974 I had begun the practice of spending Palm Sunday weekends at a Benedictine Abbey located on a hill above Mission in the Fraser Valley. It enjoys a magnificent location looking out over the valley to Mount Cheam. There was a sense of stillness and peace that provided needed respite. In the library I came across a *Dictionary of Philosophy* by Brugger and Baker. It provided a coherent vocabulary of Thomist meaning that could be verified, as indeed it had been in the course of Catholic scholarship and theology over many centuries, in the context of my own conscious reflections. It also provided an essential key to my growing understanding of Lonergan's work, not just in terms of an exercise in learning but, of vastly deeper consequence, of awakening to myself as spirit, to the world as it really is.

The conviction that started to emerge is of the same nature as that which attends upon the embarking on a familiar task with the certain knowledge that you already know how to go about it. This does not, of course, guarantee an outcome but presupposes the fullest prior employment of one's talents and abilities. How can we undertake important personal decisions when one's immediate future can never even be certain of its coming into existence? If there is a primordial ordering principle underlying the evolutionary development of the universe, the totality of existence, surely this must somehow become manifest in such circumstances. That would eventually turn out to be the case, though of the essence is that most difficult of human dispositions to acquire, patience.

It was always difficult to leave the Abbey knowing that such feelings must dissipate under the winds of secular involvement. In time, there would come the realization that the healing power that permeated the place came from the persistence of patient listening in the monastic prayer life, the Divine Office – *The Office of The Hours* that is ordained to the sanctification of the day. Purchasing the appropriate volumes, I made it a daily routine, one that remains an increasingly exciting source of inner strength and meaning. To put it crudely, it can, as it were, "zero one's mental apparatus" for the day, stilling interference by inordinate affective distractions, facilitating emergence of possible courses of action, insights and value responses.

My work was concerned with the application of fluid dynamical theory to the response of a complex coastal system under forcing by tides, winds, fresh water run-off from the land and events propagating inward from its boundaries with the open ocean, with the methodical construction of more and more powerful mathematical models, verified against observations, possessing both explanatory and predictive capabilities that have extensive practical significance. Would it ever be possible to develop a somewhat comparable body of theory, yielding explanation and some measure of predictability in the vastly more complex realm of human living? Must life consist solely of a denial of all somatic importunity in accordance with the legalism of remote and static generalities, for some sort of nebulous afterlife? Could one set up a "working model" after the manner of the Victorian physicists, a compact set of terms and relations which, like the exquisite harmonies of my beloved steam engines, could furnish, in a context of vastly greater scope, both empowerment and direction on one's voyage over the infinite seas of human existence with experimentally verifiable consequences? This would not accord with Chesterton's lines quoted above but with the possibility of once again falling completely in love, this time with the very magnificence and promise of the universe itself.

I also formed the habit of attending the daily lunchtime mass at St. Mark's College, a short walk across the University of British Columbia campus from my office. It made for very welcome moments of recollection and meditation amid the highly secular and materialistic environment of a large university. If my ambition expressed to the manager of the Harland and Wolff repair works in Southampton Docks all those years earlier had been for a university teaching position, all traces of my youthful idealism had long since vanished. Wherever you go, to a greater or lesser degree, one encounters the same old battle between good efforts of the majority and its attempted subversion, for selfish purposes, by a small minority embedded in its own venal purpose.

The university itself, once synonymous for me with the highest form of human service reaching out to ever-new realms of knowledge for the benefit of the world community, had become a glorified trade school. It was now dedicated more and more to uncritically supplying the demands of society as prompted by the social engineers, themselves hired by national assemblies and multi-national corporations to create wealth for their supporters and shareholders respectively. Thus would technical innovation and investor greed become the great driving social forces they are.

In May of 1977 I attended the 9th International Liege Colloquium on Ocean Hydrodynamics at which I presented my work on tidal and estuarine studies of the waters between Vancouver Island and the mainland. Afterwards I took leave to visit friends in England and Ireland. It was actually in the course of a visit to Oxford that, browsing in Blackwell's Book Shop, I happened on two major discoveries that would prove of immense significance to my own journey. One was Lonergan's *Method in Theology*, the other Hugo Meynell's *Introduction to the Philosophy of Bernard Lonergan*. I was delighted to find in the latter a concise glossary of Lonergan's definitions. For a non-philosopher like myself, the enormous problem was establishing an unambiguous basic framework of terms and definitions, some sort of "model" that could be helpful in establishing some sort of direction in life, what sort of questions to ask, and where meaningful answers might be found.

Slowly over the years I had begun to grasp the basic nature of my own cognitive process, its empowerment through feelings, a "self assembly" if you will, in terms of something of the nature of meaning, something that could accumulate and progress over a lifetime. Now I could at last postulate a working feedback model of the "self-assembling human spacecraft," however crude, but reasonably complete in its major parts and the relationships between them, consonant with the data of my inner experience, a strategy of deciding and acting. The key to its performance was facilitation of access to the omnipresent principle of information directing the net transformation of energy to yield new levels of order, diversity, complexity, in an overall fundamental context of uncertainty. What is happening on planet Earth is an exponentially growing field of meaning, the product of human heads. At its core is something, as publicly verifiable, that we identify as reality or truth.

A significant change in psychic attitude would be recorded in a singularly dramatically phased dream sequence. The dream ego and an engineer are watching out for fallen rock, while seated on the front of a steam locomotive at the head of a train proceeding along the bottom of an extremely deep cutting, a magnificent feat of engineering. The train stops at an opening at the cutting where there is a high steel framework carrying an elevator to the high ground above. The dream ego and engineer are carried up to find a winter resort with a frozen lake where many people are skating. The engineer warns that the place is not what the advertising makes it out to be. The dream ego starts down a road coming to a junction in the fork of which is a house from which a party of police is departing. The dream ego knows the house to be his and that he himself is the object of the police search. Pretending to take the left hand fork, the dream ego, once the police are out of sight, cuts back to the right fork. Ahead lies a long straight road leading to a great mountain enveloped in black storm clouds – the path the dream ego must take. Passing cars descending from the mountain have their headlights switched on. The dominant theme is the role of the feedback model's ability to return the dream ego, by train and elevator, to the more widely accustomed ground of the "human circle," but only as preparatory to taking a more difficult road, unpoliced by authority, but using the light of intellect and conscience to meet the challenge of the mountain and the storm.

Through dreams such as this, it was becoming apparent to me that after many years of reflection I was beginning to come to terms with some of my own questions. The foundation for this rudimentary understanding included Lonergan's analysis of human consciousness, that takes into account human thought about human thinking all the way from ancient Greece, to multi-faceted evolutionary knowledge of the universe, in particular of living systems of planet Earth, and from thence to the psychoanalysis of Freud, the analytical psychology of Jung, the personal psychology of Adler, and then the further developments elaborated by their successors.

If we are pressed by someone for an answer to the question as to what we really believe is going on in the universe and why we are here, on the one hand we may respond that there is nothing to be found, or that the question is unanswerable and we just have to get on with it. On the other hand the tension that is at the heart of human existence remains. Commonly some sort of myth is found to alleviate that tension. Thus at the beginning of his book, *A Brief History of Time,* Stephen Hawking recounts a story of how a well-known scientist, after delivering a lucid account of the solar system and its location in the galaxy, was met by a caustic rejoinder from a little old lady who proclaimed, "What you have told us is rubbish. The world is really a flat plate supported on the back of a giant tortoise."

With a superior smile the scientist replied, "What is the tortoise standing on?"

"You're very clever, young man, very clever," said the old lady. "But it's turtles all the way down."

For myself, I suppose I could not have done much better. I recalled a first year physics class in which I was told that energy, the most all-embracing concept in relating diverse phenomena, is only knowable by its effects. From then on there was always the lurking conviction that if we don't know what knowing is, we don't know what we are talking about, no matter how clever our description and explanation of the effects. I had tried my hand at philosophy and logic back on the Antarctic whaling grounds, only to find such considerations boring and inconclusive. I had the mind-set of the engineer that wanted to build models that could work and be used to produce demonstrably useful results. It never even entered my head that a conceptual model could be built, an abstract unity of terms and relations, capable of yielding the most concrete of all practical results, a growing excitement as to the present role of consciousness in the universe, and the evolutionary prospects for each entity that thinks of itself as a "me". The clue is to be found in the exponentially growing field of meaning on planet Earth, that which is produced in human heads and is both accumulative and, on a historical scale, progressive. How does it come about?

In other words: What is the meaning of meaning? Such a question is not as obscure or silly as it may sound. Human consciousness is able to think back about its own thoughts and feelings during past situations, wonder what happened, or wonder if the right thing had been done, etcetera.

Meaning is something that occurs in human heads and can be passed from one human head to another. In this manner, we can come to learn the meaning, not only of that which concerns the people and things around us, but also that of other times and places. Central to it is the notion of understanding. For example, on obtaining a box of parts from the store, when we understand the accompanying information, or instructions, we can assemble and operate the parts as a unity, whether it is a computer or a bike rack. (Often today, the same information may be expressed in several different languages.) That act of understanding is central in enabling us to fulfil some need, to do something that we were unable to do before. With that act of understanding we turn the information on how the whole unit can be assembled and used into a bit of knowledge in ourselves. It stays with us, becomes part of something we think of as "me." We must have reasonable faith, or belief, in the fact that the specialists who design and build computers and bike racks understood what they were doing. Common to all such activities, are three fundamental levels of mental operation – directing attention, questioning and judging.

An intriguing aspect of this "thinking back" is afforded by instances of neurosurgical electrical stimulation of exposed brain tissue under local anaesthetic. These could result in a sort of "dual consciousness." Thus the patient could describe events to the surgeon (Wilder Penfield), as though they were again present, and which were also recognizable as the contents of earlier experiences. The electrode could bring about such recall, produce bodily movements, but could not bring about these fundamental operations of the mind, of directing attention, questioning and judging. That could only be done by the patient (the operator) in response to a request from the surgeon with respect to the electrically-induced reappearance of the past record. It would thus appear that as the operator can experience, understand and judge, the resulting contents become a fixed accumulation of meaning.

The age we are living in is being called the "information age" because of the enormous increase in facilities for communication. There is an expanding field of more and more specialized meaning that confronts each generation. Currently, there is direct access to a vast field of global meaning at the click of a "mouse." But what are we, as individuals and as potential "meaning makers," to contribute? Generally, we have to grasp some pertinent personal level of meaning, already contained in other human heads, libraries or data banks, before we can satisfactorily decide how to make the best of whatever particular interests, skills and talents we may possess. Then we will have something worthwhile to communicate – and that is what gives rise to feelings of genuine satisfaction.

This 'working out' for myself elicited the comment: "Nobody has put it to me like that before!" Thus I started to think about how the topic might be raised and expanded in future conversations.

The really interesting thing about meaning is that it can be passed as information from one human head to another in many different ways, as long as both heads are familiar with the sort of code involved, language, strings of bits, or whatever. A particular instance of meaning can be illustrated using many different examples or illustrations. Information seems to exist independently of the physical system that carries it, though it can affect a particular system in terms of its future performance.

There is a capacity to accumulate vast amounts of meaning in a single human head over the course of any one lifetime. This comes about through asking questions about the everyday things we experience, giving rise to possible answers. This then gives rise to a further question as to whether a particular answer is certainly or probably true. It is generally exciting to arrive at such an answer since it involves a release from that tension of inquiry where there is usually much work involved, much mulling over sources, in arriving at answers. Still, such answers tend to make life easier when we decide to put our new bit of knowledge into practice. More and more we have to have faith in the specialized, publicly verified knowledge that has been passed on, acquired and augmented in other human heads. The object of generating all this meaning, which can include possibilities, imaginary beings, speculations, truth and falsity, and so on, is to arrive at an expansion of knowledge which can be publicly affirmed and commonly applied for the public good of order.

Such knowledge can be expressed in the form of classical natural laws, expressed as ideals underlying all sorts of things going on in the world, both in us and around us. Complementing such classical laws there are also statistical laws, ideals pointing to some sort of regularity in otherwise random occurrences. (Obviously, we are not meant to run out of questions, as we can always ask, "Is this the last question?") Thus, for example, a civil engineer might fulfil a social need by using the classical laws of physics and chemistry to build a highway. But it could be in later terms of traffic accident statistics that there can be shown to be a high probability of accidents at a particular location, indicating a design omission requiring corrective action. More generally, change appears in terms of statistical regularities, oscillations, schemes of recurrent events that attract attention and give rise to questions, eventually leading to the formulation of classical laws. Our great business seems to be the contribution of whatever talents we possess to the communal process of bringing about new levels of order through understanding, and passing on that understanding, answers to questions, in the form of information to our successors.

Eventually we arrive at the biggest questions of all: What's it all for? Who am I? What am I? What will happen to me? These are religious questions. They pertain to some personal view of the world. Can we understand ourselves as spiritual entities that develop? Such development must include the accumulative contents of myriads of acts involving, not only experiencing, inquiring, judging, but also of deciding on what to do, of adapting satisfactorily to something we think of as the "real world."

We don't each have to master the enormously difficult abstractions of modern physics to realize that our common sense appreciation of the everyday world around us is but the tip of a vast iceberg of something we call "truth" or "reality" which is arrived at by elaborating clever questions, in the form of hypotheses, which can be experimentally tested. Such abstractions can provide information about the universe, concretely verifiable as established knowledge, and yielding results of immense practical significance. Thus it is common public knowledge that the real world goes far, far beyond the mere data of common sense experience from which each of us must start out. Thinking about our own thinking can also yield a conviction that the "me" that results also goes far beyond the mere data of our senses. When confronted in a mortuary by a body, which seems to be all that remains of a person once loved and cared for, it is extraordinarily difficult to have faith that the real human person continues to exist in a manner to which we do not yet have access. Yet there is a probability amounting to effective certainty that such is indeed the case. Here we need a bit more science.

The most all-embracing concepts, in our present understanding of world process, are energy and information. Energy gives rise to, and performs the work of changing matter. Information directs and controls the manner in which that change occurs, the physico-chemical reactions that give rise to progressively higher, more diversified and complex forms of matter. Thus the seething universe of energy and matter, through cosmic and chemical process, through endlessly varied plant and animal life concretely displays a net evolutionary development from less to more highly ordered systems, possessing new levels of freedom to do things. The most exciting thing about it is that it is all interconnected and comes from a common source. As best we can presently understand it, that source consisted in some infinitely compacted concentration of energy, the so-called *big bang*, that in dispersing and cooling, as illustrated by the thermal history of the universe, has given rise to something that can reflect on itself, human consciousness, that which has the greatest freedom of anything we know about so far. Religion is largely a matter of the relation of human consciousness with that which has given rise to it – the cosmos. The more of the questions we can answer concerning it, then the deeper becomes our faith that there is a particular purpose for each of us being here.

Human consciousness comes about when the laws for generating a unity from an information multiplicity are assigned in a human head. Over the brief flash in space-time of that neural system, human consciousness can inform itself, live intelligently, reasonably and responsibly, thus becoming an ineradicable part of a minutely organized and carefully controlled more significant "bang" – an explosion of information. Matter can come and go, as our physical bodies, which are persistently changing, also come and go. Information seems to be the primary stuff that is evolving in the universe. If it were not doing something of the sort, we would not be here! It thus becomes highly probable that we can reasonably look forward to some discarnate involvement in an evolutionarily informed future. In the words of theologians Karl Rahner and Herbert Vorgrimler, "Historical process does not mean that an able mind vanishes without trace to make room for another which is quite foreign to it, but that mind carries the intellectual past, transformed with it into the future."

Information, insofar as it is concerned with physical systems such as a pattern or an array of items, is quantifiable in terms of the number of choices required to bring them about. At the simplest level, one choice, or one bit of information would be constituted by a "yes" or a "no" answer to a question. Throughout life, we have to make such choices. Many of these are concerned with learning some common level of meaning appropriate to our time and location in history. From that we can go on to the experiences of others in other places and at other times. Then we come to the most difficult choices of all – choices that are not quantifiable. What should we do with ourselves? Where does that information come from?

My own inclination for many years was to take refuge in the satisfactions accruing from the intellectual search for meaning, particularly in the writings of the Canadian theologian and philosopher, Bernard Lonergan, primarily his book *Insight: A Study of Human Understanding.* It was only in his later book, *Method in Theology,* that I realized that there had to be a parallel development in the spontaneities of feeling. In my own experience, it then became possible to tackle the problem of developing an authentic religious attitude appropriate to our time. This takes full account of the vast developments in science and scholarship that provides the concrete historical basis for the meaning of our time. These point ever more surely to an omnipresent information source with which we can co-operate.

How then do we decide, on that basis, what sort of action we should undertake? We must now move from the level of the intellect to reflect on the extraordinarily complex flow of feeling, or psychic energy, that brings about change in the accumulating aggregation of events, once present in consciousness that is becoming a "me." This is where the fourth level of mental operation comes into play, that of decision. Here, at the interface between past and future, of time and timelessness, there occur the spontaneities of attracting or repelling, reinforcing or conflicting, feeling responses to incoming imagery, situations, circumstances, physical or social environment, good or evil, love or hate, desire or aversion, hope or despair, joy or sorrow, courage or fear, freedom from constraint or helpless anger. Our past experiences and actions greatly influence the spontaneities of feeling in the present, often unconsciously. Our own pasts make us what we are. However, there frequently results an inability to intelligently question, and reasonably judge, what possible course of action to decide on.

Coming back to our three levels of mental operation, experience, understanding and judging, we note that our experiences are alive with feelings, with psychic energy. Thus we all share at least some strong feelings of desire and of aversion. Through understanding, we can arrive at possibilities of ordering ourselves as community to maximize individual resources and talents. This can ensure the maximal fulfilment of the needs of both our selves and others, and protection against natural hazards, including aberrant performance by self-seeking individuals and groups. At the level of judgment, a new level of spontaneity of feeling can come into play, value feelings, as the key to the net upward positive development in such spontaneities by acting in collaborative accord with the omnipresent fundamental principle of ordering in the universe. However, this is where we are most likely to encounter the need for hard work that is required to bring us abreast of the meaning of our times. It is based on the judgment that includes both the practical intellectual possibilities of succeeding in some course of action, as well as the value feelings that it accords with furthering the cosmic good of order in some particular circumstance. Then we decide to act, bring about change. This, in turn, brings about new experiences to be questioned and judged.

Such considerations lead eventually to a concrete realization of the role of meditative prayer in catalyzing the occurrence of imagery, feelings and insights conducive to the answering of questions as to what we should do with ourselves. Patience is of the essence. Complementary to these may be the interpretation of symbols occurring in dream imagery as indicative of unconscious influences leading to aberrant conscious performance. Prayer is not a matter of invoking magical intervention in the exquisitely ordered process of the universe but in seeking direction as to how one might fulfill one's own tiny role in it.

John Henry Newman described such listening in terms of the primacy of personal "conscience" as the "prophet of information." Thus, he described conscience as the "governor" optimally controlling the advancing "knowledge/feeling synthesis" that eventually leaves its disposable biological substrate behind on a mortuary slab. Bernard Lonergan turned Newman's "illative sense" into the central act of understanding, or insight, as the key to collaboration, at however a mundane or exalted level, in contributing to the emergent good of cosmic order. There results the slow but profound affirmation in the spontaneity of feeling (at the level of value feeling) that accompanies the movement from Newman's merely "notional" to "real assent" in achieving one's own personally satisfying level of meaning. One's level of knowledge and spontaneity of feeling, the overall state of a "me" that changes from moment to moment, can, over the long haul, potentially mount to an ecstatic awareness of the promise of some evolutionary future yet to be realized.

Wisdom involves a presently realizable level of understanding into the role of consciousness in a universe that is evolving, from prior less-ordered states, to later more-ordered states. There is much to be found that is helpful in the writings of the world's major religions – in their authentic moments. There is also involved a vast variety of specialist developments, scientific, technological, medical, psychological, sociological and so on. Most significantly, however, there is the wisdom literature accumulated over millennia, not least among it the works of Aristotle, Augustine, Aquinas and Lonergan, that brings assurance of effort rewarded, an evolutionary promise expressed in languages and imagery appropriate to the writer's own time, place and community. Our task is to bring together the best of the old and the best of the new. Thus we find powerful grounds for faith and hope in the authentic experience of other men and women, whether sage, prophet, apostle, scholar or scientist. Most influential of all, perhaps, are those we occasionally encounter who have met challenges and weathered great storms in life, but now radiate a sense of calmness and fulfilment that becomes a source of inspiration for others to do likewise. Whatever the circumstances, there is a meaning to be found. Intelligence and reason can be encouraged to make responsible decisions, those which accord, in particular instances, with the overall emergence of cosmic order. We are certainly not alone in that endeavour.

Perhaps the most demanding aspect of that work is acquiring the patience to attend to the spontaneities of feeling, until the time is right, at the deepest level of the psyche, and then using our essential freedom to direct attention, inquire and judge so that we may decide responsibly in bringing about something that is truly good for us, and will contribute to order both in ourselves and in assisting others to do likewise. This is a major task that often involves the hard work of bringing about the circumstances in which our own essential decisions can become effective. It is difficult to accept the fact that the spontaneity of motivating feelings in other individuals or groups may be equally reasonable but differ radically from one's own. Approval or disapproval must thus be based on an assessment of whether the actions taken by others demonstrably accord with the slowly emerging collaborative good of the planetary community, both socially and environmentally. Thus the collective field of human consciousness is authentically expanded.

So it is that we must also attend to warning feelings that something is evil, and is contributing to disorder in ourselves. This can often involve seeking the acquisition and exercise of power over others, usually furthering communal disorder. The precepts of attentivity, intelligence and reason can be used irresponsibly, giving rise to such abominations as those known only too well in recent history, global and local, and that descend into a wickedness below any mere level of animal behaviour.

The challenges set by realms of such world-scale evil can only be met by organizing the overwhelming forces of the global human good, now slowly assembling under the banner of the United Nations. In fact, the only reason for the existence of human evil in the universe would seem to be that of challenging the world population to achieve higher and higher levels of organization in the collective preparation of each human intelligence for the next phase of cosmic evolution.

In keeping with the rest of cosmic process, we have to do the work, meet the challenges, overcome the difficulties of some immediate local circumstance. The reward is a release from that driving fundamental tension of inquiry, an understanding that eventually converges in a real assent to the glory and wonder of God's own work, informing an energy/mass universe towards something that remains for us up the "evolutionary turnpike" and over our present event horizon! Stephen Hawking concluded his *Brief History of Time* with the following: "However, if we do discover a complete theory, it should in time be understandable in broad principle by everyone, not just a few scientists. Then we shall all, philosophers, scientists, and just ordinary people be able to take part in a discussion of why it is that we, and the universe, exist. If we find the answer to that, it would be the ultimate triumph of human reason – for then we would know the mind of God."

It is questionable whether we can so actually "know everything about everything." But I am convinced that faith is a matter of some such religious knowing, of rational belief. If we are prepared to do the life work of ordering our own psychic contents, the familiar words of the old carole, now so apt to be relegated to the status of a sales-boosting jingle, *Oh come all ye faithful,* carries a concretely verifiable convincing entailment, *joyful and triumphant* – provided we keep abreast with the meaning of our times!

In some such inner movement of spirit then, of *pneuma*, of a discreet entity uniquely becoming myself, of a "me/not me" that is persistently changing, a dynamic metaphor of space age proportions began to resonate.

CHAPTER XII

PNEUMOCHIP@INFORMATION.UNIVERSE

A CONTEMPORARY METAPHOR

The one thing we can't seem to get away from is change. Everything within us and around us is changing. The "us" consists of an innumerable aggregate of conscious "me's" arriving, changing, and then departing with some load of "meaning" that has come about of each individual interval of "space-time" existence. Such "meaning" can be passed, at least in part, from one "me" to another. Each conscious "me" has an extraordinary capacity to reflect upon itself, become aware of itself and the accumulative nature, both individually and collectively, of what is going on in that awareness. It is "self assembling." What sort of contemporary metaphor might be adopted to provide as to how it operates and performs the work of bringing about change?

We live in an age of extra-planetary space travel and exploration, technological advance in communication made possible by an explosion of knowledge, of better and better approximations to a "reality" as acceptable in the growing context of a publicly affirmable "truth." In that truth, the collective "us" is con-forming to a change which can be grounded in the two most widely embracing concepts of everything that seems to be going on in the universe. "Energy" enables the work that brings about change; "In-formation" directs the "form," assimilable by an "us," and which expresses, in a manner characterized by ineluctable uncertainty, a net development from lower to higher levels of order, diversity and complexity. On the one hand, no individual "me" can come any where near close to mastering the bewildering complexity of it all. On the other hand, a suitable metaphor or "working model" could provide guidance as to proper, or improper, instances of change brought about by a particular "me" in the light of the net emergence of higher levels of order bringing about new levels of freedom and new capacities to do things that we couldn't do before. I decided to call that metaphor a "pneumochip" and its server, "information universe."

Every instance of change involves some sort of "intention," of something that is to come about, of some "form" to appear. Some of the elements undergoing change will remain the same, others will not. It is only through the alteration from earlier to later states that change becomes knowable, thus introducing the notion of time. What seemed to me of particular interest is how that "me" undergoes change. What elements remain the same, what elements undergo change. This gives rise to an analysis of "intention" on the part of a "me" that can be thought of as a raising of the level of consciousness or awareness. The bits of that "me" that remain the same can be listed from reflecting on one's own thinking:

A first level involves a directing of attention to something. It gives rise to an experience which is characterized by an initial intending.

A second level involves an innate curiosity, a level of questioning that gives rise to various possibilities. This brings into consideration what we already know. Imagery from the unconscious is summoned in a manner suggestive of the sort of answer sought by the question, giving rise to possibilities.

A third level involves judging which possibility is, or probably is, the best explanation of the something that gave rise to the question. This can be expressed as part of one's individually appropriated vocabulary of words. What we had failed to understand we now understand. Thus one's vocabulary expands to accommodate higher and higher levels of meaning that have been personally appropriated through that understanding.

A fourth level concerns the course of action that will be personally most advantageous in terms of a particular "me," that will make me "feel" better, release more and more psychic energy. It is at this level that we encounter a sort of "feeling traffic light" that provides guidance as to the intentional process of the emergence of order in the universe insofar as it concerns an individual "me." Courses of action that are consistent with that ordering principle are affirmed in feelings of approval, courses of action that are contrary give rise to feelings of disapproval, ambiguity of feeling indicates the need to proceed cautiously with acquisition of more data.

Thus our conceptual model is equipped with four fundamental coupled "black boxes" that provide a sort of "running plot" of the situation in which a "me" or "human psyche" finds itself at the moment. If disengaged, there is a sort of minimal knowledge of what's going on that prevails. When engaged there can be a sort of rumination on the past record, activation of associations by which one psychic content gives rise to another, as for instance when driving on the freeway, until interrupted by some threat and full engagement of all levels is demanded. Is it "real"? It is certainly every bit as real as one's directing attention, questioning, judging and deciding on what use the fanciful notion of a "pneumochip" might be. In practical terms, it provides a strategy for getting at the role of human consciousness in an evolutionary universe, a sort of internal hygiene of questioning that has progressive, accumulative and increasingly positive spontaneities of feeling states of anticipation for what lies up the evolutionary "turnpike," provided we do our part of the work, pay the toll for use of the road. Not everyone wants to do that.

The really important thing is that the contents of the four levels of operation remain within us, each mind pursuing its own course actuated by a myriad incommunicable feelings and imaginings, of symbols that beckon or repel. The more diligently and responsibly we have employed the "black boxes," our innate talents, the more positive will be the spontaneity of later feeling states, a sort of feedback that averages out over some time scale that is not at our immediate command. We make ourselves what we become.

On the one hand, if we proceed impartially in implementing the first three levels, we know, so to speak, where "we stand" in the "real world" and are best placed to take decisions at the fourth level. On the other hand, if the "traffic light" of conscience (literally meaning "with knowledge") interferes with our primitive levels of desire and aversion, we can start to tinker with those earlier levels to justify illicit courses of action, those which do not accord with advancing the good of order in oneself, one's community, one's environment. There results a blockage of the emergence of the sort of imagery that would suggest the proper answer to the question of what we ought to do. We don't want to be bothered with accepting fundamental responsibility for our life, because it is less trouble to flow along with our pleasures and dislikes, including the prejudices of our own group. Thus there comes about the distinction between good and evil in the course of human affairs.

There is an intention of change that can ascend over a lifetime to the highest levels of release from the fundamental tensions of existence, or descend to the lowest levels of historical abomination all too familiar in our time, from the mass murderer to the home invader. There is a fundamental freedom to search

for the meaning of life, no matter how appalling the imposition of victimiza-
tion and injustice even when so dramatically experienced during three years of
incarceration in Auschwitz and other Nazi camps by the Jewish psychiatrist
Viktor Frankl. With that intention and integrity of conscience, reflecting on itself and its role in a universe of change, it can affirm itself as an entity, a person,
that perdures, transcends change. There emerges a secondary level of meaning
to be found in the primary level of the horror of that immediate experience.
Each "me" is assigned a unique task and, no matter how difficult, the energy
and the information to carry on will be there, if the meaning of one's life is
sought with every fibre of one's being.

The individual pneumochip becomes aware of itself as located at some
point in the interface between all that is known together with all that remains
to be known, the most general space we can conceive of, knowledge-space. The
relentless task of human life seems to be that, not merely of contemplating
what we already know, but of adding increments to that knowledge. All we
know is somehow present and operative within us. We make ourselves what
we are. There is an essential detachability of truth from the particular mind in
which it happens to be generated and an essential communicability from one
mind to another. This has given rise to a variety of empirical approaches to
modifying human behaviour.

It was Freud who identified that past unconscious record as a motivator
of behaviour, emphasizing the role of biological progenitors, in particular
sexuality and aggressivity. Psychoanalysis provided a means for bringing about
change in behaviour, thought and feeling. Jung saw the psyche as a self-regulating system presupposing a creative function in the flow of psychic energy that
had its source in an inherited collective unconscious. Analytical psychology
seeks to bring healing of aberrant behaviour through recovery of the meaning
of an individual life through the use of symbols that relate feeling to imagery,

particularly in the context of dreams. The individual psychology of Adler locates the source of behaviour problems in feelings of inferiority, whether conscious or unconscious, physical, psychological or social, ultimately deriving from individual differences in behaviour. Increasingly, such approaches are developed by their successors to attest to the extraordinary variegation in success and aberrancy attendant upon the conscious journey of each human psyche.

There is something going on in the universe on a scale so vast that it soars far beyond our present grasp. Its temporal development is characterized, amid all the immediate uncertainties and digressions, by a net emergence of higher from lower levels of order characterized by wholly unpredictable new levels of freedom and ways of functioning. Adverting to that source of energy and information in the revelation of earlier recorded experiences brings about the dramatic significance of the relief of prayer. This is essentially aided by reflection on the symbolic experience of others and constitutes a patient attitude receptive of the insights and feelings that direct and urge us towards the successful completion of our space-time existence.

As the years go by and the record of events once conscious lengthens that secondary level of meaning, arrived at by applying the operations in a personal reflective context, an empirical confirmation of the high practical usefulness of the conceptual model is provided. There is some fundamental progress in the spontaneity of a prevailing attitude of highly positive feelings with regard to one's individual tiny role in the universe and the prospects of one's role as a surviving "meaning-unity" after the dissolution of one's body left behind on a mortuary slab. One encounters an entirely new degree of evolutionary freedom for which one's living is but a preparation. Thus the highest levels of abstraction developed by millennia of human thought may be made concretely affirmable in a manner appropriate for each contemporary "me" in our own times, the information age, where each of us, addressable as a "pneumochip@informa-tion.universe," can interact with its omnipresent information source.

There was certainly nothing joyful and triumphant about my life in Vancouver. What had gone wrong? Freud had shown how present behaviour is affected by that of one's own past record of contents once present and conscious. Jung stressed the importance of interpreting symbols in terms of associated feelings and of dreams as indicative of aberrant conscious performance.

With my slow growing understanding of the above, came the ineluctable challenge of putting my understanding into practice – a thoroughly frighten-ing task to be sure, for it meant facing my own failures and shortcomings by patiently and without prejudice assembling the data, from within and from without, to understand and judge rationally, then to seek responsibly what was truly good for both myself and others. True conviction as to the enduring authenticity of Lonergan's work would eventually be found in increasingly pos-itive spontaneities of feeling occasioned by prolonged implementation of the transcendental precepts. The hardest lesson of all would emerge in the course of that implementation – be patient. We cannot command our own situations but we can respond when such inner and outer circumstances are constellated in a manner propitious for action, even though there are no guarantees of im-mediate gratification.

Thus, in November 1977 I told Ellen that we should formally separate, a course of action with which she refused to agree. On Christmas Day of that year, instead of appearing for dinner as formerly required at her mother's, and overcome by a sense of utter repugnance at that customary hypocritical subser-vience to the "love and largesse" of Grandmother, I instead left home to spend the entire day walking in the rain. My wanderings took me from the Marpole neighbourhood of South Granville, around Point Grey, by the sea below the University of B.C. campus to Spanish Banks, Locarno and Jericho Beaches to

Kitsilano to home again – a distance of some thirty-five kilometres. The anticipated response was one of fury. The next and last time I visited the Kearney house was on the occasion of Mrs. Kearney's funeral in November 1978.

For myself, the inability to cope with Ellen's exclusive subjection to her mother's wishes and refusal to entertain any other professional advice in relation to our marriage, had taken their own toll. Who knows what influences from the past, such as Ed's "falling from his pram" or what family or business adversities had given rise to the woman whose eyes had filled with an implacable anger when I refused to comply with her orders as did her own children and grandchildren? I have no doubt that anger which is not dealt with can turn into hate, however, actions inspired by hatred are intrinsic to the nature of human evil in the world. The degree to which any one of us can be held responsible for our own actions involves a vast and complex database, one that we can only hope to access in terms of our own self-appropriation. Defending ourselves and others against such actions is at the heart of our moral endeavours. Such actions accord with an omnipresent principle of ordering which directs the employment of energy to bring about new levels of diversity and complexity, with new levels of freedom to function, in order to bring about change in the cosmic drama that constitutes development.

My occasional visits to England and Ireland over the next several years were times of great joy, when I could throw open the windows of the spirit in the presence of old and cherished friends to survey our varied progressions through the years from a time and place once held in common. It had long been my conviction and consolation that a return to that environment would answer all my problems. It had become apparent from my fragmentary grasp of Lonergan's work that prayer played an important role, not in producing "magical interventions" in the exquisitely crafted mechanisms of the universe, but in that stilling and informing of the mind that is preparatory to whatever role one is called to play.

Once understood, the latter enabled me to appropriate the basic nature of the thoughts and feelings that make up the conscious flow of my experience. Thus I was able to confirm that the essential array of terms and relations that equipped my symbolic representation of the human spirit as a sort of craft travelling in knowledge space was, though simplistic in one major regard, correct. The problem that really had me stuck was the matter of its empowerment! Not only would Lonergan provide the explanation, in terms of the essential diversity of feeling, but also the essential "instrumentation" of how they may be monitored in terms of peace or disturbance of conscience. This turned out to be an old friend of my early boyhood fascination, the "pictures on my pillow"! Dreams of high significance to one's way of living I had found to remain remarkably active and memorable. So I started on a review of my own dream record.

In 1979, on one of my visits to the Benedictine Abbey overlooking the little town of Mission in the Fraser Valley, a momentous event occurred – I was in my fifty-third year. I had been reflecting on the only remaining alternatives to getting through the remainder of my life: returning to England or to my beloved Howth Head, or perhaps to Liverpool as soon as I could qualify for early retirement and had the means of putting a continent and an ocean between myself and this city of exile. A specifically articulated spontaneous question formed itself within my own consciousness, "Do you want these things or do you want Me?"

It was difficult to trust some caring presence in the darkness that surrounded my own limited horizon of thought and sense, difficult to shed the crutches of a fearful mind, above all to challenge the self-proclaimed authority over one's living and dying imposed by the religion in which I had been raised. Within these limitations, I formed a firm intention to seek out whatever I could best determine as a manifestation of the Divine Will. I could not know then, that moment for what it was, a turning point, a pivot bearing some balance of my days. It was a moment of deep conversion, an unquestioning conviction to the role of conscience as the key to spiritual development. John Henry Newman was absolutely right. So was Bernard Lonergan. In his phrase it could be expressed as a "virtually unconditioned," that is as a personally appropriated truth because its conditions have been fulfilled. Looking back over the years, further confirmation would come in terms of a constructive eclecticism, that which supplied an intellectual formation sanctioned by an escalating development in positive spontaneities of feeling. Thus would be marked a dramatic moment in the mystical journey, as emphasis shifted from the purgative to the illuminative.

In another context, it would become increasingly clear that the mother's iron will, the emphasis on "Catholic Duty," responsibility for Edward, the crucial role of the family funeral business in "helping the bereaved" and, presumably, a more than adequate source of income, ensured absolute authority over Ellen on the part of the mother.

The nature of Edward's medical problem I never heard referred to by the rest of the family, other than, as previously mentioned, being due to an early childhood accident. The only comment I ever heard from a knowledgeable source came from a nurse familiar with the family who persuaded Ellen to allow him to use the facilities available for such patients at a local hospital. Later this nurse told me that it was the unanimous opinion of the staff who worked with such patients that he could have lived a much more normal life but that his condition was largely due to his mother. She also stressed the importance of my standing up to the latter. In fact, Edward would long outlive his mother, and his siblings Frank and Ellen, living comfortably with my eldest son and his family.

I was reminded of the character Claudius in Robert Graves's dramatization of his survival through taking refuge in his physical disabilities from the deadly machinations of intrigue at the highest levels of power in the ruling family of ancient Rome, of his being dismissed as an idiot of no consequence. In the limited opportunities for interaction between Ed and myself over the years, I would nevertheless remain impressed by the awareness he showed of his surroundings, especially when others of his family weren't present.

Attending to recurrent dream symbolism, there was insistent warning of the persistence of extant psychic deterioration. There would eventually occur a momentous insight into a paralyzing underlying matrix of fear stemming from those early days of catechetically enjoined simplistic ideals of responsible human behaviour, the pernicious legalism of static generalities. A first dream, my only experience of a somnambulic character, involved a tremendous storm in which violent winds were crashing and banging the double gates in the back fence of the Dogwood house that led down a short driveway to the carport at the back of the house. I put on my robe and was halfway down the driveway when I realized that it was an absolutely still night. There was no doubt as to the significance, the existence of a major threat to my own psychic defences.

The crucial turning point, however, would come in the second dream. In this, the black Cadillac pulled up outside the house on Dogwood and Mrs. Kearney, Ellen and the poodle started coming up the path to the front door. My dream ego was absolutely paralyzed with terror. Seeking my own associations with the source of that grotesque and completely irrational terror, a further insight revealed the extent to which the inexorable role of Catholic duty had been assimilated from my childhood imaginings of the excruciating pain of unending hellfire, its imposition symbolized by experiences of a ruthless Latin master and the dreaded "ferula room."

It was an insight that released an immense accumulation of psychic energy from its entombment in a terrible complex formed of such earlier consciousness contents. It seemed that these were of so painful a nature that they warranted deliberate protective concealment from normal conscious process to permit at least some level of viable adaptation to the demands of living. In the absence of the worldview afforded me by Lonergan's work, it was clearly a time when the assistance of the informed and balanced objective assessment of a counsellor was required. In the recorded transcripts of his introductory lectures to the book *Insight* back in 1958, Lonergan noted that imposed ideals of religious instruction can give rise to the notion that by sheer effort, right choices and self-discipline, one can win through to some sort of spiritual perfection: "There results psychological breakdown, a nervous breakdown of some sort." Our old friend and neighbour back in Nanaimo, Dr. Cosgrove, had been right. My personal relationship with Ellen was unlikely to change. The only recourse now was to undertake what had been up to now the unthinkable, launching a full action for divorce.

This involved a difficult coming to terms with my earlier childhood indoctrination. However, according to a document of Vatican II, "Man's dignity demands that he acts according to a knowing and free choice. Such a choice is personally motivated and prompted from within. It does not result from blind internal impulse or from external pressure." Further, Pope John XXIII had written: "A bishop who is himself holy will have a following of holy priests, whose holiness will redound to the religious perfection of the whole diocese." On the other hand, at the first session of Vatican II, the Bishop of Bruges became famous for his reference to an ecclesiology that had become clericalist, juridicist and triumphalist. Certainly such a statement conformed with my own experience.

Living an essentially solitary life during these years, and with a new and growing threat to my research program, I was becoming more and more enmeshed in an attitude of resignation, of finding a minimally inconvenient way of getting through the rest my life. Such an affective state was, however, clearly inconsistent with my "working model." My crude grasp of Lonergan's thought, of its clearly extraordinary level of scholarship stemming from the best of Catholic theology and philosophy in terms of its relevance to the problems of contemporary technological society, of its capacity to provide answers to my deepest and most difficult questions, carried highly practical psychological implications.

CHAPTER XIII

CHOICE

The choice to avoid the challenge and to remain mired in some sullen round of discontent or to do something about it was up to myself. In 1980, having been legally married for twenty-five years, I initiated a prolonged and costly process of litigation to free myself from a union that had been merely nominal in character for many of those years. My own inner struggle with freeing myself from the legalistic enmeshment in archaic and static Catholic doctrine was further augmented by an awareness of the psychological and secular power that would be martialed against me – and it was.

All the spiritual courage and consolation that could be mustered would be badly needed for the many dreary months of preparation, the pain and humiliation of the two days of pre-trial discovery proceedings for divorce followed by four days in the Supreme Court. At last, however, the terrible legal ligament was severed. In the following months there was a great weariness, no sense of new direction. Where would I find the strength to face a future dark with menace; to face my declining years in an isolation potentially more lethal than anything I had known?

In 1982 I started attending the Benedictine Abbey of Mount Angel in Oregon, located some 350 miles south of Vancouver. I had become increasingly aware of a rigidly conservative atmosphere at their affiliated monastery in Mission. The last two Palm Sundays that I had attended there, the homilies delivered in each case by senior members of the community were so suffused with resentment, if not hate, for the "glass and concrete towers" of a secular world that "wouldn't listen to Holy Church," that I found myself questioning the authenticity of their own vocations.

Attending again to dream symbolism, it became clearly apparent that my habitual way of life was in some manner deficient. In an existence precluding any real sense of deep companionship, my solution was an intellectual preoccupation with finding a satisfactory worldview. There was need to attend to that other great sphere of psychic development without which genuine growth cannot occur, the affective, the sensitive, the proper feminine counterpart of the masculine. If my mother and my old friend in Shalbourne had always been cherished confidantes and supporters of my earlier efforts and adventures, it was clearly evident from the dream material that there had been a significant deterioration in that aspect of myself.

The crucial dream in this context placed the dream ego on top of an enormously high steel framework of the design that would normally support a vast office tower. I was assembling another layer of steel when I looked up above to the open sky, an interminable expanse which could never be scaled by any human structure. The view was magnificent but the predominant feeling was that sense of immense frustration. Seeking associations, it became evident that my excessive intellectual emphasis on seeking a solution to the problem of life and the universe was the source of this frustration. One cannot "live" in a steel framework, no matter how marvellous the view from the top!

A second major association was the occasion when Kitty brought me to the parrot house of the London Zoo. I was completely fascinated by a bird of magnificent plumage which watched me and then, to my amazement started to call me by my name: "Pat! Pat!" Later I realized that Kitty was calling me and the bird must have picked this up. The evocative beauty of the plumage symbolized the association with the feminine as the appropriate route for bringing about new levels of spontaneity of feeling through the very risky business of letting go of my obsession with duty as defined by my childhood formation.

Once again the insight into the dream symbolism brought about a release of psychic energy entombed in another complex of earlier consciousness contents associated with a source of temptation so terrible it must never be mentioned. It concerned the authentic growth in my own spontaneity of feeling, discernment of symbols which must transform and transvalue over life. In short, the intellectual aspect must be complemented by such discernment of values in symbols that bring about genuine development. I now had to learn to "fly," a realm that I had rigidly excluded in the name of my "Catholic duty." I had even coined my own motto for this practical attitude. "It's the discipline that makes a Guards regiment!" Every action must be put before the bar on intellectual moral judgment! The implication of that flight involved entering into the highly dangerous region of the feminine. I was afraid of releasing a torrent of feeling from the unconscious, a torrent of destructive power that I could not handle in entering into another relationship. The only solution was total reliance on some primordial ordering power in the universe that would provide me with the affective guidance, aware of my own vulnerability in entering something with a totally unforeseeable outcome.

Given such a diagnosis, I had to do something about it. That meant entering into a relationship after many years of rigid self-discipline in keeping my own affairs to myself, other than in matters of professional consultation. No academic or psychological experiment, I feared the torrent of feeling that might be released that could overwhelm and destroy. It would perhaps be wiser to keep to myself, avoid risks and be content with my private devotions in the Divine Office. But there is no refuge there, for it is vitally concerned not with any retreat from life but with the "how" of going about it – for prayer is the balance on which to weigh the metal against the dross of one's intent. At about the same time I tackled another major problem, and undertook the thoroughly distasteful, but ineluctable, course of public confrontation over an unwarranted interference in my research program. The outcome was entirely satisfactory.

In such matters as the latter, attention to data, particularly that elicited in the course of prepared questioning in front of others, was of the essence. The problem was to maintain objective detachment in the heat of confrontation, again a matter for prior mental stilling in prayer. I could never guarantee the outcome. Without the courage to accept the consequences, whatever they might be, there would have been a tacit failure to apply the working model, that is, failure to act in accord with the basic norms of my own conscious procedures. It was thus, in some such manner, that I sought the gift of "personal prophecy" in that it furnished an interpretation of the present in the light of its dynamism for the future.

Thus it was, with an inner attitude set as best I could manage in the context of prayer and inner listening, that I set out upon such a course, consciously overriding such guilt feelings as remained from the legalism of early catechetical instruction. I would find that I was far from alone in my encounters with the vicissitudes of life. All too often religious attempts to force ideals of behaviour, without regard for the genuine and the proper needs of the human subject, are apt to lead to neurosis and breakdown. All too readily can "Tartuffean" excess conceal the manipulation and use of others in order to avoid the demanding task of genuine spiritual development.

The immense problem in dealing with the issues of good and evil that so permeate our lives is that the latter is primarily concerned with maintaining a facade of good intention so that it can exploit the innate decency of the majority of ordinary people. On occasion, the mask can slip, though, for the most part, there is required a level of critical attention that may extend over many years. The outcome can only assert a coherent pattern of acts consistent with evil intention and recognize that they have no place in any community and must, if at all possible, be stopped. As to whether the perpetrator is intrinsically evil we cannot know. The most difficult task of all is searching out one's own failings that are hidden from ordinary conscious perception except with the relaxation of what Freud called the censor that admits or fails to admit materials into consciousness.

For myself, concomitant dream sequences would bring out aspects of myself of which I was totally unaware, which had to be faced up to and let go. It was to discover in heart and mind the falsity of apparent loving which is ultimately a need to possess and the genuine article that finds its ground in the need to give. It would be difficult to overemphasize the healing power of such encounters, the climactic distinction between the ephemera of transient satisfactions and the enduring nature of response to value.

The change in direction that resulted I would later find amply presaged in a poem by W.B. Yeats called *The Choice*;

> *The intellect of man is forced to choose*
> *Perfection of life, or of the work*
> *And if it take the second must refuse,*
> *A heavenly mansion, raging in the dark*
> *When all that story's finished, what's the news?*
> *That old perplexity an empty purse,*
> *Or the day's vanity, the night's remorse.*

Sadly, a materialistic society all too often forces some such choice upon many.

PART FOUR

RETIREMENT

CHAPTER XIV

CHANGES IN TIDAL FLOW

A CAREER ENDS AND A MARRIAGE BEGINS, VANCOUVER, B.C. (1988–1995)

I had now completed over thirty years of pensionable service with the Canadian Government. Further, the economic situation had led to extensive cuts in research funding and there were those who had spent many years of training for the diminishing number of research positions. It seemed time to complete the writing up and publication of my own work.

My professional activities, therefore, drew to a close with the publication, as senior author in collaboration with two colleagues, of *Mathematical Modeling of Tides and Estuarine Circulation* published by Springer-Verlag in 1988. It essentially drew together, into a single perspective, my research activities over the preceding twenty years. An earlier practical outcome was the *Current Atlas*, originally published in 1983 and now in its fifth reprinting. It remains in common use for the waters between Vancouver Island and the mainland and received the 1986 National Award for Applied Oceanography from the Canadian Meteorological and Oceanographic Society. The mathematical model used in that work would subsequently be adapted and employed for oil spill predictions in the 1991 Gulf War. All in all, it seems a very modest showing for the effort expended.

On the 15th April 1988 I retired from the Department of Fisheries and Oceans and in the following June set out on a prolonged visit to England and Ireland. It would prove to be my final visit to see my old friend Marguerite de Beaumont at Shalbourne Manor.

Over the years my visits to Shalbourne Manor would be marked by a shift in character, for with some slow descent into age, infirmity and isolation, evil days would come upon that house. But the sensitivity and perceptive acuity of my old friend remained undimmed and I knew that she would command the manner of her own going. Now, rather than coming to receive, I could bring something of my own journey that would again find expression before the smouldering logs on that great Tudor hearth, but this time through the high symbolic promise in the familiar measured phrases of Vespers and of Compline.

On this occasion, of what would be my last visit, she did indeed never speak but gestured to me to come closer and listened as I read the prayers that are appropriate to the ending of the day. I left the house for the last time to some gratuitous sneer from a local nurse about my exploitation of hospitality. I was reminded of the words put by Robert Graves into the mouth of the failing emperor Claudius, surrounded by the intrigue of the household; "Let all the poisons that lurk in the mud hatch out." During other visits she had told me of her plan for the estate, that "there were all sorts of things going on about the place," but that she never said a word. I sensed the unease of those who would attend the impending dissolution of her long-standing household and the presence of some unknown influence from the past. It seemed to me that her priorities concerned the care and well-being of her beloved horses and to that end she preferred to remain in her home and not end her days in hospital.

She died in September 1989. In 1992, I would visit her grave in the little parish churchyard. In the church, St. Michael and All Angels, it seemed entirely appropriate that the Scout Flag under which we used to gather in the scout loft at the Manor, almost fifty years previously, now was mounted on one of the pillars of the nave. If the flag hung motionless in the dim light filtering through the ancient windows, the real power and ineluctable intention that it symbolized remains increasingly vibrant and gloriously active in the ever-expanding field of human consciousness. For such is the way of a highly dynamic evolutionary universe that now finds its most advanced shoot, oddly enough, in us!

Though the deposit of the wealth of that estate would achieve high media attention, there was no mention of the true enduring legacy, one that proliferates and moves outward and onward from those ineradicable early days when so many, like myself, were helped to find meaning, direction, hope, purpose through the guidance of that good spirit.

It was during this time in my life that a meaningful friendship had developed over some several years between Wendy McFeely and myself. A rich relationship would lead to an authentic civil marriage, one that would carry its own remarkable capacity for healing and development, much in accord with Lonergan's insistence on genuineness in the enlarging of consciousness, for it is, as I discovered, at one's psychic and spiritual peril that one ignores Cardinal Newman's celebrated toast 'to conscience first.' The crucial element now became avoiding my own past shortcomings and genuinely respecting the freedom of conscience of another human being.

On the 23rd May 1995, in the presence of her grown children, Brian and Loraine, Wendy and myself exchanged our vows on board *Fintan,* a Pacific 30 sailboat moored in a False Creek marina against the backdrop of Vancouver's downtown metropolis. Enjoying a picnic supper in the cockpit on that beautiful

Wendy and myself enjoying a social gathering in Vancouver in November 1991.

May evening presaged the joys of the shared years ahead. In the days immediately following, we purchased the condo beside my sixth floor home of some ten years, the mirror image to mine, and both with majestic views of Burrard Inlet and the North Shore mountains. With municipal and strata permits in hand, we soon commenced the renovations required to make the two suites into one, so symbolic of our union.

Finding, restoring, naming and launching *Fintan* was a project of the initial months of my retirement. It had been a long-held dream to own a sailing craft of my own with which to explore the San Juan and Gulf Islands, the mainland coast, Desolation Sound, Princess Louisa and Burrard Inlets and the reaches of Indian Arm. For so many years the subject of my research projects, now I found sheer delight in puttering about *Fintan* when dockside, and exploring the beautiful inlets and bays of these waters on leisurely holidays – myself charting our

At the helm of Fintan, *a retirement restoration project that I named after St. Fintan, an Irish monk who shared my deep love of the Emerald Isle.*

course and Wendy at the helm. We would be joined on adventures such as these by Wendy's children and old friends from the Pacific Oceanographic Group. There were also boat picnics on day outings with friends and family living locally and on visits from Wales, England and China, and even a memorable boat-cleaning-bee with family donning their diving tanks and gear to scrape *Fintan's* barnacle-encrusted hull.

For a number of years our destination was Degnan Bay, Gabriola Island, where we anchored near our friend aboard *Duc en Altum* and, following morning prayer on one boat and breakfast on the other, made our way by dinghy 'round Indian Point for glorious visits with our friends summering there. These many years later, with *Fintan* now in my son's name, it is a B.C. ferry which takes us across the Strait to stay with these treasured friends each summer. With every passage the years of tension seemed to drift away in the wake of

*Wendy and myself sailing the waters of Howe Sound near Vancouver, B.C., in our
30-foot sloop designed and built on Vancouver Island some twenty years earlier.*

Fintan's steady progress, leaving only a deepening sense of peace and authenticity as to my life's many evolved and evolving pathways.

These years were also profoundly enriched by many meaningful relationships as a community of friends and family expanded beyond our wildest imaginings. Our social life was to fill with visits with Wendy's family, old friends, and many dear friends from our beloved Catholic community of St. Ignatius of Antioch near the UBC campus. Opportunities to gather with my sons and their growing families would also emerge with the years, further profoundly blessing our lives with the affection and lively energy of their presence. Each in our own way, Wendy and myself had weathered the storms and vicissitudes both of our own making and those that life had thrown our way. Whatever darkening clouds might gather over the distant horizon in the years to come, we would, God willing, chart a course together. Julian of Norwich had written, "all will be well", and she was right, but not without facing into the difficult task of addressing our own shortcomings in light of the data of consciousness that is ours only to appropriate, and from which we glean for ourselves and for those we hold most dear, the best of the old with the best of the new.

CHAPTER XV

SMOOTH SAILING

A CREW OF TWO, VANCOUVER, B.C. (1995–2011)

Spring 2010 dawned with the long delayed decision to complete the aesthetic uniting of our condo homes with new flooring. We correctly anticipated a major upheaval. My mobility somewhat impaired due to a deteriorating back condition, Wendy was on her own to organize not only the project itself with an occasional yea or nay asked of myself, but a two-week hiatus *somewhere* so the renovation team had open access for removing and laying floors, gluing baseboard, painting, and sanding concrete balconies. The month of June arrived, along with the renovation team, and while our home with its several hundred books was turned upside down and inside out, we took to the road on a memorable circuit of some 2500 kilometres through the Fraser Canyon, Golden, Lake Louise, Radium Hot Springs, Kelowna, Harrison Hot Springs for my delightfully anticipated thermal wallow, and home, visiting with warmly welcoming and delightful friends along the way.

Through an organizational feat previously not even entertained, let alone thought possible, order was gradually restored to our beautiful new setting. From myriad corners, stacks, and filing cabinets, Wendy gathered together my writing efforts of some twenty-five years into one, unliftable tote. The hard copy evidence of the years of unrelenting effort to understand how it is the human spirit comes to know what knowing is, sat on the floor before me, the "me"∘ I had been attempting, in the very process, to know. Despite not given to dating my writing, much to Wendy's chagrin, including the many old letters that chaos had thrust into view, we could now piece together a pattern of development to which these many jottings and finished essays attested, a story within a story, if you will.

Much to my surprise, it would seem that the first appearance of an autobiographical nature was as early as 1985 with the penning of *The Human Journey.* Encouraged by Abbot Bonaventure of Mt. Angel Abbey in Oregon, a Lonergan Symposium was subsequently organized and attended by some three hundred people in the autumn of that same year. I presented this little essay at that time, albeit self-consciously, alongside the soaring scholarship of the plenary speakers. It was an extraordinary event affirming, as it did, the years of my solitary effort to grasp the enormity of Lonergan's genius and engineer the resulting understanding into a practical working model applicable to daily living. Thus, Wendy unearthed *The Secular Contemplative: A Practical Introduction to the Thought of B.J.F. Lonergan*, a very early version of what eventually became the more detailed manuscript *Science, Self-Knowledge & Spirituality: A Feedback Model of Bernard Lonergan's Philosophy of Human Consciousness*, itself completed, for all intents and purposes, by the mid-nineties. (Published in tandem with this autobiography in 2011.) It was this latter work that Lonergan scholar Fred Crowe, S.J., would describe as "all Lonergan in a nutshell!" These and other writings, including the 1981 essay *The Divine Office*, informed a series of lectures I gave for several years at St. Mark's College on the University of B.C. campus from 1988 through 1996 under the title *The Religious Vision of Bernard Lonergan*. Other essays such as *Pneumochip@Universe.ca*; *O Come All Ye Faithful* – a Christmas letter; *Pax Vobiscum*; *Science As Religion: Minds Search for Faith, Good and Evil In Our Time*, followed in mostly unrecorded fashion, each nevertheless contributing to a crystallizing of perspective, the long-sought worldview.

During these years Wendy continued her employment with a major Vancouver newspaper while fulfilling her own long dreamed of university education, a process she began the autumn of 1988 at the age of forty-three. Many were our conversations and book sharing throughout these years and high was the joy on her graduation day, nine years later, from Simon Fraser University. The bagpipes she had yearned to hear for her own walk across the academic quadrangle played *for her* on the 3rd October 1997. The baccalaureate joint major she earned in English and the Humanities had served to open, and challenge, horizons of thinking, of feeling, of knowing. It was a grand celebration with family and friends whose unceasing encouragement had spanned the years. Deep in the wonder of this 'mountain top' experience, it didn't occur to either of us that further education would beckon a year later.

For some years we had been attending Father Albert Zsigmond's Sunday mass with the community of Saint Ignatius of Antioch. It had long attracted a far-flung congregation as a source of authentic spiritual inspiration. This did not appear to include the senior officials of the Roman Catholic Archdiocese of Vancouver, however. One of the latter stepped in as a replacement on the occurrence of Father Zsigmond's untimely death in late 1991.

Our accustomed homiletics of a holy man now sharply contrasted with the practiced jargon of a public relations man. It would transpire that his apparent mission was to move St. Ignatius' community home of nearly thirty years from St. Anselm's Anglican Church to the new chapel at St. Mark's College. I had met him at an earlier social occasion and on mentioning my interest in Lonergan studies he triumphantly declared his complete ignorance of the subject. I eventually found that on topics concerning the minutiae of ritual or the colours appropriate for priestly apparel on particular feast days he was thoroughly at home, on familiar ground, and happy to dispense enlightenment to the ignorami. Subsequently when he announced his appointment to a senior post in the diocese, I found a paraphrase of W.S. Gilbert's satirical verse irresistible:

> *I mastered all the rubrics so carefully*
> *That now I am the ruler of the Chancery!*

In terms of homiletics I was reminded of George Eliot's description as: "The cock that thought the sun had risen just to hear him crow!" Personally, I made a point of having nothing much to do with him.

My lectures at St. Mark's College, though, had apparently not gone unnoticed. Without disclosing the agenda behind his casual questions, he asked a family member about where we had married, concluding that it was unlikely Wendy and myself had sought to involve the Diocese in our marriage through the so-called "dissolution" and "annulment" procedures, respectively. With the earlier de facto involvement of my former mother-in-law in the marriage tribunal, and my own numerous experiences with local clergy in marital matters, any such pretension no longer existed for myself, nor did it for Wendy, who eschewed the dissolution procedure out of her own convictions many years prior to the friendship that developed between us. Accosting Wendy at the funeral reception of a friend, he advised her of his findings and of his intentions. When we ignored him, we were formally suspended, by couriered letter, "let there be no mistake about it..." from receiving communion.

It seemed, however, that though the reason given was our civil marriage, it would become apparent that the Diocesan disquiet was more in regard to my

Lonergan lectures, a fact imparted to the principal of St. Mark's College. All this emerged when the next series of lectures came up for discussion. Anxious to avoid any embarrassment to the College, I volunteered to cancel the 1997 Spring Term lectures, to the principal's evident relief. He attributed his concern to the possibility of adverse publicity, an event to be avoided at all costs.

While neither Wendy nor myself doubted the sacredness of the vows we had exchanged in the presence of the marriage commissioner, family and friends, the opportunity arose many years later for our marriage to be *officially* blessed by a knowledgeable and compassionate parish priest who knew all too well the emotional cost of following one's own conscience in the Roman Catholic tradition, particularly so in such matters of divorce and re-marriage, even though explicated, as it were, in canon law's *internal forum*. He also knew the spiritual and emotional healing integral to a couple remaining in full communion with their established community and how rare it is to be otherwise, all factors which the public relations man, who himself would eventually add canon lawyer to his clericalist resume, had somehow omitted to consider.

Thus ended any formal sense of allegiance to the pomp, circumstance and spiritual vacuity of institutional Roman Catholicism. The best of its millennia of prayer and scholarship had been distilled by Lonergan into an intellectual compass that pointed to the eventual evolutionary solution of the world's problems, not in terms of a legalism of static generalities but as an evolutionary model of both the individual and collective development of the human spirit, a development that can be verified and tested in the laboratory of one's own consciousness. As Lonergan observed, "The chair of Moses stands but it is occupied by scribes and Pharisees" – a viewpoint that accords with my own experience. However, history, and eventually Divine Providence, judges the authenticity of a tradition and, I have no doubt, will take its course!

For Wendy, however, this thoroughly repugnant occurrence in our otherwise spiritually enriched lives, would result in new and persistent questions regarding the Christianity in which her life had been steeped, and the interconnected questions regarding the origins of such destructive dogma, the self-serving application of which we were witness. The call to which she responded in September 1998 saw her enrolled in graduate studies at the Vancouver School of Theology located in the theological corner of the UBC campus. She would be challenged on every front even as she was inspired, edified, illumined, in every cell of body, heart, mind and spirit. Her studies would have the side effect of taking her further into the mystical tradition of Christianity that had long been a wellspring of guiding inspiration, affirming an ever-deepening appreciation for the parallels inherent within the heart of mystical spirituality, be it within the ecumenical or interfaith spectrum. The never-failing Love and Presence found therein would, along with a growing appreciation for the edicts of ancient councils, many of which had long since failed to pertain to serious seekers of the twenty-first century, become the pivots upon which she would judge for herself the authenticity of dogmatic pronunciations from within the hierarchical lock-down, and the largely absent compassion shown by those few whose own career aspirations are dependent on the dispatching of same.

For myself, with my old emotionally guarded way of being more and more a guise of the past, it was my delight to welcome Wendy home after her long days of classes and studying, to bridge the gap between our individual worlds and that which we shared, to initiate and plan our travels, to begin what felt like a finale to my writing, to serve up one of my by now infamous one-pot-dinners, making up in sustenance what was utterly lacking in gourmet presentation and taste. The exigencies of life continued to demand the fullest of our attention and our prayers yet, even so, peace and joy found their own expression.

As such, there was an agreeable ease in the daily commerce of our shared

life, a reflection of our love to be sure, yet also a reflection of a more settled unconscious, indicated by the absence of disturbing dream imagery. I could recall
a similar unselfconscious ease from the long ago innocence of my childhood
explorations in Pope's garden and grotto by the Thames, the far-ranging bicycle
and scouting adventures throughout Berkshire and beyond, and the many rambles with friends in the Wicklow Hills as a young man at university.

As Wendy had introduced me to the Vancouver neighbourhoods of her
childhood and youth, I was now introducing her to those of mine. Our overseas visits included walks in the neighbourhood of my father's Macklin Street
school in central London, South Kensington's Imperial College and the Science
Museum, long walks along the tow paths from Hampton Court past my childhood homes in Strawberry Hill, in Twickenham, and on into Richmond – the
paths I walked so many years before with Uncle Joey, with my father.

On one memorable occasion Wendy and I visited Sister Maurus at the convent by the Thames who, as our visit drew to a close, peremptorily sent me off
to the bathroom, whereby, motioning Wendy closer, she proceeded to quiz her
as to her "intentions... as he has had a difficult life." Satisfied by Wendy's hasty,
albeit surprised reassurance, she hugged us warmly and bid us on our way.

Such was the tone of these visits, whether the extraordinary times with old
friends or new or the wonderful visits with my niece and her family, whether
walking in Kew Gardens or Greenwich, whether at theatre in the West End
or at chapel in Hampton Court, St. Paul's Mary Chapel or St. Martin's in the
Field, or whether simply being a photographed and photographing tourist as
evening fell on the scene spread out along the Thames below the slow turning
of the *London Eye*.

As unforgettable as our visits to England and Wales, as well as a memorable
visit with dear friends in Bejing, it was Ireland's soul that still held mine within
her own, the spirituality of the life deep within her mystic isles and so within

On a visit to Twickenham, England, I introduced Wendy to my old friend, Sister Maurus (sitting to my left), at the Convent of the Sisters of Mercy.

her people. Here, I was truly home and introducing Wendy was a joy unconfined, one her own joy clearly reflected. Sometimes our visits would begin in Dublin where we stayed at the cottage on Howth Head, then owned and being lovingly and meticulously restored by Mick and Kitty's youngest daughter and her husband. We'd take magnificent walks around the head and down into the harbour town of Howth itself. On occasion we stayed with their eldest son and his family just down the road. Other times we flew into Shannon to a warm welcome by Mick and Kitty, and were soon happily settled into the home they'd built and in which they lived their entire married life, in Ennis, County Clare. The years of friendship with Mick and his family now spanned some sixty years, and throughout each of them, himself and Kitty were beacons of affectionate acceptance that blazed across the miles. Now Wendy was warmly welcomed, as had been my mother and on at least one occasion, Ellen and the boys.

No matter where our flight touched down, the centre of every visit was Mick and Kitty as we joined in their retirement routines with delight. The mid-morning coffee and the daily newspaper to be read at the kitchen table under the watchful gaze of the iconic picture of the Sacred Heart of Jesus, or, if the weather was fine, sitting in the delightful conservatory looking out through a thick array of sweet peas to rows of vibrant colour along the low stone wall, be it emanating from dahlias or daisies or roses, against the green expanse of side lawn.

There would be visits from their children and grandchildren or neighbours stopping by for a chat, and then, after dinner at noon, incomparable drives through the Irish countryside. Many were the short excursions to Lahinch and the long sandy stretches of low tide beach for wind-blown walks, and the Cliffs of Moher, a little further down the road where on one particularly windy day Mick's cap was lifted from his head and sent on a wild flight down the cliff face. The longer drives would take us 'round the Ring of Kerry, or to the Burren with its ancient Poulnabrone burial sites, or to bleakly beautiful Connemara and afternoon tea in the lovely setting of Kylemore Abbey. We would walk among the stories engraved on solemn tombstones and Celtic crosses in the ruins of Quinn or Corcomroe Abbeys, where the spirit of the ancient monks' voices, raised in the singing of the Psalms, could be heard in the music of the wind.

Throughout, Mick would regale us with history and politics, stories of in-dividuals, of properties changing hands or abandoned to the elements. Kitty's stories would be of families, who lived where, when, of hearing and heeding the Banshee's cry as she cared for patients as a young nurse, all the while pulling 'sweets' from tucked away places and handing them around the car. In Galway with their younger son's family, it would be the Aaran Islands and small coun-try roads with a lakeside stop where construction workers informed Wendy

Wendy captured a treasured moment between three old friends in this photo: myself with Mick and Kitty Torpey following a long beach walk at Lahinch near the Cliffs of Moher, Ireland in 2004.

she must be a "planter," a designation laughingly explained by the Torpeys and myself on the soft drive home.

Newgrange, the Hill of Tara, Saint Oliver Plunkett's shrunken head, the ancient atrocities of Cromwell's battle on the field alongside the River Boyne, and so much more while staying with their eldest daughter's family in Drogheda. Then there were the evenings back home in Ennis at the close of these remarkable days. Retiring to the sitting-room and stretching our legs out before the fireplace, perhaps a little nip of Kitty's favourite Bailey's Irish Cream on-the-rocks, or a chocolate, the nine o'clock BBC World News, the day's final cup of tea with buttered bread or a cracker before succumbing to sweet dreams in hot water-bottle or electric blanket heated beds. So many soul-stirring and

*On another Irish adventure with Wendy, we arrive at the cottage on Howth
Head for a visit with the daughter of Mick and Kitty to whom I sold the home
that meant so much to my parents and myself.*

deeply treasured memories, so much delight in the company of these ever-
faithful friends.

On one of these oft' remembered occasions Wendy and myself rented a car
to drive the long way around to Mick and Kitty's in Ennis. Our route took us
from Dublin to Derry, down the energetically spectacular coast of Donegal,
under the table top mountain of stark Benbulbin to walk the little village of
Drumcliff and pay homage at the grave of its famous bard, William Butler
Yeats. It also led to an exploration of my Crean ancestors' graves lying within
the ruins of Sligo Abbey and of which I'd read many years before in W.G.
Wood-Martin's *History of Sligo*, and on to a delightful visit with my old friends,
Aleck and Joan Crichton. The setting of their home was as pastoral as I had

long remembered and every bit as beautiful as the welcome extended to Wendy and myself. With fascination we would watch Aleck's sheep dog, Dash, who, even when he was apparently sound asleep, would be instantly alert if Aleck so much as raised an eyebrow or shifted in his chair. It was remarkable to see such attentiveness and utter devotion in this beautiful working dog. While my visits with the Crichtons were infrequent through the years, the respect and affection established with our first meeting at the Irish Mountaineering Club and our many shared hikes in the Wicklow Hills and climbs on such as the cliffs of Lugalore or Dalkey Quarry, stayed true to the original set of that course. It was remarkable to be with them, to walk the fields by the bay with Wendy at my side, for her to meet them and know of whom I spoke so fondly when first we began to share the people and places of our lives.

While the riches such as these were many, they were not lived in isolation,

Aleck Crichton and Dash at the edge of their property on Ballysadare Bay near Sligo on the west coast of Ireland.

rather they formed the backdrop and foundation for the daily come and go and attendant challenges that the cycles of life present. Wendy would know the grief of losing the daily presence of her much loved parents, her father not long after our marriage, and then her mother some eleven years later. Together we would grieve with Michael and his young family the tragically early and

In our apartment workshop, working on the Myford Lathe given to me by my mother during my doctoral studies in Liverpool.

A Christmas celebration with Tom and Jo-Ann and their three children, and with Mike and Dianne and their five children.

Tom, Mike and myself at a family gathering in our home in 2009.

Our Christmas brunch in 2010. Back row: Wendy, Jo-Ann, Caitlin, Mike, Jake Power (husband of Christie), Christie, Patrick, Kelly-Ann, Jennifer (wife of Ryan), Ryan, Tom. Front row: Catherine, myself, Sean and Trevor.

Wendy and her three granddaughters, Maude, Beatrice and Edith, mid-April 2011.

Wendy and myself welcome our first great-grandchild, Owen Michael, at the end of April 2011!

unanticipated death of his wife Dianne from complications of rheumatoid arthritis. How to comprehend such a tragic loss as we joined my sons' and Dianne's families and friends gathered around her bed that awful day? To write of those moments even these five years later, is to experience again not only the absolute sorrow and profound loss of her presence to each family member, it is to recall the unshakeable depth of faith and peace surrounding her still form.

For Wendy and myself Dianne was the jewel-in-the-family-crown as it was she who encouraged a more frequent participation in hers and Michael's family life. There had been lovely Christmas gatherings mid-December, invitations to the high school graduations of their eldest children and the confirmation of a younger, as well as delightful overnight stays near their campground in the

Fraser Valley where we joined them in delicious corn fests and campfire sing-a-longs that were happily inclusive of Tom and Jo-Ann and their children. My gratitude was, however, not only for the invitations they extended. It was also for the sense of their acceptance, tangibly present within each gathering, of the years in which such engagement in their lives had not been feasible.

With faith and courage and the support of family and friends, Michael would face into the years ahead without his loving wife at the heart of their long shared household. There would be more graduations to come in both Michael's and Tom's families, the marriages of Michael's son and daughter and his warm and enthusiastic welcome of their new spouses and families, summer gatherings around campfires, new Christmas traditions. Certainly, for myself, for my sons, as for all generations of human spirits, past events and relations create complex challenges, both conscious and unconscious, of response and questions as to values, worldview, of relationships of all dimensions. The joy for me is that in these my later years, Wendy and I are part of the lives of her children, grandchildren, extended family, wonderful friends, as we are part of my sons' and their families, friends and extended family. For me, these relationships are those for which I had long hoped, yet knew nothing of how to bring about. With the birth of our first great-grandchild in April 2011, hope springs eternal that it is the essence of such love that truly lives on beyond the limitations of our incarnate selves, as G.K. Chesterton observed:

> *My friends, we will not go again or ape an ancient rage,*
> *Or stretch the folly of our youth to be the shame of age,*
> *But walk with clearer eyes and ears this path that wandereth,*
> *And see undrugged in evening light the decent inn of death;*
> *For there is good news yet to hear and fine things to be seen,*
> *Before we go to Paradise by way of Kensal Green.*

EPILOGUE

The seemingly unanswerable question that formulated itself in my schoolboy days, in the grey morning light of a pre-war London railway platform, as to whether life had any meaning or not would eventually turn out to have an answer. For myself, the real reward is somehow meeting and surviving the challenge of my time, its revelation of a universe, filled with promise, that soars magnificently beyond my wildest early imaginings. Basically, energy is informed to give rise to the myriad manifestations of existence. Meaning is, both individually and collectively, a product of human heads through attending, informing and acting. At its core is an exponentially growing fund of publicly verifiable knowledge.

We are each called upon to use whatever talents, with which we have been endowed, in whatever personal circumstances, to utilize, and contribute to, however minutely, directly or indirectly, this fund of available knowledge in our own time. It was arrived at by grasping the experimental nature of a "feedback model" applicable to human conscious process which should be verifiable in the averaged context of progressively improved positive-feeling states or diminishing of negative-feeling states.

The term "model" implies a replica of something that is useful in solving problems, and permits some measure of realizable anticipation. For the Victorian physicist something could properly be said to be understood if a conceptual mechanical model could be built of it. Science was certain knowledge of things from their causes.

Though still valid for many practical applications, science has developed more powerful mathematical theories that can be verified in instances and suggest new levels of experimental exploration. Outcomes are not certain but probable. The aim is an ever better approximation towards truth, towards reality, that can eventually be settled by appeal to sensible data. In some such manner, the "feedback model," if employed in a proper context of attending to spontaneities of questioning and of feelings, generally consistent with advancing the good of order in ourselves and in others, should be susceptible of longer term verification in some averaged context of spontaneities of feeling.

Attempts to avoid this arduous and demanding task on the part of the world community in present times are all too evident in, for example: ruthless economic exploitation, environmental abuse, substance abuse, fantasies of sexual excitation and release, violence, discordant rhythmic noise and light effects, high-speed driving, shopping and chatter, and so on. Too late it is often found that "negative feedback" from the real world can exact a price that urges return to greater authenticity in living.

Authentic performance results from putting into practice those aspects of mind that distinguish our range of knowing from the merely animal range of knowing. Thus we are called upon to attend, not just to what is pleasant, but also to those aspects of existence that we would rather avoid. We must be honest in raising the questions that result, even though they reflect badly on one's own performance. We must judge the possible answers fairly on the basis of all the evidence. We must then decide on a course of action that is consistent with furthering the good of increasing order in the universe, that is, of authentic loving as an intrinsic manifestation of the raw material of the universe as best we can describe it, energy. One must start with oneself in an attempt to become a positive influence for others.

If the road is apt, for most of us, to be long and arduous, there can be a powerfully experienced growth in personal meaning that is both accumulative and progressive. It is marked by changes in the spontaneity of questioning, but most dramatically of all in spontaneities of feeling, the sheer joy of living as, and awakening to, the superb promise of an evolutionary universe yet to be disclosed. The alternative view is that the universe is a formless chaos, which it obviously isn't, or that nothing can be known beyond merely material phenomena. Thus, indeed, was my old problem in physics!

Energy is knowable by its effects hence, if we don't know what knowing is, we don't know what we are talking about. The extraordinary capacity of the mind to reflect on the nature of its own operations and the accumulative nature of what accrues through performing the operations, affirms that we can at least know enough about knowing to affirm, with a very high probability of being correct, that what is being formed now has some key role in the future evolutionary development of the universe, at least for practical purposes in encouraging us to do our best with whatever has fallen to our lot.

This appears to occur through "closure," a term that is now in common use. Thus, for example, some horrendous tragedy, such as the fatal crash of an airliner, the relatives and friends gather to experience in common, the violent sundering of a major part of their own living experience.

This meaning of the word would seem to originate in Gestalt psychology and carries with it the notion of "completing something" so we can move on with our lives. For myself, this would seem to be essentially identical with the practical meaning of Lonergan's "virtually unconditioned," that which is satisfactory for practical purposes, that which removes the tension of potentially unlimited questioning for solving some immediate problem.

With respect to the problem of life itself, as viewed from a London railway platform, it would turn out to be the meaning of Newman's movement from "notional" to "real assent." At a more esoteric level of mathematics, the closure of a set (a collection of any kinds of objects) by inclusion of its own limit points which might be crudely interpreted for present purposes as "more of the same." Note that the meaning of the word is not exhausted but there is suggested a convergence of meaning as yet to be disclosed.

There is involved an encounter with classic meaning that is to be found in the writings of others, and can be verified in one's own conscious experience. The term "classic" implies some instance of meaning that is singularly important, writings that can never be fully understood, and therefore invite constant return in the light of one's accumulating knowledge in a progress to higher and higher levels of appropriated meaning. Thus they constitute motivating symbols that give rise to further questions and open up new vistas of feeling as yet to be experienced. Authentic religious texts can be read as powerfully symbolic of the evolutionary destiny of the human spirit.

The early symbolism of the waiting crowd on the other platform of Twickenham Station, to the insistent sound of transforming energy from the electrical power house all those years ago, and the question as to the meaning of human existence, would eventually be found in the advancing meaning of meaning itself as produced in human heads, for each a matter of some unique temporal transition that enters into timelessness, of accumulative and progressive meaning. Thus from its solar source, is energy informed and manifesting itself in myriad forms of existence. The most significant of these is that which lies at the core of meaning, that is knowledge, or being – everything that is in the past, is in the present, is in the evolutionary future.

The role of "meaning" is central to the development of the human spirit. There is something that is accumulative, and can be, to a greater or lesser extent, progressive over a lifetime, something that is of the nature of "thought content" that wasn't there at the beginning of one's life. Optimally, it is brought about by putting into practice those attributes that make us human rather than animal; by acquiring that hygiene of thought which involves being attentive, intelligent in questioning, rational in judgment and responsible in decision with respect to both the short and the long term consequences of our decisions.

A useful practical indicator of progress or decline is available through the symbolic certification of dream symbolism. The criteria of success lie in the ease and readiness of implementation of the precepts: be attentive, be intelligent, be reasonable, be responsible. These lead to the final precept, be in love.

It is important that one assess one's progress in terms of knowledge and affective spontaneities, against the recorded experiences and understanding of others. A dominant influence in my early years was my father's respect for the scholarship of his Jesuit friends. It had never occurred to me to question some implied omniscience, or indeed, that the term "jesuitical," as carrying a connotation of dissembling, ambiguity, false reasoning, was anything other than merely pejorative. Certainly my own experiences during my last two years at the Jesuit College in London had left me with a morbid and stultifying scrupulosity in terms of religious formation.

It was, however, the lifelong labours of two remarkable Jesuit scholars, Pierre Teilhard de Chardin and Bernard Lonergan, who showed me the way through my own fascination with the physical universe, with science and engineering as being wonderfully consonant with some underlying fundamental principle of ordering that effect change from lower to higher states of order, diversification, complexity, functioning. This I was able to eventually systematize for myself in terms of a "feedback model", essentially powered by feelings deriving from symbols, whether immediate, or deriving from others around us or gone on before us.

The net result should be a parallel development of both heart and mind over one's life which constitutes a preparation for the next major evolutionary phase of the universe, that which we encounter now as "spirit." If the feedback model is a reasonable approximation to what is basic to this development of the human spirit, it should carry the hallmark of public verification in terms of the experience of others. This should best be reflected in artistic symbolizations appropriate to roughly one's own span of years and the changes that were occurring therein.

The manner in which each operator can perform the operations in accord with an authentic drawing towards the meaning of some overarching unity, expressed and shared in words as so clearly delineated by Bernard Lonergan, himself standing on the shoulders of millennia of like-motivated predecessors. In view of the publicly verifiable nature of reality, it is well to find expression, not only of the cognitive, but also of affective aspects of my own journey to be held in common with others. Though the work of many sources could be adduced, two stand out as being particularly apposite to my own experience. In terms of early religious formation in a fine tradition that had ceased to be authentic, the salient symbolic aspects of that journey are best expressed, for myself, by the word-pictures drawn by Evelyn Waugh in *Brideshead Revisited*. In terms of discovering for myself the significance of meaning as the real world into which the human spirit can expand over a lifetime, preparatory to its entering into the next major phase of evolution in the universe, that which would seem to be of the nature of consciousness itself, the words of T.S. Eliot in the closing verse of the *Four Quartets* contributed immensely to that movement from "notional" to "real" assent as described by J.H. Newman.

Brideshead Revisited chronicles the life of an aristocratic Catholic family between the world wars, and the divisions occasioned by militant convictions based on a sort of "mad certainty" on the one hand, and varying degrees of uncertainty and antagonism without any ability to critically articulate objections on the other. Thus the former would be bound by a complete subjection of feelings to the rule of mind, a sort of "emotional castration." While for the latter, a "religious complex" that precluded any critical and discerning release from the troubling tension of questioning with respect to the deep feelings that should motivate to higher levels of personal growing of both heart and mind, would dominate.

That Catholicism, so vividly eloquent of my own formative years, was simply an arid legalism of static generalities into which the incredibly varied and immensely demanding exigencies of human lives must be fitted. If they didn't, one was told to offer it up, the Lord would understand and there would presumably be "healing"! It seemed that almost every word and phrase coming from the varied cast of characters awakened echoes all too familiar in my own past. The institutional Catholicism of that era would later be criticized at the Second Vatican Council as clericalist, juridicist and triumphalist.

I was well on the way to breakdown before, with the aid of the "feedback model" and role of psychic indications of deterioration, that I was able to realize the role of authentic prayer as a preparation of the heart and mind for the patience, insights and feelings that provide authentic timing and guidance for entering into the events that become one's lived conscious record, a "you" or a "me." The human spirit expresses itself in symbols before it knows. Thus it was, that with growing excitement, I would eventually find a record of a very similar journey in the poetry of T.S. Eliot, best summarized at the close of his *Four Quartets* – an account employing a powerful symbolism of words quite independent of Lonergan's intentionality analysis.

What we call the beginning is often the end
And to make an end is to make a beginning.
The end is where we start from. And every phrase
And sentence that is right (where every word is at home,
Taking its place to support the others,
The word neither diffident or ostentatious,
An easy commerce between the old and the new,
The common word exact without vulgarity,
The formal word precise but not pedantic,
The complete consort dancing together)
Every phrase and every sentence is an end and a beginning,

(The sources of "meaning" are all the conscious acts, and the contents that are produced, in human heads. At the end of each life there is some personal accumulation of "meaning" which can be regarded as a human "spirit," uniquely ordered to some role in the next major phase of evolution in the universe, that which would seem to be constituted as an evolving field of love and meaning. Its most powerful, flexible and diversifying expression is to be found in words, expressions that can be passed on from one human head to another.)

Every poem is an epitaph. And any action
Is a step to the block, to the fire, down the sea's throat
Or to an illegible stone: that is where we start.
We die with the dying:
See, they depart, and we go with them.
We are born with the dead:
See, they return, and bring us with them.
The moment of the rose and the moment of the yew tree
Are of equal duration. A people without a history

> *Is not redeemed from time, for history is a pattern*
> *Of timeless moments. So, when the light fails*
> *On a winter's afternoon, in a secluded chapel*
> *History is now and England.*

("Meaning" is accumulative and progressive so that each of us is uniquely called to make our own tiny contribution to "communally solving" the great puzzle of the universe. We must be attentive, intelligent, reasonable and responsible in mastering such aspects of prior meaning that already exist and then "listening" for the affective grace and spontaneity of questioning in prayer that guide the process of personal discernment.)

> *With the drawing of this Love and the voice of this Calling*
> *We shall not cease from exploration*
> *And the end of all our exploring*
> *Will be to arrive where we started*
> *And know the place for the first time.*
> *And the end of all our exploring*

(Later, in a life authentically lived, there has usually been traversed, not only some appropriate advance in the field of knowing, but also a much expanded range of spontaneities in feeling, through attentively responding to persisting changes in one's own temporal evolution of personally motivating symbols. Thus we can begin to grasp the diversifying role others, differing widely in age and vocation, have contributed so much to one's own formation.)

> *Through the unknown remembered gate*
> *When the last of earth left to discover*
> *At the source of the longest river*
> *The voice of the hidden waterfall*

And the children in the apple tree
Not known because not looked for
But heard, half-heard, in the stillness
Between two waves of the sea.
Quick now, here, now, always -
A condition of complete simplicity
(Costing not less than everything)

(Through the labour of authentically implementing the precepts, we find that transformation in the spontaneity of feeling which accords with the final precept, that which is constituted by an overpowering falling in love with a mysterious creator and a magnificently evolving universe, that which is made accessible to us by the gift of consciousness.)

And all shall be well and
All manner thing shall be well
When the tongues of flames are in-folded
Into the crowned knot of fire
And the fire and the rose are one.

(And which has become the personal path to that level of "meaning," in one's time, and which has become a genuine lay mysticism of exciting anticipation.)

In the context of my own present experience, this would seem to manifest itself as a re-experiencing of the fascinations, the interests, the excitements, the wonder, of those early childhood years but which had succumbed to the harsh realities of what we call the real world. It seemed to have been summed up on the occasion of my last visit to Sister Maurus, then in her nineties and living in a nursing home in Saint Albans. As she was being brought to the reception room, I overheard her remark to the nurse in the corridor, "He's a big professor out in America, but he hasn't changed since he was a little boy!" However inaccurate the former assertion, I would like to think that there was a grain of truth in the latter.

What were the formative influences? Was it the life of those early days in Twickenham, of my parents and my friends across the road, the nuns? Was it the influence of my old friend in Shalbourne? Was it the power of science as religious symbol? Was it the prayer life of a monastic community? Was it the lingering presence about his grotto by the Thames of a little deformed genius? One who wrote: "Know thyself, presume not God to scan. The proper study of mankind is man."

Was it Bernard Lonergan who showed me the way of going about it? It matters not, for all are cut from a common fibre, one from which may be woven on the loom of time the fabric of a life, which in God's great mercy, may find appointment in the making of His Kingdom.

PATRICK B. CREAN
1926 – 2011

Patrick Bernard Crean was born in London, England, 14th August 1926 and was raised in Twickenhan, the Borough of Richmond upon Thames. During WW II, Patrick apprenticed as a marine engineer at the Admiralty shipyards in Cowes, Isle of Wight. After graduating with a Bachelor of Science and Diploma in Chemical Technology from University College Dublin, he became a junior chemist with United Whalers Ltd. This appointment placed him onboard the whale factory ship Balaena of the British Norwegian Fleet in the Antarctic for three off-shore expeditions including a summer season at a South African shore station.

Following his whaling adventures, Patrick immigrated to Canada in 1953 to further his education with a Master of Science in Chemical Engineering from the University of Toronto. These studies led him to employment with the Fisheries Research Board of Canada and a number of projects conducted by Fisheries Technological Laboratories on the West and East Coasts. During this time, he married, began a family and settled on the West Coast. Eventually Patrick accepted a position with the Pacific Oceanographic Group and completed a Doctorate in Physical Oceanography through the University of

Liverpool, England. He would remain a scientist with this group and then with Fisheries and Oceans Canada until his retirement.

Patrick and Al Ages* were responsible for collecting and publishing the first comprehensive measurements on seasonally variable oceanic conditions from the entrance of Juan de Fuca Strait to the northern end of the Strait of Georgia. This volume of reports (P.B. Crean and A. Ages, 1971, *Oceanographic records from twelve cruises in the Strait of Georgia and Juan de Fuca Strait, 1968*, Department of Energy, Mines and Resources) was the standard for all oceanographers for over three decades. In the late 1960s, Patrick moved to Vancouver to use the UBC computer to model the hydrodynamics of southern Inside Passage of British Columbia. The result a few years later was the first, highly accurate numerical simulation of tidal heights and currents of an inland sea.

In 1983, the Canadian Hydrographic Service published Dr. Crean's *Current Atlas: Juan de Fuca Strait to Strait of Georgia* that remains in common use to this day. In the past 28 years this publication has sold almost 100,000 copies and still sells 1,300 per year. Patrick proposed this publication and prepared the maps of current vectors, which were based on his own numerical model of these waters. For this effort he received the 1986 National Award for Applied Oceanography from the Canadian Meteorological and Oceanographic Society. He was also a senior author in collaboration with two colleagues of *Mathematical Modeling of Tides and Estuarine Circulation: The Coastal Seas of Southern British Columbia and Washington State* published by Springer-Verlag in 1988. The mathematical model used in that work would be adapted for tidal current models of the entire BC coast and the Gulf of St. Lawrence and subsequently employed for oil spill predictions in the 1991 Gulf War.

---

*Alard Ages, 8th October, 1924–10th August, 2011

In 1988, after thirty years of service, Patrick retired from the Canadian Government to sail the waters he had spent so many years studying and concentrate on writing up his years of personal study in the areas of theology, philosophy and psychology. He subsequently completed *Science, Self-Knowledge & Spirituality: A Feedback Model of Bernard Lonergan's Philosophy of Human Consciousness* followed by his autobiographical account which integrates this work with his life, entitled *Pictures on My Pillow: An Oceanographer's Exploration of the Symbols of Self-Transcendence*, both published by Agio Publishing House in 2011.

CPSIA information can be obtained at www.ICGtesting.com
Printed in the USA
LVOW010842050112

262421LV00002B/1/P